CHINA'S SOCIAL V

China Today series
Greg Austin, *Cyber Policy in China*
David S. G. Goodman, *Class in Contemporary China*
Stuart Harris, *China's Foreign Policy*
Elaine Jeffreys with Haiqing Yu, *Sex in China*
Michael Keane, *Creative Industries in China*
Joe C. B. Leung and Yuebin Xu, *China's Social Welfare*
Pitman B. Potter, *China's Legal System*
Xuefei Ren, *Urban China*
Judith Shapiro, *China's Environmental Challenges*
Teresa Wright, *Party and State in Post-Mao China*
LiAnne Yu, *Consumption in China*
Xiaowei Zang, *Ethnicity in China*

CHINA'S SOCIAL WELFARE

THE THIRD TURNING POINT

Joe C. B. Leung and Yuebin Xu

polity

Copyright © Joe C. B. Leung and Yuebin Xu 2015

The right of Joe C. B. Leung and Yuebin Xu to be identified as Authors of this Work has been asserted in accordance with the UK Copyright, Designs and Patents Act 1988.

First published in 2015 by Polity Press

Polity Press
65 Bridge Street
Cambridge CB2 1UR, UK

Polity Press
350 Main Street
Malden, MA 02148, USA

All rights reserved. Except for the quotation of short passages for the purpose of criticism and review, no part of this publication may be reproduced, stored in a retrieval system, or transmitted, in any form or by any means, electronic, mechanical, photocopying, recording or otherwise, without the prior permission of the publisher.

ISBN-13: 978-0-7456-8056-9
ISBN-13: 978-0-7456-8057-6 (pb)

A catalogue record for this book is available from the British Library.

Library of Congress Cataloging-in-Publication Data

Leung, Joe C. B.
　China's social welfare : the third turning point / Joe C. B. Leung, Yuebin Xu.
　　pages cm
　Includes bibliographical references and index.
　　ISBN 978-0-7456-8056-9 (hardback : alk. paper) – ISBN 978-0-7456-8057-6 (pbk. : alk. paper)　1. Public welfare–China.　2. Public welfare administration–China.　I. Xu, Yuebin.　II. Title.
　HV418.L482 2015
　361.951–dc23
　　　　　　　　　　　　2014030422

Typeset in 11.5/15 Adobe Jenson Pro
by Toppan Best-set Premedia Limited
Printed and bound in the United Kingdom by Clays Ltd, St Ives PLC

The publisher has used its best endeavours to ensure that the URLs for external websites referred to in this book are correct and active at the time of going to press. However, the publisher has no responsibility for the websites and can make no guarantee that a site will remain live or that the content is or will remain appropriate.

Every effort has been made to trace all copyright holders, but if any have been inadvertently overlooked the publisher will be pleased to include any necessary credits in any subsequent reprint or edition.

For further information on Polity, visit our website: politybooks.com

Contents

List of Tables	vi
Map	vii
Chronology	viii
Preface	xii
List of Abbreviations	xvii
1 Overview	1
2 From Socialism to Modernization	17
3 Social Challenges under Market Reform	39
4 Urban Social Protection	68
5 Rural Social Protection	98
6 Social Care for Older People	125
7 Innovating Social Governance: The Emergence of Social Work Organizations	144
8 The Third Turning Point	172
References	185
Index	211

List of Tables

3.1	Basic population information in the 2000 and 2010 censuses	40
3.2	China's Gini coefficient as compiled by the NBS	56
3.3	Annual urban per capita disposable income and rural per capita net income (in yuan)	58
3.4	Poverty line, numbers in poverty and headcount rate, 1978–2013	66
4.1	Funding and coverage of *dibao*, 1998–2013	90
4.2	Average thresholds and payments of *dibao*, 2006–2013	91
5.1	Coverage and funding of rural *dibao*, 2007–2013	106
5.2	Average assistance standard and actual payment of rural *dibao* (yuan per person per month)	109
5.3	Coverage and funding of the NCMS, 2005–2012	122
6.1	Provision of beds, number of residents and occupancy rates, 1990–2013	133
7.1	The development of social organizations	151

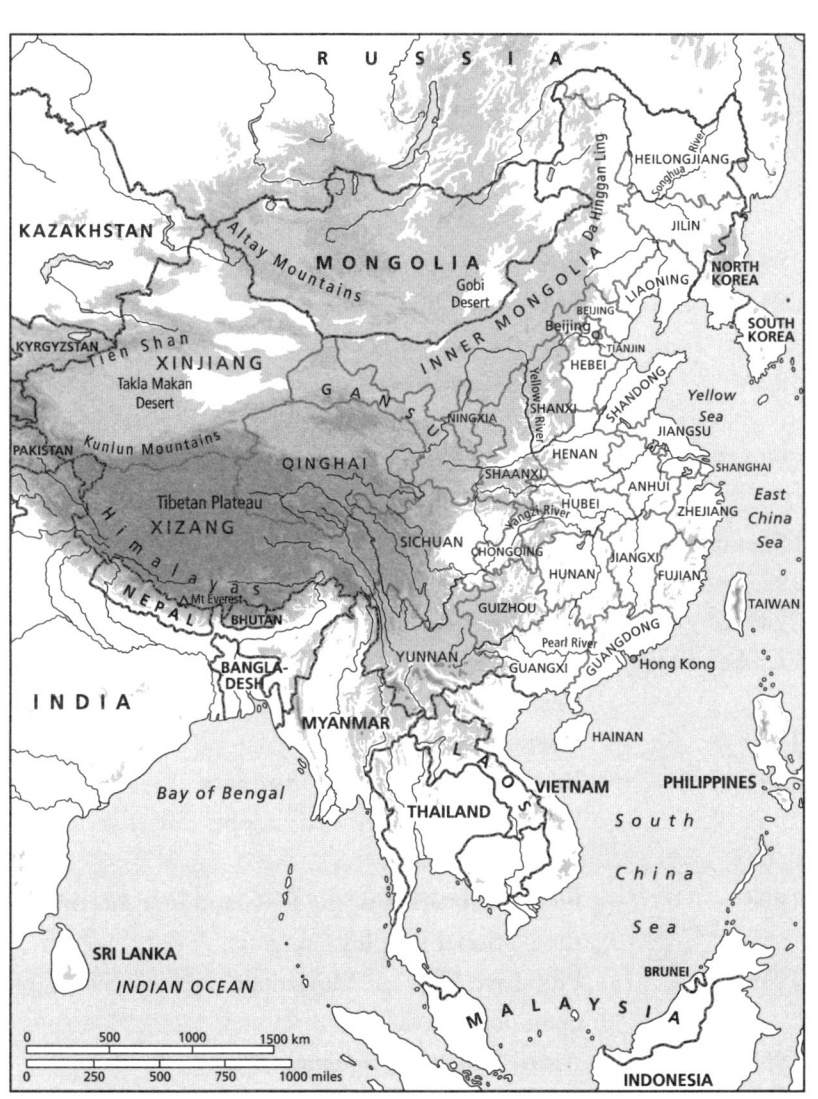

Chronology

1894–5	First Sino-Japanese War
1911	Fall of the Qing dynasty
1912	Republic of China established under Sun Yat-sen
1927	Split between Nationalists (KMT) and Communists (CCP); civil war begins
1934–5	CCP under Mao Zedong evades KMT in Long March
December 1937	Nanjing Massacre
1937–45	Second Sino-Japanese War
1945–9	Civil war between KMT and CCP resumes
October 1949	KMT retreats to Taiwan; Mao founds People's Republic of China (PRC)
1950–3	Korean War
1951	Regulations on Labour Insurance
1953–7	First Five-Year Plan; PRC adopts Soviet-style economic planning
1954	First constitution of the PRC and first meeting of the National People's Congress
1956–7	Hundred Flowers Movement, a brief period of open political debate
1957	Anti-Rightist Movement
1958–60	Great Leap Forward, an effort to transform China through rapid industrialization and collectivization

March 1959	Tibetan Uprising in Lhasa; Dalai Lama flees to India
1959–61	Three Hard Years, widespread famine with tens of millions of deaths
1960	Sino-Soviet split
1962	Sino-Indian War
October 1964	First PRC atomic bomb detonation
1966–76	Great Proletarian Cultural Revolution; Mao reasserts power
February 1972	President Richard Nixon visits China; 'Shanghai Communique' pledges to normalize US–China relations
September 1976	Death of Mao Zedong
October 1976	Ultra-leftist Gang of Four arrested and sentenced
December 1978	Deng Xiaoping assumes power; launches Four Modernizations and economic reforms
1978	One-child family planning policy introduced
1979	US and China establish formal diplomatic ties; Deng Xiaoping visits Washington
1979	PRC invades Vietnam
1982	Census reports PRC population at more than 1 billion
December 1984	Margaret Thatcher co-signs Sino-British Joint Declaration agreeing to return Hong Kong to China in 1997
1986	Bankruptcy Law
1989	Tiananmen Square protests culminate in June 4 military crackdown
1992	Deng Xiaoping's Southern Inspection Tour re-energizes economic reforms
1993–2002	Jiang Zemin, new president of PRC, continues economic growth agenda

1994	Regulations on the Work of Rural Five-Guarantees Households
1997	Decisions on Establishing a Unified Basic Pension System for Enterprise Employees
1998	Decisions on Establishing the Basic Medical Care Insurance System for Urban Employees
1999	Regulations on Unemployment Insurance; Regulations on the Guarantee of the Minimum Living Standard System for Urban Residents
November 2001	WTO accepts China as member
August 2002	World Summit on Sustainable Development held in Johannesburg; PRC ratifies 1997 Kyoto Protocol to the United Nations Framework Convention on Climate Change
2002–12	Hu Jintao General-Secretary of the CCP (and President of the PRC from 2003)
2002–3	SARS outbreak concentrated in PRC and Hong Kong
2006	PRC supplants US as largest CO_2 emitter
2003	Third Plenum of the 16th Party Congress endorsed the concept of 'Scientific Development'
2003	Proposal on Establishing New Cooperative Medical System
2005	Decisions on Perfecting the Pension System for Workers in Enterprises
2006	Sixth Plenum of the 16th Party Congress: Decisions Concerning the Construction of the Socialist and Harmonious Society
2006	National People's Congress announced the plan of Building a New Socialist Countryside
2007	Decisions on the Pilot Medical Care Insurance System for Urban Residents

2008	Labour Contract Law
August 2008	Summer Olympic Games in Beijing
2010	Shanghai World Exposition
2010	Social Insurance Law
2012	Xi Jinping appointed General-Secretary of the CCP (and President of PRC from 2013)
2013	18th Party Congress pledged to build a moderately well-off society and achieve major results on economic and social reforms by 2020

Preface

Having been born in Hong Kong, I found that my understanding of the changes under socialist China was limited. As a child, in 1958, I made my first visit to Guangzhou, China, a city 120 kilometres from Hong Kong. It took a day of travel by train (now it is a two-hour journey), and we were interrogated thoroughly at the border checkpoints at Shenzhen by Chinese immigration and customs officials. Looking hostile, a People's Liberation Army soldier holding a machine gun guarded the bridge between Hong Kong and Shenzhen. My family had taken along as many essential basic goods as we could carry, such as cooking oil, canned food, used clothing, shoes, etc., as gifts for our relatives. We had to pay a tax on items that were considered to be beyond personal use. In order for us to stay with our poor relatives, our names had to be registered with the neighbourhood police. Food was terrible and in extremely short supply. My relatives had to seek special permission to obtain some eggs for me. However, when we were treated by another relative, who worked in the customs office, we had lots to eat, including meat and soup. That was my first experience of inequality in China.

After the Cultural Revolution I made occasional tour visits to southern China. My impression was that China was extremely poor, underdeveloped and secretive. We had to live in specified hotels for foreigners and purchased goods with foreign exchange certificates from the friendship stores. My journey of academic exchange and research on social welfare in China began in the mid-1980s, when I was a junior lecturer at the University of Hong Kong. The Department of Social Work and Social Administration received invitations from the reinstated Sociology Department of Sun Yat Sen University in Guangzhou to introduce social work education into China. Under the leadership of Professor Richard Nann of the University of Hong Kong, I was responsible for initiating three major projects in 1986: setting up a social work programme at Sun Yat Sen University with courses taught by teachers from Hong Kong; introducing summer social work fieldwork placements for Hong Kong social work students in work units (neighbourhood offices, youth services, schools and non-governmental organizations); and introducing a course on social welfare in China at the University of Hong Kong (most likely the first of its kind inside or outside China since 1949).

Teaching social work and developing fieldwork placements was difficult, as no one in China at that time seemed to know what social work was. After listening to my lecture 'What is Social Work?', one student challenged me, saying that Chinese workers and peasants were also social workers, as they 'served the people'. I still remember that, in 1987, one of my masters' students from Hong Kong was detained for hours and warned by the Guangzhou city police for carrying out a survey on the welfare of industrial workers.

Inspired by Professor Nann, in 1995 I co-authored with him the book *Authority and Benevolence: Social Welfare in China*. Initially, it was difficult to find a publisher interested in our manuscript. China was perceived as a backward and somewhat isolated country, particularly after the Tiananmen protest and crackdown in 1989. World interest was based largely on curiosity rather than on the need to engage China. There were hardly any books or journal papers published internationally on this topic. The questions 'What is Social Welfare?', 'What is Social Policy?', and 'What is Social Work?' did not seem to receive a great deal of attention within China. China studies were dominated by Sinologists, who were preoccupied mainly with political and economic change. Limited publications on social welfare provisions were based chiefly on travel logs, visits and interviews with Chinese scholars rather than on empirical research. In 1994 I was able to publish a paper on social welfare reforms in China in the *Journal of Social Policy*. Presumably, this was the first time this journal had published a paper on social welfare reforms in China. In the early 1990s, the University of Hong Kong began to enrol PhD students from mainland China in social welfare courses.

In 2002, the University of Hong Kong was able to set up two masters' programmes, in social work and social service management, a collaborative project with Fudan University, Shanghai. This was the first social work programme registered under the Ministry of Education to be operated by an outside university. Because of the lack of reference material, we had to provide hundreds of donated books on social work from Hong Kong. Even in the early 2000s, university facilities were poor and teachers were poorly paid. We had to contribute an overhead projector for teaching purposes. Teachers at that time lived on the campus with students, and everyone owned a bicycle. Today, most professors live outside the campus in their own purchased house and drive to the office in their own private car. Parking is now a big problem at most universities in China.

The late 1990s saw the beginning of a thriving interest in studying social policy in China, particularly among scholars in Hong Kong. We could obtain Hong Kong-based research grants to carry out research in China, often in collaboration with our partners or with University of Hong Kong graduates. By that time, the study of social policy had emerged under different disciplines, namely sociology, political science, public administration, geography, economics and social work. The appearance of Chinese social policy scholars trained overseas had stimulated a proliferation of related publications. They often collaborated with their Western colleagues to carry out research and publish papers and books. Besides being more open, with the publication of policy documents and key statistics, the Chinese government has sponsored social policy research by local research institutes. There is also growing interest among international organizations, such as the World Bank, the Asian Development Bank, the United Nations Development Programme and the Organization for Economic Cooperation and Development, to provide consultancy to the Chinese government, and joint reports and working documents have been published. One of the major difficulties arising from studying social policy in China is that one can easily miss key publications and research studies published locally and internationally. However, internet searches for publications and information have become convenient and expedient.

In recent years, I have been more preoccupied with the provision of training to social work students and government civil servants from China. In 2006–9, supported by the Hong Kong University Grant Committee, I headed a longitudinal study on social assistance recipients in three cities. I was the international consultant for the Asian Development Bank, evaluating the impact of rural social assistance (2010–11). Since that time my focus has been on the government purchase of welfare services from non-governmental organizations, particularly in Guangdong province. As such, I was appointed as an advisor to the Committee for Social Affairs of the Guangdong Provincial Party Committee, an organization working to promote service innovation and maintain social stability.

Finally, I was honoured to be invited by Polity Press in autumn 2012 to submit a book proposal. It was indeed a formidable challenge for me as I approach my imminent full retirement, and I invited Professor Xu Yuebin of Beijing Normal University to team up with me. He has contributed the two chapters on urban and rural social protection systems. Locally, he works closely with the Ministry of Civil Affairs on welfare policy evaluation. Overseas, he has been contracted by a number of international organizations, including the Ford Foundation, the

World Bank and the Asian Development Bank, to carry out social policy studies.

Inevitably, we may easily have missed out key readings, references and perspectives and committed factual mistakes. To be sure, the study of China now involves not only a tremendous amount of reading from a variety of sources but also contested interpretations. We are fully responsible for all omissions, mistakes and misinterpretations.

Joe Leung
July 2014

List of Abbreviations

ADB	Asian Development Bank
AFEPH	Assistance for the Extremely Poor Households
BMISFUE	Basic Medical Insurance System for Urban Employees
CASS	Chinese Academy of Social Sciences
CDRF	China Development Research Foundation
CHARLS	China Health and Retirement Longitudinal Study
CMS	Cooperative Medical System
CNCA	China National Committee on Ageing
CNC	China News Centre
COEs	collective-owned enterprises
CPC	Communist Party of China
DRC	Development Research Centre
EOAPS	Employee Old-Age Pension System
GDP	gross domestic product
MCA	Ministry of Civil Affairs
MISFUE	Medical Insurance System for Urban Employees
MISFUR	Medical Insurance System for Urban Residents
MOHRSS	Ministry of Human Resources and Social Security
NBS	National Bureau of Statistics
NCMS	New Cooperative Medical System
NGO	non-governmental organization
NROAPS	New Rural Old-Age Pension System
OECD	Organization for Economic Cooperation and Development

PMIS	Public Medical Insurance System
POS	purchase of services
PPP	purchasing power parity
PRC	People's Republic of China
ROAPS	Residents' Old-Age Pension System
SOEs	state-owned enterprises
SWOs	social work organizations
TVEs	township village enterprises
UNDP	United Nations Development Programme

Chinese currency is in yuan; in July 2014, the exchange rate was approximately US$1 to 6.2 yuan.

1 Overview

THE RISE OF CHINA

Indisputably, China now is a political and economic superpower. The economic achievements resulting from the market-oriented reforms begun in the 1980s are widely considered to be phenomenal. With continuous high growth rates for three decades, China became the second largest economy in the world in 2010, and with expected continuous growth, albeit at a slower rate, it is predicted to become a high-income economy by 2020 (*Caijing*, 2013) or 2030 (World Bank, 2013; OECD, 2013d).

However, China's nominal per capita GDP in 2012 was only US$5,430 (based on US$ at 2014 rates), ranking 91st in the world; in terms of Purchasing Power Parity (PPP) it was $10,900, ranking 89th in the world (World Bank, 2014). As an 'upper-middle-income economy', China has economic wealth similar to countries such as Ecuador, Jamaica, Algeria, Belize and the Maldives. Its strong economic growth is attributed partly to high investment and savings rates. High saving rates and low consumption expenditures imply that the Chinese people are feeling insecure and uncertain about their future social expenditure needs. Therefore, they consume less and save more.

In terms of social development as presented in the Human Development Index compiled by the United Nations Development Programme (UNDP), China ranked 101st out of 185 countries in 2012, being considered as a 'medium human development' country

(UNDP, 2013a). The Human Development Index comprises three dimensions, namely life expectancy at birth, mean years of schooling and expected years of schooling, and per capita GDP. China's poverty alleviation efforts have been considered by international organizations to be a successful learning example. Between 1981 and 2010, over 680 million people were lifted out of extreme poverty (based on the World Bank poverty threshold of US$1.25 a day), and the poverty rate dropped from 84 per cent in 1980 to 10 per cent in 2013. Over the past three decades, China alone has contributed to three-quarters of the world's total decline in extreme poverty (*The Economist*, 1 June 2013, p. 11). Between the 1980s and 2000s, life expectancy increased from 67 to 73 years, and child mortality under the age of five years declined from 65 to 18 deaths per 1,000 (Zhuang et al., 2012, p. xi). Overall, economic growth has inevitably brought with it a general improvement in the standard of living.

Despite these remarkable economic and social achievements, however, marketization has triggered a wide array of social issues, leading to a new set of risks for the people. China's current model of development has been described as 'unstable, unbalanced, uncoordinated and unsustainable' (Wang and Zheng, 2013, p. 104). For one thing, improvements in living standards have not been evenly distributed. While China's income inequality levels may remain lower than those of South American countries such as Brazil and South Africa, they are well above the average of most OECD and Asian countries (OECD, 2010a). The crux of the problem is the speed at which China has changed, from being a relatively egalitarian society in the 1970s into one which today faces wide income disparities. Such inequality has now unquestionably become a threat to social stability and social cohesion.

Some Chinese people have found themselves facing higher risks of income loss because of social dislocation, insecure employment, poor health and inadequate social protection (Leung, 2005; Shue and Wong,

2007; Zhang et al., 2007). Facing a more pluralistic employment structure, accompanied by marketization reforms of social security, the emerging social protection system has increasingly shown itself to be inadequate, segmented, ineffective and even regressive (Leung, 2003; Wong and Flynn, 2001; Saunders and Shang, 2001; Leung and Xu, 2009; Gao and Riskin, 2009; Gao, 2010; Gao et al., 2013).

Public anxiety and dissatisfaction with declining pension benefits and the rising cost of medical care, housing and educational expenses is mounting. According to the 2009 annual report of the Chinese Academy of Social Sciences (CASS), the relative slowdown of economic growth resulting from the global recession has sharpened social inequalities in China (Ru et al., 2009). Based on public opinion surveys, more people were feeling anxious about income disparities, food safety, environmental deterioration, labour protection, violation of the rights of vulnerable people, and corruption (CNC, 6 November 2012). All told, individuals are more and more worried about the increasingly competitive and costly educational system, unaffordable housing, environmental deterioration, and the lack of protection in old age.

In consequence, the determinants of Chinese social policy will need to shift focus, from a primary concern with facilitating economic growth towards a more balanced development that addresses the needs of vulnerable groups. China has to formulate an innovative model to guide future development in the face of profound and unprecedented challenges. Welfare scholars have asked whether the country's social policy experiences can be classified into some existing social welfare typologies and regimes, or whether these represent a completely new model. What are the key lessons for developing countries?

TURNING POINTS

Throughout the process, China's experiences of reform have been substantially different from those of other countries, both former socialist countries and those in the West. Since the establishment of the People's Republic of China (PRC) in 1949 there have been two major transformations or social revolutions (Whyte, 2010a, ch. 1) – the turning points at which the country achieved major restructuring of its developmental direction, priorities and institutions. These turning points involved extensive and comprehensive changes to the socio-economic system and, to a lesser extent, the political system. In making the transformation, the Chinese are convinced that maintaining social stability is paramount.

At the first turning point, in 1949, China became a socialist country, which brought a new regime and national unity. By 1954 the construction of the socialist command economy and society was almost complete. But attempts to deepen socialist reforms during the Great Leap Forward and the Cultural Revolution left the country in chaos and disarray. The avowed egalitarian society promised people a relatively stable livelihood at the expense of economic development and civil liberties. Despite being largely egalitarian, the economy was inward-looking and underdeveloped.

After almost thirty years, in 1978, China took another turn, to incorporate by degrees a market mechanism into its economic and social service systems. The country was opened up to foreign investment, technology and trade. Without pursuing radical reforms of privatization and liberalization, economic and administrative decentralization incentivised local governments, state-owned enterprises (SOEs), industrial workers and peasants to enhance efficiency and productivity. Yet, despite initial economic success, the pro-economic growth and decollectivization development strategy gradually dismantled the traditional social protection system, creating a profound welfare gap. More importantly, it has produced widening income and regional disparities, including inequality in access to social protection and social services and the increasing marginalization of vulnerable sections of the population.

In contrast to the two earlier turning points, the third turning point is more diffuse and does not seem to have an exact starting point or year, although this is generally recognized as 2006, when the then General Party Secretary, Hu Jintao, announced a new developmental directive to construct a harmonious society. Since then, China's economic and social development has seemingly entered a new stage, described as 'changing gear'. Together with an inevitable slowing down of economic growth, the country is facing a new economic and social environment involving an increasingly globalized economy, labour shortages and rising labour costs, population mobility, environmental deterioration, an ageing population and rising income inequality. Facing new challenges and economic slowdown, China requires a radical shift in its development priorities and strategies, not only in the economy but also in social welfare. With such a shift, quality of growth becomes more important than quantity.

In the new turning point, new social welfare programmes, including pensions, health-care insurance and social assistance schemes for both urban and rural residents, as well as social care programmes for older people, have been embarked upon. Social spending has showed significant increases, and central government intervention has become more active. The government has promised a move from a pro-market social policy towards a more balanced and inclusive model of development (Zhao and Lim, 2010; Shi, 2012; World Bank, 2013; OECD, 2013d, 2014; L. T. Zhao, 2013; Ngok, 2013a, 2013b; Gao et al., 2013; Li et al., 2013; Besharov and Baehler, 2013).

The Chinese government has designated the year 2020 as its target to accomplish a number of objectives, among them the attainment of a moderately prosperous society (*xiakang*) and the establishment of a comprehensive social protection system; 2020 is also one year before the 100th anniversary of the establishment of the Communist Party of China (CPC). In addition to the Five-Year Plan on Economic and Social Development, all government initiatives are strategically aimed at 2020, as specified in the communique of the Third Plenum of the 18th Party Congress in November 2013. By 2020, if successful in achieving a series of developmental objectives, China will have accomplished the third turning point and transform into a modernized and high-income nation, with a mature and sustainable economy supported by a universal social welfare system. As advances in social welfare have been lagging significantly behind economic achievement, China has to pursue a more vigorous strategy in its social welfare system in this new stage of development.

The World Bank published a report in 2013 entitled *China 2030: Building a Modern, Harmonious, and Creative High-Income Society*. This highlights the need for China to adopt a new development strategy to rebalance the role of government and market, private sector and society, in order to reach the goal of becoming a high-income economy by 2030. Facing changing social and economic circumstances, the pro-economic growth model, which has apparently been successful in the country's phenomenal economic performance, needs to be replaced by a more inclusive model (OECD, 2013a, 2013d, 2014). China's development is at a crossroads, and further structural reforms are needed to ensure broad, sustainable and equitable growth in the years to come.

China's new social welfare system should have wide coverage; it should be accessible to all, and eligibility should be based on rights. In order to be pluralistic, the country needs to construct a new governance system with shared responsibility between different levels of government, as well as between civil society, the state and the market. Effective social welfare programmes can not only meet mounting social needs but also mitigate social conflicts and promote social cohesion. If China fails to make this turning point, the result may be declining living standards and rising political and social instability. The legitimacy of the CPC to rule continuously will be based on its ability to deliver to the people the promise of a more shared and inclusive growth.

CONCEPTUALIZING CHINA'S SOCIAL WELFARE

The term 'social welfare' has been used in tandem with other terms such as 'well-being', 'social security', 'social services', 'social development' and 'social policy'. In a wider perspective, it is the collective response to social problems (Segal, 2010, p. 3). It can include public and social policy addressing poverty, social deprivation, and inequality in resource distribution. Accordingly, social welfare would cover programmes on social security, human services and social assistance. In a narrow sense, it can be referred to as the provision of social care services and programmes, and support for those in need. Social welfare policy is defined as 'collectively defined rules, regulations, procedures, and objectives to address social problems and those institutional problems that affect the implementation of specific policies' (Jansson, 1990, p. 18).

Under the socialist regime in China, social welfare was considered to be a feature of the capitalist countries. Together with social science disciplines, the subject of social welfare was banned in universities and research institutes in 1953. Since it was an alien concept, government ministries possessed no such term or scope of work. After the market-oriented reforms the concept was, in a narrow sense, referred to as relief work assisting vulnerable groups within the social security system. The term 'social security' embraced employment-based social insurance programmes, social welfare for the vulnerable such as the elderly and the disabled, social relief for the poor and victims of natural disasters, and preferential treatment for ex-soldiers (Leung and Nann, 1995, pp. xx–xxi). In recent years, it has been considered in a broader sense to include provisions for retirement, health care, education, employment, social assistance and special disadvantaged groups (CDRF, 2012). Overall, social welfare has been largely state-centred, with underdevelopment of the private and non-profit sectors.

Traditional measures on welfare, well-being and poverty would involve composite indicators on income, jobs, education, the environment and health. In this book, many of these social and economic indicators will be deployed to indicate the level of social development, where possible, in comparison to the development of other countries. In China, because of its vast landmass and large population, 'averaged' figures may cover up wide variations across regions. The accuracy and reliability of its official figures have been challenged from time to time (Orlik, 2011, p. 6). Equally important, the use of subjective measurements or indicators is becoming popular to inform social policy performance (Deeming, 2013). These often rely on self-reported surveys that capture personal experiences, psychological functioning, attitudes and cognitive assessments – preferences of 'how people think about and experience their lives' (OECD, 2013b, p. 10). The significance of subjective welfare implies that there are effective channels for people to express their views and feelings, as well as to influence the policy-making process.

Admittedly, the Chinese government has largely monopolized most of the mass media and actively shaped public opinion. Apparently, ordinary people may not have secure and open channels to articulate their genuine interests and dissenting views. Yet, the Chinese government has been increasingly sensitive and, to some extent, responsive to public opinion in policy-making so as to mitigate social tensions (Tang, 2005). The CASS has published its annual public opinion surveys on the quality of life since 1993 (Ru et al., 2013). Ironically, opinion surveys often indicate that the Chinese people are on the whole satisfied with the government and the progress being made. However, there is more dissatisfaction expressed in the form of petitions, protests and violent disturbances.

China's development is often regarded as unique and distinct, though it is difficult to compare China with other countries in terms of agreed yardsticks. Admittedly, it has been difficult to conceptualize China's welfare development, which has been contested. Classical studies on welfare in East European socialist countries (George and

Manning, 1980; Adam, 1991; Deacon and Szalai, 1990) and modernization theories expecting all contemporary welfare states to converge in development (Rimlinger, 1971; Wilensky, 1975) have become less relevant.

Drawing on the experiences of East Asian countries, popular concepts to capture China's development include 'developmental state' (Johnson, 1982; White and Wade, 1988; Weiss, 2000; Stubbs, 2009), 'Beijing consensus' (Ramo, 2004; Halper, 2010; Kennedy, 2010; Hsu et al., 2011) and 'middle-income trap' (Zhuang, 2008; Zhuang et al., 2012, p. xii; OECD, 2013d). These conceptualizations are based largely on economic rather than social development and all point to the need for a strong and active government having a close relationship with the private sector. The success of East Asian countries may provide a number of loosely constructed models and experiences by which to guide China's development, though China's large demographic and geographical size and the complex relationship between local and central government make direct application difficult (Xia, 2000; Naughton, 2010).

Studying Western welfare states, Esping-Andersen (1990) formulated three types of welfare regimes, namely the liberal, the democratic and the corporate. His typology did not take in Asian countries, as most, with the exception of Japan, were not perceived as welfare states per se. Following the economic success of East Asian countries, world attention has been drawn to understand their social welfare policy. Subsequently, there have been efforts to develop a welfare regime model which can aggregate the experiences of East Asian countries (Rose and Shiratori, 1986; Jones, 1993; Goodman and Peng, 1996; Goodman et al., 1998; Wilding, 2000; Holliday, 2000, 2005; Gough, 2002, 2004a, 2004b; Holliday and Wilding, 2003; Aspalter, 2005, 2006; Lee and Chan, 2007; Haggard and Kaufman, 2008; Hwang, 2011; Izuhara, 2013). These efforts at classification were often focused on selected countries and territories, notably South Korea, Japan,

Taiwan, Hong Kong and Singapore, and the developmental experiences of China are often excluded. In short, the strategic role of the state is found not only in economic development but also in social welfare development.

The East Asian welfare model can also be described as a 'Confucian welfare state' (Jones, 1993; Leung and Nann, 1995; Goodman and Peng, 1996; Lin, 1999; Walker and Wong, 2005). Confucian values emphasize social stability and order over conflict, collective over individual interests, obedience to authority, family obligations, a work ethic, and the importance of education. In justifying state authoritarianism, social justice, social rights and redistributive policies are neglected (Holliday and Wilding, 2003). In counteracting Western influences, the concept of Asian values has been widely used by some Asian leaders to promote the uniqueness of Asian culture rooted in traditional Chinese Confucianism and Asian religions. Despite the setback during the 1997 Asian financial crisis, the resilience of the East Asian Tigers and China in regaining their strength seems to have reinvigorated the concept of Asian culture. The rise of China has also increased the value of Asian culture as an alternative to wholesale Westernization.

The East Asian Tigers are classified as 'productivist welfare regimes', where social policy is subordinate to economic policy (Holliday, 2000, 2005). Despite low social spending, these countries invest highly in education, health care and workfare. On the whole, redistribution for greater equality is not a developmental priority. Social policy serves to enhance labour productivity. These countries can hardly be called 'welfare states' as their political leaders are often found to be 'anti-welfare' (Walker and Wong, 2005). With their low social spending and selective focus, East Asian countries are often seen as marked by segmented and underdeveloped social welfare programmes (Midgley and Tang, 2009, p. 4), although they have reasonably good social outcomes in health, education and equality indicators. They seem to provide a model of the welfare state that is quite distinct from those of Western countries (Jacobs, 2000; Holliday, 2000). In fact, in terms of the Human Development Index, these East Asian countries and territories are all regarded as 'very high human development' economies (in 2012 Japan ranked 10th, South Korea 12th, Hong Kong 13th, and Singapore 19th) (UNDP, 2013a). Not surprisingly, Holliday and Wilding (2003, p. 8) challenged the argument that the social welfare of East Asian countries is 'underdeveloped'.

In a loose sense, as an ideal-typical category, China has adopted some of the key features of the East Asian welfare regime, including low social spending, strong occupational welfare, limited government intervention, a low redistributive function, and the subordination of social policy to economic growth. In a real sense, East Asian countries vary significantly in terms of the structure and finance of their social protection systems, benefit levels and coverage. As an illustration, the Social Protection Index (total social protection expenditures per total reference population divided by a regional poverty line) of 27 Asian countries, developed by the Asian Development Bank (ADB), showed a wide variation. In terms of expenditure on social protection as a proportion of total GDP, Japan's spending (19.2 per cent) more than doubles that of South Korea (7.9 per cent), and is almost four times that of China (5.4 per cent) and more than five times that of Singapore (3.5 per cent) (ADB, 2013). South Korea and Taiwan have state-financed social insurance systems in pensions and health care, whereas health care and retirement in Singapore is largely dependent on personal savings accounts in the Central Provident Fund. In Hong Kong, the savings accounts of the Mandatory Provident Fund are for retirement protection, and hospitalization is largely publicly financed (Wagstaff, 2005; Park, 2012). Following the economic success and democratization movement of the East Asian countries, a common trend among them is their continuous welfare expansion (Izuhara, 2013, p. 2).

Like other East Asian countries, China faces rising social risks and expectations because of economic prosperity coupled with an ageing population. It is ready to increase social spending and intervention to establish or restructure its 'welfare state' with universal coverage and need-based entitlements. However, China is too large and its welfare system too segmented, and there are substantial differences in living standards both between regions and between rural and urban areas. The subnational dimension of policy is often either ignored or sidestepped in the classification of welfare regimes (Hudson, 2012). One can hardly group the developmental experiences of the coastal provinces, such as Guangdong and Zhejiang, with those inland, such as Tibet and Guizhou. On the whole, social policy is still considered to be 'supporting and not hindering economic growth' (Aspalter, 2006, p. 297). However, there is a clear recognition that increased social welfare provision is an attempt to maintain social stability and the legitimacy of the CPC.

Notwithstanding the wide variation in socio-economic and political situations across the East Asian countries and territories, some common elements and differences in social welfare responses are apparent. It is misleading to think in terms of one homogeneous, overarching 'East Asian welfare model' (Goodman et al., 1998, p. 14). Overall, the debate on East Asian welfare regimes has not yet reached a clear consensus, and the concept is still loosely constructed, largely imprecise and incoherent. More importantly, China may have learned from the experiences of East Asian welfare states, but its low economic development is yet too immature for it to be grouped with Japan and the Asian Tigers. The East Asian welfare model is potentially useful both for pointing out important differences from traditional Western approaches and for indicating significant similarities in social policy aims, objectives and priorities within the region. Overall, the developmental experiences of East Asian countries are particularly relevant to guide China's post-socialist economic, political and social reforms.

At issue is whether the Chinese model can replace the Western model of modernization (Zhao and Lim, 2010). Overall, China has neither a learning model nor a blueprint for other developing countries. It emphasizes that each country should have its own unique road to development, with reference to its own socio-economic and political situation; there should be no universal or one-size-fits-all model. In essence, emphasis is put on the strong role of the state in policy and legislative formulation and reform, provision of resource support, regulating, directing and monitoring policy implementation, and building the innovation and governance capacity of local government.

By stressing its distinctiveness in building up its socio-economic system, China also actively learns from others and at the same time makes incremental, piecemeal and bottom-up modifications. Social reforms are guided more by pragmatic concerns than by a clear visionary direction or a comprehensive developmental blueprint (Leung, 2000; Wan, 2014). Assuming the role of macro-control at the top, the central government delineates broad guiding principles for reforms. These reforms are indicative rather than mandatory and universal. At the local level, government is encouraged to experiment with different solutions and models according to local circumstances and financial capacity. Meanwhile, policy adjustments are made based on adaptive learning from research studies and advice from international organizations and consultants. After some years of continuous experimentation and evaluation, the government, often through legislation, attempts to unify diversified practices by promoting one of the more successful models.

The strength of this decentralized approach is that it can minimize resistance and facilitate readjustments through feedback from programme implementation. The shortcoming is that regional disparities in social service development are substantial. Given the decentralized and segmented system, access and entitlement to social services and social security benefits is differentiated primarily among occupational groups, economic sectors and geographical regions.

OBJECTIVES AND CHAPTER OUTLINE

As international interest in understanding the social life of China increases, the major objective of this book is to provide an objective and wider perspective on China's critical and interrelated social issues, policy responses and prospects. It is aimed at social welfare scholars and students enrolled on courses relating to social policy, social welfare and social development in China. We have chosen to give a broad overview, the background and analysis rather than going deeply into an examination of individual issues and policy programmes. Indeed, each of these social issues and programmes, such as pensions, medical care, migrants, poverty, rural development and inequalities, is deserving of an independent study. In the last decade, several edited volumes on China's social policy have focused mainly on macro-level social policy development rather than specific social welfare services (Chan et al., 2008; Zhao and Lim, 2010; CDRF, 2012; L. T. Zhao, 2013).

In order to provide a better understanding of social welfare issues in China, analysis has to relate to the changing socio-economic and political background, drawing references from various disciplines. The study of social issues, such as income inequality and poverty, social protection, demographic transition, population mobility, non-governmental organizations (NGOs) and community governance, involves research and publications from various disciplines, including social welfare, sociology, demography, economics, geography, history, public administration and political science. In fact, relevant references in social welfare publications are still limited relative to other disciplines. To make an objective analysis, both international and local references must be tapped and compared. Notwithstanding the fact that China studies often involve contested and controversial interpretations, it is important for the analysis to be evidence-based, including, where possible, major perspectives and arguments.

The rise of China has led to a proliferation of publications on its economic and social reforms; book series, special journal issues, and papers in discipline-specific journals are becoming popular. International bodies, such as the World Bank, the OECD, the UNDP, the International Labour Office and the ADB, have been active in collaborating with research partners in China to produce reports on the country's economic and social issues. For example, the UNDP has published the *China Human Development Report* every two to three years since 1997 (a total of seven reports). Up to June 2014, the World Bank had produced a total of 459 publications on China, second only to India (646 publications). By June 2014, the OECD had issued 213 publications related to China, even though China is not a member of the OECD. Admittedly, a community of Chinese scholars trained locally and overseas has emerged, and they have become more active, often in joint authorship with Western scholars, in publishing internationally in academically refereed publications.

The Chinese government has pledged to move away from an economic growth model towards one that considers inclusive growth. As social welfare is one of the primary institutions addressing income inequalities, the key concern of this book is to examine whether social welfare in China is redistributive or regressive. The first chapter provides the background and conceptual issues in analysing social welfare in China. Chapter 2 presents the historical development of social policy from the establishment of the PRC in 1949 to the beginning of the 12th Five-Year Plan for National Economic and Social Development in 2011, as well the beginning of a new era under the leadership of Xi Jinping. Chapter 3 presents selected key social challenges under market reforms, including demographic transition, rural migrants, left-behind children, income inequalities and poverty. Chapters 4 and 5 review the social protection reforms in urban and rural areas, respectively. The universalization and harmonization reforms of the social insurance and social assistance programmes are considered. Significant improvements in social insurance coverage, including pensions and health care, particularly in the rural areas, are registered. Chapters 6 and 7 attempt an analysis of the social welfare services for older people and the emerging development of social work professions and welfare NGOs – an area in which international publications are still limited. These two chapters provide readers with a general picture of the rapidly changing landscape of social welfare provision in China. The final chapter draws conclusions on the strengths and weaknesses of China's development, specifically in tackling income inequalities, suggests how the country can move towards a relatively well-off society, and advocates the need for a more comprehensive and structural transformation.

2 From Socialism to Modernization

This chapter traces the transformation of social policy and social welfare in different periods after 1949 in the context of socio-economic and political development. Changes are often attributed to the dominant influence of CPC leaders, including Mao Zedong (1949–76), Deng Xiaoping (1978–92), Jiang Zemin (1989–2002), Hu Jintao (2002–13) and, recently, Xi Jinping (from 2013). It is noteworthy that the policy-making process in the PRC is not in the hands of a single individual. In reality, members of different factions within the leadership of the CPC influence policy decisions, and the implementation of policies is in the hands of bureaucrats who are known for protecting their own interests in translating policies made at the centre to action at lower echelons (Lieberthal and Oksenberg, 1989, pp. 16–18).

THE FIRST TURNING POINT: ESTABLISHING THE IRON RICE BOWL

On coming to power on 1 October 1949, the CPC leadership undertook the formidable task of rebuilding a nation still reeling from the aftermath of the Second World War and a civil war. After gaining full control and achieving the national unity so long desired, there was an urgent need for the CPC to maintain social stability through the establishment of new political and government structures and to revitalize the economy. As described by Mao Zedong, the 'Great Helmsman', China was 'one poor and two blank', meaning that it was lacking material resources and underdeveloped in culture and science. Facing near economic collapse and international blockade, China relied heavily upon aid from the Soviet Union in the form of trained technicians and capital loans. More importantly, the Soviet model of socialism for political, economic and social development was thus the logical choice. Equipped only with its previous administrative experience in governing the guerrilla bases in the countryside, the CPC's challenge in rebuilding China was profound. The social construction of a new China involved the removal of the 'three big mountains' – imperialism, feudalism and bureaucratic capitalism.

Among mounting social problems were unemployment, drug addiction, crime, prostitution and poverty. For example, the number of unemployed had reached almost 5 million, or 24 per cent of the working-age population (Seldon and Lippit, 1982, p. 4). Initially, the Chinese government provided a mixture of aid, including cash assistance, mutual help through material and financial donations, the promotion of neighbourhood-based self-salvation economic production groups, assignments to public work projects, and reduction of taxes to assist the unemployed and poverty-stricken. The principal approach was through job placements and close supervision supplemented by heavy political education (Riskin, 1987, p. 61; Leung, 1994). Enterprises were not allowed to dismiss employees.

Social science teaching was withdrawn from the university curriculum in 1953, and welfare services provided by foreign missionaries and local charity organizations were either nationalized or closed down. The Marriage Law, enacted in 1950, provided the freedom of marriage, divorce and gender equality. Parental authority over marriage-related decisions was restricted. 'Holding up half of the sky', women were encouraged to work and engage in manual labour like their male counterparts. Family policy served to shift the traditional loyalty of individuals from the family to the country as a whole. Divorce rates soared dramatically in the early 1950s (Leung and Nann, 1995, p. 21).

Under the centrally planned economy, full and lifelong employment, the extensive rationing of basic commodities (food and clothing), job creation and assignment, and restricted labour mobility were regarded as the superior features of socialism. Modelled after the Leninist model of social security, the 1951 Labour Insurance Regulations prescribed the need for work units to provide comprehensive social security benefits covering retirement, health care and work injury. Following Marxist–Leninist ideology, the working class was accorded a privileged status in China's socialist society. In the rural areas, wholesale land reforms in the early 1950s eliminated former rich landowners and landlords and redistributed plots to the poorer peasants. Gradual collectivization of agriculture involved the formation of cooperatives in 1956 and communes in 1958. The 'Five Guarantees' scheme was introduced in 1956, providing food, clothing, medical care, housing and burial arrangements for the destitute.

The urban-biased policy is described as 'primitive accumulation', in which peasants were forced to sell their grain at low prices to the state. While the peasants lived at subsistence level, urban residents were guaranteed a food supply and were able to live on low wages (Spence, 1990, p. 544). Since social welfare was employment-centred, each work unit functioned as a self-sufficient 'welfare society'. As such, urban residents were guaranteed jobs and were provided with heavily subsidized food, education, housing, medical care and consumer goods, as well as retirement protection. Based on distribution decisions made by the local administration, a basic, egalitarian security network – the so-called iron rice bowl – was established, with high employment, high welfare and low wages (Leung, 1994). In contrast, peasants faced the plight of the price differential 'scissors problem', in which the procurement prices of agricultural products were kept low while the prices of industrial products for agricultural use, such as fertilizer, pesticide and farming equipment, kept rising (Whyte, 2010b, p. 10).

The process of nationalization of the industries was largely completed by 1956 and the collectivization of rural farming by 1960. Being impatient with the pace of reform, Mao Zedong launched the Great Leap Forward (1958–60). Through increased collectivization, communes were set up in rural areas. Under the three-tier structure of people's commune, production brigade and production team, incomes were shared out according to work points, based on contribution and needs. Social services, such as public canteens, sewing stations and nurseries, were provided centrally. Peasants were not allowed to have private plots. Through the use of low-cost paramedical personnel – 'bare-foot doctors' – during the Cultural Revolution, the Cooperative Medical System (CMS) emphasized preventive health care and public hygiene improvements.

In 1950, life expectancy was only around 35 years and infant mortality stood at 265 per 1,000 live births. By 1982, life expectancy had increased to 68 and infant mortality had decreased to 35 per 1,000 live births (Hsiao, 1984). Following the general improvement in the quality of life, China experienced the first phase of demographic transition. High birth rates, declining mortality rates and a strong growth rate meant that China's population structure was marked by a large proportion of young people. According to the first national census in 1953, the population stood at 588 million. The birth rate was 37 per 1,000, while the mortality rate had declined to 14 per 1,000 and the natural growth rate was 23 per 1,000 (NBS, 2014). As a result, the structure of China's population moved from a stage of 'high birth rate, high mortality rate, and low increase', typical of an underdeveloped society, to a stage of 'high birth rate, declining mortality rate, and high increase'.

The proposed New Population Theory in 1957 to control population increase, made by a Malthusian demographer, Ma Yinchu, was criticized by Mao Zedong as an attempt to discredit the superiority of socialism (Freeberne, 1964). The 'man–mouth' theory (having more people will make feeding them more difficult) was replaced by Mao's 'man–hand' theory (having more people will create more resources). Under a pro-growth population policy, the fertility rate was around five children per woman. Under the 'first wave' of population increase, the natural growth rate between 1953 and 1957 reached a height of over 20 per 1,000. In 1960, because of the disastrous Great Leap Forward, the natural growth rate had dropped to a negative figure. However, it began to rise again, to 21.4 per 1,000 in 1962 and to 33.5 per 1,000 in 1963. This period was regarded as the 'second wave' of population increase. Because of the introduction of the family planning campaign in 1973 to promote late marriage, spacing out the years of childbirth and having fewer children, in 1978 the natural growth rate declined to around 12 and fertility to 2.3 (Leung and Nann, 1995, p. 12).

Under socialism, China was often perceived as an egalitarian society. The Gini coefficient in Chinese cities in 1978 was only 0.19 (Khan and Riskin, 2001). Rather than genuinely egalitarian, the socialist system built up by Mao was described by Whyte as feudalistic, 'socialist serfdom' (2010b, p. 20). Even the egalitarianism of the Cultural Revolution was segmented and partial. Inequalities in income, housing, schooling and other resources across work organizations, locales, villages and regions were still substantial. In fact, over half of the population lived in a state of subsistence poverty (CDRF, 2009, p. 3). Despite the claim to be building up an egalitarian socialist society, Mao Zedong created a dichotomy in Chinese society, dividing the rural and urban areas. Under socialism in the 1950s, people were classified into different social categories, such as landlords, poor peasants, workers and capitalists, based on class origin. Later, people were classified into cadres, workers, peasants, army and intellectuals. These labels affected people's access to education and employment, as well as their social status.

Work units (danwei)

Under the socialist system, the state controlled major social and economic resources. People were assigned to work units in the urban areas and cooperatives, later communes, in the rural areas. On the one hand, work units were appendages of the state. They relied on the state to provide resources (raw material and finance), assign personnel, set wages, purchase products, reimburse losses and claim profits. In other words, there was no open and competitive commodity and labour market. On the other hand, work units enjoyed the autonomy of self-government.

As the employing organizations, which included the state-owned enterprises (SOEs), government offices (government ministries, departments and bureaus), public institutions (government-administered institutions, such as universities, schools, hospitals and research units) and collectively owned enterprises (COEs; enterprises owned by township governments), work units were 'mediating organizations', serving not only economic but also political, administrative and social functions. In other words, a person could obtain not only their wages but also their social status, identity and social protection from the work unit. From receiving education, medical care, housing, cultural activities, social security benefits, food rations and family planning advice, to seeking certification for travel, marriage and the right to give birth to children, to political education and mobilization, recruitment of Party members, the mediation of disputes, and the disciplining of criminals – the work units were central (Walder, 1986; Whyte, 1974; Leung and Nann, 1995; Lu and Perry, 1997). Under the socialist system, one could not imagine living without the patronage of a work unit.

As a summary, the work unit provided the following.

+ *Social security* Non-contributory social insurance schemes covered medical care and retirement support. Expenses were counted as

operational costs of individual work units. Unemployment insurance was considered unnecessary.
* *Subsidies* State subsidies in cash and in kind covered food, travel, fuel, electricity, etc.
* *Collective welfare* Financed as operational expenses, facilities and services managed by the unions included schools, libraries, cultural centres, barber shops, clinics, canteens, hospitals, kindergartens, nurseries and sports centres.
* *Personal welfare* Among individualized services were social assistance and poverty alleviation, family planning, re-employment services, mediation of family disputes, care of the disabled, and disciplining of delinquents. They were provided by Party cadres from the Communist Youth Leagues, unions and the Women's Federation.

In short, the work unit functioned as a 'mini-society' in itself, providing 'three irons': the iron rice bowl (job security), the iron wage (wage differential low and adjustment rare) and the iron position (transfers were not possible). It provided secure protection for its employees, but there were no incentives to encourage productivity.

Household registration (hukou)

The first Chinese Constitution in 1954 provided people with the freedom of settlement and movement. But industrialization drew rural peasants into the cities throughout the 1950s. The urbanization rate increased rapidly, from 10.2 per cent of the population in 1949 to 15.4 per cent in 1957 (Kamal-Chaoui et al., 2009, p. 7). In 1955, Chinese people held either agricultural (rural) or non-agricultural (urban) status, based on their parents' status. To prevent peasants from moving into cities and to facilitate population management, the government introduced the household registration system (*hukou*) in 1958. Under this system, urban enterprises were not allowed to employ rural migrants. The neighbourhood police would keep detailed information of the members of each household. Any person who wished to leave their place of *hukou* had to report to the local police for permission. In principle, an individual could change their *hukou* through marrying someone with different *hukou*, getting a job in an SOE, joining the army, graduating from university or, in the 1990s, buying a house in the city. In reality, however, it was extremely difficult to change one's *hukou* status (Chan and Zhang, 2009).

In essence, the social welfare system in the urban areas was modelled after the welfare state, with full guaranteed employment, social insurance coverage and extensive state subsidies. The government was responsible only for taking care of the 'three nos' – those who could not work, had no family support, and had no other source of income. These were mainly orphans, childless older people and the disabled. In contrast, rural social welfare was largely residual, based on family and collective protection for the destitute. The social problems found commonly in Western societies, such as drug addiction, prostitution, sexual diseases, youth offenders, unwed mothers, welfare dependency, child poverty, obesity, etc., were almost entirely absent in this socialist society.

In summary, in a closed society with limited internal and external mobility, poverty and deprivation were not considered an issue at all. Chinese people relied mainly on information and interpretation from the official channels and were not informed of what was happening outside the country. The state monopolized and controlled most of society's resources. Reliant on their work units and collectives, people were on the whole guaranteed a basic livelihood and security. In return, they had to give up the basic freedoms and rights of employment, faith, movement, education, lifestyle and organization. Moral judgements on what was right and what was wrong were provided by the Party. People were told to accept commands and were mobilized in campaigns passively. They were accorded better social status and privileges through Party membership, family background (parental status), *hukou*, SOE employment or being a member of a government cadre. In other words, China was not particularly egalitarian under socialist rule.

THE SECOND TURNING POINT: TRANSITION TOWARDS A MARKET ECONOMY

After the Cultural Revolution, China's economy and social situation were in complete disarray. The Chinese leadership under Deng Xiaoping, the 'Chief Architect', fully understood that the previous socialist model did not work; but there were no clear successful models to copy. Overseas trips to the West and Japan facilitated the leadership in being more open to adopting the idea of a market economy (Vogel, 2011), and the years of market-oriented reforms after 1978 were marked by gradualism and readjustment. Deng's development theory prioritized economic construction and growth, replacing Mao Zedong's emphasis on self-reliance and class struggle. Though Deng did not hold the top position in the Party after 1978, his influence on the adoption of market-oriented reforms had been well calculated.

The role of the market in the economy was gradually strengthened through the introduction of market models in different years. Central planning mechanisms in job assignment, job protection, wage differentials, regulating SOEs and price determination were gradually replaced by market mechanisms. In short, competitive manufacturing and the labour market re-emerged gradually. In 1980, Deng envisioned the 'three-step strategic development'. Step one was to double GDP between 1980 and 1990 and meet the basic living needs of the people in terms of food and clothing. The second step was to quadruple GDP by the year 2000, and the third step was to achieve a moderately wealthy country (*xiaokang*) by the middle of the twenty-first century. At this point, it is expected that the Chinese people will have achieved a high standard of living and modernization. Growth in GDP was perceived as central to modernizing China (Leung, 2000).

All reforms were introduced incrementally and pragmatically. The approach was often described as 'feeling for the stones in crossing the river', 'seeking truth from facts', and 'it doesn't matter whether a cat is white or black, as long as it catches mice'. Because of the emphasis on 'inequality or imbalanced development strategy' by 'allowing some people and regions to get rich first' and on decentralized administration and finance allowing local governments increasing discretion and responsibility to achieve economic growth, there was uneven development, leading to growing inequalities between urban and rural areas, different occupations and geographical regions (coastal and inland) (Leung, 2000, 2005).

Major reform initiatives in the 1980s included the introduction of the household responsibility system, relaxation of rural–urban migration, development of township village enterprises (TVEs), diversification of industrial ownership, reduction of state control on commodity prices, and setting up of special economic zones. Economic reforms focused on the gradual liberalization of the economic structure and increases in the production and management autonomy of SOEs. The introduction of the taxation system in 1983 provided an incentive for SOEs to make, retain, reinvest and share profits and enhance efficiency. After meeting government quotas they could sell their products at the market price. The 'iron rice bowl', which involved 'everyone eating from the same big pot', began to be regarded as impeding economic efficiency, labour mobility and productivity by acting as a disincentive. By the mid-1980s, the government was aware that a restructuring of the social security system would be an indispensable part of the whole process of market-oriented economic reform (Leung, 1994, 2003).

In 1986, the Bankruptcy Law was announced, and loss-making SOEs were, in principle, allowed to declare bankruptcy or be sold to the private sector. To reduce the welfare responsibility of SOEs, the contract workers' scheme was introduced in 1986. New employees were to be on contracts rather than permanently employed, and both contract workers and SOEs were required to make contributions to pension funds. As employees could now become unemployed as a result of the bankruptcy of their employers and the termination of contracts, the contributory unemployment insurance scheme was introduced at the same time, as was the pooling of pension funds to share the responsibility of the pension burden. Participating SOEs were not required to shoulder all the expenses (Leung, 2003). All these reforms aimed to enhance the competitive advantages of SOEs by reducing and sharing responsibilities.

During the 1980s, de-collectivization reform in the rural areas was considered successful. Peasants' income had improved significantly and poverty rates had reduced dramatically. But the collective schemes in health care and education were rapidly eroded, followed by the declining capacity of local governments to raise funds for public and social services. In the urban areas, the iron rice bowl protection system was gradually weakened. Instead of life-long employment, new employees were on contracts, and jobs became less secure. In short, in the 1980s the socialist collective social protection system, particularly in the rural areas, was becoming eroded. Since a new social welfare system was only beginning to be formulated, significant social welfare gaps in both urban and rural areas emerged. Overall, the primary aim of this period was economic growth in a stable political environment, and the basic task of the primary stage of socialism was to develop productivity.

When Jiang Zemin, 'the Chief Engineer', took over the Party leadership in 1989, China was facing a political crisis. Jiang continued to give development priority to maintaining political stability and economic growth. The process of deepening the transition towards a market-oriented economy has been described as the 'restoration of capitalism' (Naughton, 1995, 2007; Brandt and Rawski, 2008). It has been argued that Deng Xiaoping did not originally intend to effect wholesale market reforms by completely dismantling the socialist system. But, as the reforms proceeded, China, under Jiang Zemin, introduced more radical reforms, learning from the successful experiences of East Asian countries (Whyte, 2010a, p. 25).

Facing a more competitive environment, many of the SOEs, including those in the mining, textiles, transport and engineering sectors, which were found mainly in the northeast and central provinces, were heavily in debt, loss-making and overstaffed. In 1996 the government implemented the strategy of 'keeping a tight hold on the larger entities while letting go of the smaller ones'. Large and strategic SOEs were modernized, separating out the functions from the government. Many were listed on the stock market. Small SOEs were allowed to dismiss employees and to be reorganized, sold, merged or declared bankrupt.

The employment issue became critical during this period, largely because of the large number of young people entering the labour market, the continual massive layoffs of surplus labour from loss-making SOEs, and the migration of excess rural labour into cities. As the number of SOEs declined, millions of workers were made redundant. During the Asian financial crisis in 1997–8, the number of employees in SOEs and COEs declined by 32 million (Lu and Feng, 2012, p. 50). Between 1998 and 2000, SOEs laid off a total of 23 million employees (Tang et al., 2007).

Even though unemployment insurance was introduced in 1986, its coverage was limited. Until 1993, unemployment was officially not recognized, as there were only 'people waiting for employment'. By the late 1990s, the 'three lines of defence' for the unemployed were established: basic subsidies, unemployment insurance and social assistance. Urban social assistance (*dibao*) was organized in all cities in 1999. The unemployed were called *xiagang* or 'off-post' employees, meaning that they were not exactly unemployed. They could still maintain a relationship with their (former) employers and live in the staff quarters. Not being regarded as unemployed, they were not eligible for unemployment insurance. However, they could receive financial subsidies, contributions to social security insurance, and retraining from the re-employment service centres which had been set up by local governments financed by employer contributions, unemployment insurance, and local governments. Following a maximum *xiagang* period of two years, they could receive unemployment insurance benefits. After completing the insurance coverage period (one to two years), they could move to social assistance. However, there were severe pitfalls involved in these re-employment projects, including resource scarcity and administrative incapacity (Solinger, 2002). Many of those laid off were reported to engage in informal jobs (Tang et al., 2007). By 2001, most of the centres were closed down.

Thereafter, newly laid-off employees were obliged to terminate their relationship with their work units with immediate effect and to seek assistance directly from unemployment insurance or social assistance programmes. In practice, the unemployment insurance programme offers only a basic living allowance, which is approximately 80 per cent of the local minimum wage and for only a defined period. Officially, unemployed people included only those with urban *hukou*, registered in the local labour offices for jobs. Even though the official unemployment rate was around 3 per cent in the late 1990s, Chinese and international analysts have estimated that the actual rate was double or triple this (Cai, 2006; Naughton, 2007; Herd, Koen and Reutersward, 2010).

Economic restructuring and rising unemployment have contributed to the increasing risk of urban poverty (Guan, 2003; Sato and Li, 2006; Saunders and Sun, 2006; Chen et al., 2006; Liu and Wu, 2006; Wang, 2007). When someone loses their job, they not only lose their wage income and their status as a permanent employee but they can also be simultaneously excluded from a variety of social welfare benefits, such as social insurance coverage and housing subsidies. The key challenge for the social security system is to reintegrate laid-off and displaced workers.

Employment growth has been fuelled largely by the expansion in 'informal or irregular employment', which refers to rural migrants who cannot work in registered enterprises because they were not registered to an urban *hukou* and to workers laid off from state enterprises who take up temporary, informal employment while still remaining nominally attached to their previous work units for the purposes of receiving unemployment allowances and re-employment opportunities. Informal employment means that employees are not protected by the labour laws and cannot enjoy social security benefits. With the relaxation of the *hukou* system, more and more rural peasants have been moving into cities to find jobs. However, the *hukou* system still discriminates against them in terms of access to basic social services and formal jobs (Li, 2006; Gagnon et al., 2009).

Under the directive of 'socialization' and the principle of 'efficiency first, equity second', social policy was marked by the streamlining of the public sector, retrenching public expenditures, reducing the role of government in welfare provision, and encouraging social service marketization (Ngok, 2013b, p. 105). Given this increased vulnerability, the market-oriented and fee-driven reforms of social services and social security have aggravated the inequalities between rural and urban areas, regions, and different income groups. Social security reforms in urban areas centred on the establishment of partially funded retirement and medical insurance schemes, as well as the establishment of individual accounts, moving away from the previous pay-as-you-go systems. Based on local pilot projects, the basic structure of the retirement insurance scheme for enterprise workers was formulated in 1997. Since then, retirees have been able to receive their pension benefits from the unified accounts, which are linked to the local average wage, and personal savings accounts, which are linked to the amount of individual contribution. Facing an ageing society, the pension system in China is riddled with problems such as insufficient funds, narrow coverage and inadequate benefits (Leung, 2003; Beland and Yu, 2004; Sin, 2005; Salditt, et al., 2007).

Similarly, the restructured medical insurance programme has lower coverage and is more reliant on fee payments (Duckett, 2001, 2011a; Gao et al., 2001; Chen et al., 2004; Gu and Zhang, 2006; Wong et al., 2007; Brixi et al., 2011). According to a study by the State Council's Development Research Centre (DRC) in 2005, the medical care system and associated reforms have turned China's medical services into the exclusive privilege of the rich. More people are facing poverty because of their inability to pay high medical expenses (CNC, 27 July 2005). With the phenomenal increases in medical fees, even people with health insurance may find the charges unaffordable. Even though health services remain largely publicly provided, they are increasingly privately financed (Herd, Hu and Koen, 2010a).

The government introduced the Basic Medical Insurance System for Urban Employees in 1998 to combat declining medical insurance coverage. The reformed medical insurance scheme comprises a unified and an individual account, both of which receive contributions from employers and employees. Medical expenses are shared between the accounts (Liang and Langenbrunner, 2013). In 2000, the World Health Organization ranked China 144th out of 191 countries on overall performance. In terms of equity, China was 188th, almost at the bottom (Herd, Hu and Koen, 2010a). Overall, the restructured health-care system is marked by high inequity and inefficiency. From 1978 to 1999, central government's share of national health-care spending fell from 32 per cent to only 2 per cent (Hu et al., 2008). Even worse, cooperative health insurance in rural areas was dismantled. It is noteworthy that the Chinese health-care model was once praised by the World Bank (World Bank, 1984). With reduced government subsidies, the financial expenses of the Chinese on health care increased substantially, and health insurance offered very limited protection. In essence, the health-care system has become increasingly inequitable.

In the 2002 Government Report, the former Chinese Premier Zhu Rongji recognized, for the first time, the emergence of 'vulnerable populations' in China. This refers to those disadvantaged groups outside the traditional employment-based social protection system, such as the unemployed, rural migrants working in the cities, and low-income families (Zheng, 2003).

THE THIRD TURNING POINT: BUILDING A HARMONIOUS SOCIETY

By 2002, the new Party leader, Hu Jintao, faced a society in which people were feeling increasingly insecure and worried about the rising cost of social services. Both urban and rural residents had to shoulder higher expenses in retirement, education, medical care and housing services. Unemployment rates remained high, rising to 4.3 per cent in 2003, from only 3 per cent in the 1990s (NBS, 2014). More importantly, regional and rural–urban inequalities continued to widen. Social security coverage was still low, particularly for rural residents and migrant workers. While continual improvement was made in poverty reduction in rural areas, urban poverty emerged as a critical issue. Estimates of the size of the urban poor in the early 2000s ranged from 12 million to 30 million (Zheng, 2003). Marketized and privatized health care had generated widespread dissatisfaction and anxiety. People were complaining that health care was both too expensive and inaccessible. The segmentation and decentralization of the welfare system make profound variations in social protection and social welfare programmes inevitable. More importantly, the social welfare system seemed to give greater protection to the privileged, such as civil servants, urban residents and the formally employed, than to the deprived, such as migrant workers, rural villagers, the informally employed and the unemployed. Overall, development has been largely uneven, uncoordinated and unsustainable.

With the further relaxation of restrictions on residential mobility, a massive number of rural peasants moved into cities looking for jobs. Migrant workers can no longer be treated as 'second-class' citizens or 'guest workers'. They are increasingly demanding equal access to social services similar to those with urban *hukou* status. The environment is deteriorating. Cadre corruption is widespread. Rising social protests and disturbances, often involving violence, have been triggered by urban redevelopment and the appropriation of farmland without fair compensation, environmental pollution and industrial disputes. Social stability is at risk and social cohesion undermined (Perry, 2002; O'Brien and Li, 2006; Walder, 2009; O'Brien, 2009; Perry and Selden, 2010). Even though the economic performance of China in the 2000s remained impressive, the World Bank warned in 2006 that social issues, including inequality and environmental sustainability, seemed to have worsened. Continuous economic growth will be jeopardized if not matched by the quality of growth (Yusuf and Nabeshima, 2006, ch. 4).

To maintain the Party's legitimacy and social stability, there was urgent need for a different developmental approach, an approach distinct from the previous dominant emphasis on the quantity of economic growth. The 2003 Party document of the Third Plenum of the 16th Party Congress, *Decisions Concerning the Perfecting of the Socialist Market Economy System*, endorsed the concept of 'scientific development'. The concept incorporates a 'people-centred' development perspective, egalitarian on property rights, business opportunity and employment, and focused on coordinated and unified economic and social development both between regions and between rural and urban areas (Fewsmith, 2004). Scientific development is intended to achieve 'Five Balances': to balance urban and rural development, development among regions, economic and social development, human and natural development, and domestic development and opening up to the outside world. Scientific development attempted to redirect and reprioritize the direction of the country in a more balanced, coordinated and sustainable way. This is the first time a Chinese policy document had proposed a concept of balanced development. The SARS (Severe

Acute Respiratory Syndrome) crisis may also have warned the new Chinese leadership that a balanced development is important (Fewsmith, 2008, p. 252; Ngok, 2013b, p. 105).

At the 6th Plenum of the 16th Party Congress in 2006, the *Decisions Concerning the Construction of the Socialist and Harmonious Society* envisaged the building of a harmonious socialist society which could balance the conflicting interests of different social groups. A harmonious society features democracy, the rule of law, equity, justice, sincerity, amity and vitality. It gives full scope to people's talent and creativity, enables everyone to share in the social wealth brought by reform and development, and forges ever closer relationships between the people and the government. It is a vision of a modern educated and affluent society guided by principles of honest, friendly and cordial relationships and just, fair and open competition between social members (*China Daily*, 29 September 2007). In fact, the concept draws on the Confucian ideal of harmony, in which all the people can share in the social wealth brought about by reform and development.

The *Decisions* pledged to ensure that all Chinese people could enjoy equal rights to education, employment, medical care, old-age care and housing. Based on a 'people-first' strategy, the *Decisions* called for perfecting the public financing system, gradually achieving the equalization of public services through increased investment in education, health care, culture, re-employment, social security, environmental protection, public infrastructure and public security. To achieve this, a pluralistic social protection system covering both urban and rural residents and comprising social insurance, assistance and welfare, together with charity work, should be gradually established. It is clear that the CPC faces a formidable challenge to maintain social and political stability and enhance the quality of life of the Chinese people. The *Decisions* aim to achieve a harmonious society by 2020. Now, narrowing income inequality has been put on the government agenda.

In the 2010 Government Report, ex-Premier Wen Jiabao reiterated the need to invest more in active employment policy through job creation and job training; to unify the pension system at the provincial level and facilitate the portability of pension funds for urban workers, including rural migrants; to launch a pilot project for a new rural pension insurance system; to increase social assistance for the poor; and to build low-income housing for the poor (Wen, 2010). At the 18th Party Congress in 2012, China pledged to achieve the building of a moderately well-off society (*xiaokang*) in all respects by 2020 (to celebrate the Party's 100th anniversary in 2021) and the creation of a 'rich, democratic, civilized and harmonious modern socialist country' by 2049 (the 100th anniversary of the founding of the PRC). Hu Jintao adopted the concept of 'inclusive growth' as the objective for balanced economic and social progress, a concept that has been actively promoted by the Asian Development Bank and the World Bank. According to Hu, inclusive growth includes four proposals: giving priority to human resources development, implementing a strategy of full employment, improving the quality and competence of workers, and building a social security system that ensures sustainable development (*Global Times*, 2010).

During this period, a number of new social initiatives were introduced which have been regarded as a significant departure from the previous growth-oriented policy (Zhao and Lim, 2010, ch. 1; OECD, 2012; World Bank, 2013; Giles et al., 2013; Liang and Langenbrunner, 2013; UNDP, 2013b; L. T. Zhao, 2013). These included the New Cooperative Medical System (NCMS) in 2003; Medical Assistance for Rural Residents in 2005; the Social Insurance Scheme for Migrants in 2006; the Urban Resident Basic Medical Insurance in 2007; Medical Assistance for Urban Residents in 2007; the Rural Social Assistance Programme in 2007; the Labour Contract Law in 2008; the New Rural Old-Age Pension System (NROAPS) in 2009; the Social Insurance Law in 2010; the Urban Residents' Old-Age

Pension System (ROAPS) in 2011; and the Urban and Rural ROAPS in 2014.

Facing the global economic recession in 2008, the government rolled out a 'four trillion yuan' spending package to stimulate economic growth and create jobs. The package focused on affordable public housing, environmental improvement and upgrading rural infrastructure (Zhao and Lim, 2010, p. 6). To tackle the hot issue of the 'three rural' – namely agriculture, rural communities, and farmers – the government had announced the plan of 'Building a New Socialist Countryside' in 2006. Coordinated economic and social development through increased investment in agricultural production, infrastructure development (roads, electricity and water supply, postal services, education and health care), financial services (credits), environmental protection and democratic governance has been promised (OECD, 2009, p. 128).

The 18th Party Congress in November 2012 pledged 'two doubles' and 'two similar steps'. First, total GDP and personal income is planned to double between 2010 and 2020. Second, increases in urban and rural residents' income should be matched similarly by an increase in economic growth, and workers' wages should be matched by productivity. China has certainly reached a new turning point and entered a new stage of social development. The questions are whether the momentum of social reform can be sustained and whether these initiatives can produce real impacts on promoting the welfare of the Chinese people.

Xi Jinping, shortly after becoming General Secretary of the CPC in 2012, conjured up the 'Chinese dream' as 'the great revival of the Chinese nation' (*The Economist*, 4 May 2013). The concept is still vague, lacking specific elaboration and policy initiatives. To be sure, Chinese society needs inspirational appeals to build up its national identity and cohesion. During 2013, Xi issued several directives: the overwhelming control of the CPC has been stressed; China's development must follow its own path; there has been a call for the full implementation of the constitution. Indeed, China is now facing new challenges, including the slowdown of economic growth, a more divided society, a declining workforce, an ageing population, rapid urbanization, and an increasingly mobile population. The rise of the middle class and information society has put mounting pressure on the government to address new social challenges. All along, the use of grand ideological appeals to unify the country and drive economic growth remains a signature governing tool of the CPC. The key concern is how people perceive and interpret these illusive concepts and visionary promises. Chinese people are increasingly looking for a better quality of life and the shared benefits of economic growth.

To acknowledge the urgency of rising income inequality, the State Council, in 2013, issued the *Opinion Concerning Deepening the Reform of the Income Redistribution System*, claiming that 'the urban–rural gap and difference in citizen's [sic] income is relatively large, income is irregularly distributed, there are obvious problems of grey income and illegal income, and some of the masses live in difficult conditions' (Salidjanova, 2013). To tackle rising inequality, the government blueprint recommends an increase in the minimum wage to at least 40 per cent of average wages, loosening controls on lending and deposit rates, and greater spending on education and affordable housing, as well as the requirement for SOEs to contribute more of their profits (State Council, 2013).

Described as a landmark for charting a roadmap for deep and comprehensive economic and social reforms, and as another 'turning point for reform', the Third Plenum of the 18th Party Congress in November 2013 has given rise to great expectations for the transformation of China into a country that is more open, more equitable, more liberal, and based on the rule of law. Social reforms are expected to cover land ownership for peasants, social security, financial responsibility between central and local government, and *hukou*. China's reform process has entered 'deep water areas' in which mistakes will be disastrous. Without further reforms, the country will reach a 'dead end' (*The Economist*, 21 November 2013, p. 36).

Yet the *Communique on Decisions of the CPC on Comprehensive Deepening of the Reforms* seems to have placed a high future priority on economic reforms, particularly in acknowledging the increasing importance of the market in relation to the state. The role of the market is 'decisive'. Political reforms have hardly been mentioned at all. There are moves to improve governance and coordination on strengthening internal and external security. In stressing the independence of the judiciary and the rule of law, as well as the anti-corruption mechanism, the Party hopes that social conflicts and social injustices can be reduced.

In social policy, the general direction is to accelerate reforms in education, employment, income distribution, social security and public health. Farmers in the rural areas will enjoy the same benefits as urban residents. Peasants will be granted more property rights and there will be equal resource allocation between urban and rural areas. There are also directives to relax the one-child policy and abolish labour camps. Overall, however, the commitment to social reforms remains uncertain. The Party is expected to achieve decisive results in key areas by 2020. The overemphasis on the role of the market and the lack of specific commitments on social protection reforms are disappointing.

In facing these new challenges, it is well recognized that the Chinese model requires a turning point. Social welfare is now considered an integral part of the overall development of China as it moves towards becoming a high-income society. The aim is towards a more universal, fair, accessible social welfare system based on equal rights. The strategic direction, objective and strategy have been formulated; the remaining issue is the strengthening of local governance and policy implementation issues. Admittedly, China is known for having idealistic and desirable policy directives, yet policy implementation gaps and failures have led to disappointing outcomes.

3 Social Challenges under Market Reform

In this chapter, selected social challenges are presented and analysed: demographic transition (the demographic dividend, the one-child policy, the skewed sex ratio and the ageing population), rural migrants, left-behind children, and poverty and inequality. This is not to say that other social issues, such as disabilities, physical and mental health, the environment and gender, are not important, but those presented here are seemingly more controversial and are high on the government's policy reform agenda. Taken together, they are interrelated, and they have exacerbated the economic and social inequalities in China.

DEMOGRAPHIC SHIFT

China's population stood at 1,360.72 million by the end of 2013, 6.68 million more than at the end of 2012. The total number of births was 16.4 million, and the natural growth rate was 4.92 per 1,000 (CNC, 20 January 2014a). Between the two censuses in 2000 and 2010, the population increased by 73.9 million, with an annual growth rate of 0.57 per cent. The growth rate declined from 0.645 per cent in 2002 to 0.479 per cent in 2011, and the net number of people from 8.26 million to 6.44 million over the same period (Ma, 2011).

Currently, the fertility rate is below 1.8 children per woman. Because of declining fertility, it is estimated that India will overtake China as the country with the largest population by 2028. According to this prediction, China's population will increase only slightly, from 1,360.72

million in 2013 to 1,395 million in 2050, and then decline to 1,181 million by 2100 (CNC, 10 May 2013a). Overall, China has reached a development stage marked by low birth rate and low population increases. The structure of the population is facing a number of changes, including declining overall growth, an ageing population, and the end of the demographic dividend (see table 3.1).

Table 3.1 Basic population information in the 2000 and 2010 censuses

	2000 CENSUS	*2010 CENSUS*
Population size	1,265,825,048	1,339,724,852
Family size	3.44 persons	3.1 persons
Age structure		
0–14	22.9%	16.6%
15–64	70.1%	74.5%
Over 64	7.0%	8.9%
Life expectancy	71.4 years	74.8 years
Proportion of Han population	91.59%	91.51%
Natural growth rate	7.58/1,000	4.79/1,000
Urbanization rate	36.22%	49.68%
Working population	720 million	764 million
Employment (by industry)		
Primary	50%	37%
Secondary	22%	29%
Tertiary	28%	35%
Unemployment rate	3.1%	4.1%
Education/100,000 persons		
University	3,611	8,930
Secondary school	11,146	14,032
Primary school	35,701	26,779
Illiteracy	6.71%	4.08%
Floating population	144.39 million	261.39 million

Source: NBS (2014).

The demographic dividend

One of the outcomes of the draconian family planning policy, introduced in 1978 but officially enforced in 1980, was the creation of the demographic dividend. The low dependency ratio has been attributed to the rapid decline in the number of children, while the proportion of older people has not yet become critical. The large segment of the population of working age also produces the indirect effect of high savings and investment rates (ADB, 2011, p. 37). The increased labour supply is a result of the massive transfer of surplus rural labour into non-agricultural jobs. The demographic dividend has been considered one of the drivers contributing to China's continuous economic growth during the reform period.

However, this population structure is likely to change soon. The working population will decline and the dependency ratio increase. It is argued that China has reached a 'Lewis Turning Point', where the previously apparently unlimited labour supply begins to present shortages (Cai and Zhao, 2012). The cheap and abundant supply of rural labour on which a low-income economy relies to gain economic success will eventually disappear. The shortages in the labour supply will be followed by inevitable wage increases. However, whether China has indeed reached the turning point is still contested. Some have claimed that the surplus number of rural workers is still substantial (Zhang, Yang and Wang, 2011). In 2012, for the first time, the size of the economically active population declined. It was 930 million, or 69.2 per cent of the national population – 3.45 million, or 0.6 per cent, fewer than the figure in 2011. The National Bureau of Statistics (NBS) has predicted that the working-age population will decline by 29 million between 2012 and 2020 (CNC, 28 January 2013). It is notable that the total workforce in 2013 reached 769.77 million, representing an increase of 2.73 million over the previous year (CNC, 20 January 2014a).

The demographic dividend that has supported the economic growth of the past three decades appears to have departed, leaving a 'demographic deficit' or a 'demographic tax'. In essence, the shift caused by a rapidly ageing population and declining fertility rates will severely undermine China's labour supply and competitive advantage. Facing the imminent decline of the workforce, China has to increase labour participation and productivity in order to maintain continuous economic growth. In other words, substantial investment in the quality of human capital is required.

One-child policy

Because the baby-boomers born in the early 1960s were approaching marriageable age by the early 1980s, the government perceived the need to cut down population growth drastically immediately after the introduction of market-oriented reforms. The one-child policy, officially implemented in 1980, attempted to limit each family to only one child. Due to strong resistance, the policy was revised in 1984 to allow a more flexible implementation. In practice, the birth-control policy prescribes 'one child', 'one and a half children', 'two children' or 'three children' in different regions. In urban areas, the one-child policy is strictly enforced. In rural areas, families can have a second child if the first is a girl. In ethnic minority regions, families can have two children. In some remote mountainous and pastoral areas, three children are allowed. For example, family planning has not been introduced to 77 per cent of the Tibetan pastoralists and nomads (CNC, 30 May 2011). In 2001, the Population and Family Planning Law prescribed that family planning is a fundamental state policy.

According to the estimates of the Health and Family Planning Commission, the one-child policy has avoided over 400 million new births. The birth rate dropped from 33.4 per 1,000 in 1970 to 12.1 per

1,000 in 2012. In the same period there were also decreases in the natural growth rate, from 25.8 to 4.95 per 1,000, the fertility rate, from 5.8 to around 1.7 children, and the net population growth, from 23.2 million to 6.7 million (CNC, 12 November 2013). Those who violate the birth-control policy pay high 'social maintenance fees'. According to the *Methods on Managing the Maintenance Fees* (2002), incomes from maintenance fees should be used to subsidize public services and for environmental protection. In 2012, the maintenance fees from 24 provinces reached 20 billion yuan (CNC, 5 December 2013a). But a recent review by the National Audit Office showed that there is massive misuse of the fines (*South China Morning Post*, 20 September 2013, p. A5).

Resistance and non-compliance to the one-child policy were common. There are also accusations that forced abortions, induced labour and contraceptive operations (the use of low-cost intra-uterine devices without regular check-ups afterwards) have harmed the physical and mental health of women (Scharping, 2003; White, 2006). Because of the strong traditional preference for sons, incidences of abandoning female babies and infanticides have been reported. In fact, the majority of the abandoned babies found in orphanages are female or disabled.

There are 350 million people, aged under 30 and born after the implementation of the one-child policy, who are the only child in the family. This generation has now given birth to another 120 million children, who are also the only child in the family. China has produced a new generation of young people (little emperors) who seem to be less trusting, less competitive, more pessimistic, less conscientious and more risk-averse than children born before the policy was implemented (Cameron et al., 2013, p. 131). The lack of interaction with siblings has created a generation of young adults who don't know how to communicate effectively with their peers. *Time* magazine calls them the 'Me' generation. As beneficiaries of China's economic prosperity, they are self-interested, apolitical and obsessed with consumerism (Elegant 2007).

The one-child policy has been controversial and contested. In the early years, it was criticized on the grounds of human rights and for the coercive measures required to ensure compliance, as well as for the abandoning of female babies. In recent years there have been pressures to relax the policy, as it has generated some undesirable consequences, including an ageing population, a decline in those of working age and a skewed sex ratio.

Officially, the Chinese government has been persistent in maintaining the one-child policy. Officials claim that the birth rate might rebound dramatically once the policy is relaxed. The other argument is that low fertility can enhance the quality of new births through strengthening investment in maternity care. The government is convinced that a high level of economic and social development can be maintained by keeping the fertility rate below the current level of 1.6 children per woman (*People's Daily*, 14 January 2013). From another perspective, the one-child policy has been considered unnecessary, as the birth rates in China in the late 1970s were already falling fast. Rapid urbanization, industrialization and rising levels of education will in fact lower the fertility rate further. The current rate is already well below the replacement level and, in the long-term, China's overall population is on the decline.

In recent years, revisions in the population policy have included the cancellation of the need to make birth applications; allowing families in which both spouses come from one-child families to have a second child; the elimination in some provinces of the requirement to space out the time period between births (the mother must be aged over 30 to have a second child and there must be more than three or four years between the first and second child); and permitting remarried couples to have children (*People's Daily*, 14 January 2013). In short, the policy has been revised and there is no longer an overall one-child policy in China.

The Third Plenum of the 18th Party Congress in November 2013 further announced a policy allowing families in which just one parent is a single child to have a second child. It is estimated that 20 to 30 million couples will be affected by the policy, and that about 50 to 60 per cent of them might desire to have a second child (CNC, 18 November 2013). By May 2014, 29 provinces had already introduced the new policy. Presumably, relaxing the one-child policy would produce an immediate small baby boom, but there were only 270,000 couples seeking permission to have another child (*China Daily*, 11 July 2014). With the new policy, the proportion of the population aged over 60 would decline only slightly, from the originally estimated 24.1 per cent (without the relaxation of the one-child policy) to 23.8 per cent in 2030, and further from 34.1 per cent to 32.8 per cent in 2050. The economically active population would increase from the projected 875 million to 877 million over the same period (CNC, 18 November 2013). Overall, the impact remains small, and further relaxation is expected.

Skewed sex ratio

In 2013, the sex ratio among births was 117.6 males for every 100 females (CNC, 20 January 2014a). Following the implementation of the one-child policy, the ratio increased from 111.4 in 1990 to a peak of 120.6 in 2008, attributable to the traditional preference for sons over daughters. In practice, parents may use selective abortion to ensure that their children are boys. The ratio can be as high as 140 in Henan and Jiangxi provinces, whereas the ratios are normal in those western provinces where the family planning policy has not been enforced. The Population and Family Planning Law forbid the unnecessary use of medical technology to identify the sex of the foetus and selective termination of pregnancy, but with little success.

According to the estimates, China will have between 24 and 30 million more men than women of marriageable age by 2020 (*China*

Daily, 24 August 2013). Other estimates put the male population in the 20 to 49 age bracket in excess of 20 million in 2015, 30 million in 2025, 40 million in 2035 and 44 million in 2040. Between 2020 and 2050, some 15 per cent of Chinese men will fail to find a spouse, prompting a 'marriage squeeze' (Chowdhury, 2013, p. A4; Guilmoto, 2012). Unmarried and childless Chinese males are known as 'bare branches'. Most likely, they belong in the lowest socio-economic class, are unemployed or underemployed, and lack stable social bonds.

There is also the phenomenon of 'missing girls', which may be attributed to selective abortion and infanticide. The skewed sex ratio may lead to the increase of violent crime against women, including abduction, forced abortion and trafficking, mainly involving the sex and entertainment industries (Hudson and Den Boer, 2004).

Ageing population

With the drastic reduction in birth rates after the implementation of the one-child policy in the 1980s, China experienced rapid population ageing. In 2013, the number of people aged over 60 reached 202 million, or 14.9 per cent of the total. For those aged over 65, the number was 132 million, or 9.7 per cent of the total (CNC, 20 January 2014a). The baby-boomers – those who were born in the 1950s and 1960s when the birth rates were high – are currently entering or coming up to retirement. The ageing process will accelerate further in the future, the elderly population reaching over 243 million by 2020, 300 million by 2025, 400 million by 2034 and 450 million by 2050, or 33 per cent of the total. The median age is projected to increase from 32.6 in 2005 to 44.8 in 2050. By then, the number of people aged over 80 will have reached 100 million (CNC, 19 August 2013a).

The major characteristics of China's ageing population are its extent, the rapidity of the overall ageing process, and the significant regional, gender and rural–urban differences. As the urbanization rate continues to speed up, rural–urban migration, particularly among the young, will further increase the age-dependency ratio in the rural areas. By 2050, the proportion of older people in rural areas may exceed 60 per cent (versus 30 per cent in urban areas) (Herd, Hu and Koen, 2010b). The differences in the dependency ratio between rural and urban areas will widen from 4.5 per cent in 2008 to a projected 13.3 per cent in 2030 (Cai et al., 2012, p. 2).

In terms of income support in 2010, around 70 per cent of the older people in cities had pensions, compared with only 4 per cent in rural areas. The main sources of income for older people in the rural areas were either continuing to work or being supported by their family (Banister et al., 2012, p. 130). The *China Health and Retirement Longitudinal Study* (CHARLS, 2014) led by Chinese and international academics, which covered 17,708 individuals across 28 of China's 31 provinces, indicated that 38 per cent of older people live with children, 37 per cent with a spouse, 16 per cent with others and 9 per cent alone. Key findings provide a profile of China's older people on physical health, social insurance coverage and financial support.

MIGRANTS

Under the socialist *hukou* system, residential mobility was strictly restricted, separating the rural and urban areas in China into two different worlds. Rural land reforms in the early 1980s had created tremendous surplus labour, and agricultural work was still low paid. Meanwhile, rapid urbanization and the development of labour-intensive industries in cities and towns had created a great demand for labour. Surplus numbers of agricultural workers were encouraged to become industrial workers through migration to towns. Township policy in the mid-1980s can be summarized as encouraging peasants to 'leave the land but not the villages, entering the factories but not cities' (Kamal-Chaoui et al., 2009, p. 10). As such, in addition to the traditional rural–urban inequalities, there arose a 'new dualism' of social division between local *hukou* and the migrant population (World Bank and DRC, 2014, p. 49).

With the gradual relaxation of the *hukou* system through a number of policy documents in 2001, 2003 and 2006, more rural peasants have been able to live and work legally in cities. Migrants are often not included in assessments of the formal city population and urban planning. They have always had difficulties gaining urban *hukou*, no matter how long they have worked and lived in the cities. Migrants are presumably perceived as temporary, or 'guest workers', and are expected to move back to their villages in the future. Thus city governments had no responsibility to provide them with any support.

According to the official definition, the term 'floating population' refers to those people who live away from their place of *hukou* for more than six months (person–*hukou* separation). In the 2010 census, the size of the floating population reached 261.39 million, 17 per cent of the national total. Compared with the figure of 144 million, or 7.9 per cent, in the 2000 census, this represents an increase of 81 per cent (Ma, 2011). By 2012 the floating population had expanded further, to 263 million. Among this group, 160 million were migrant workers. In the coming three decades, another 300 million peasants will aim to move to cities for jobs, around 15 million migrant workers each year (Mok, 2013, p. A13). China's massive transfer of rural labourers, from primary industry to secondary and tertiary industries, in recent decades has been described as the greatest internal migration in world history (Li, 2013, p. xx). Coastal provinces, such as Guangdong, Shanghai, Beijing, Fujian and Zhejiang, are host provinces, while central provinces, such as Anhui, Sichuan, Henan, Jiangxi and Hunan, are major sending provinces. In many large cities, migrants can account for one-quarter to one-third of the population. Currently, it is estimated that migrants contribute around 20 per cent of China's GDP (CNC, 6 February 2013).

Despite relaxation of the regulation on residential mobility, the *Regulation on the Custody and Repatriation of Vagrants* (1982) strictly forbade rural migrants from living in cities without official permits based on employment, permanent living address and legal identity. Those 'three nos' would be detained and sent back by force to their place of *hukou*. Migrants could come to work in cities only through authorized channels. In an incident in 2003, the university student Sun Zhigang was mistaken for a vagrant and was beaten to death by officials in the reception centre in Guangzhou. The incident triggered a national movement defending the rights of migrants against repatriation. Under pressure from strong public criticism of the unconstitutional nature of the 1982 regulation, within five months the government had introduced a new policy to provide assistance to vagrants and beggars without means of livelihood. Reception centres were set up which would provide food, lodging, medical care and transportation to those in need (Li, 2006). The incident was regarded as a landmark case in the reform and public awareness of human rights and the rule of law (Hand, 2006).

The *Report on the Development of the Mobile Population 2012*, published by the China Population Planning Commission, offers a profile of migrant workers: 69 per cent came from western and central provinces; 72 per cent worked in eastern provinces; their average age was 28; those born after 1980 constituted 45 per cent; 30 per cent had already lived in their host cities for over five years and been engaged in their present job for over four years; and they returned home on average less than twice a year (CNC, 7 August 2012). The first generation of migrants, who moved for jobs in the 1980s and 1990s, saw working in the cities as temporary. After accumulating sufficient savings, they would return to their villages. The second generation of migrants, who moved after 2000, are younger, more educated, came with family members, aspired to live and develop their career in the cities, and are more conscious of their rights. Some 58 percent of all migrant workers

(85 million) were considered second generation. Some 59 per cent of them lived with their spouses. Over half desired to settle down in cities for better job opportunities, incomes, educational opportunities for children and job prospects (CNC, 12 April 2013). Their employment was still insecure, consisting mainly of short-term or temporary contracts. Affordable housing, the care of children left behind, and emotional needs were their major concerns. The issue of providing equitable educational opportunity for migrants' children became more prominent.

Whenever their labour rights are violated, migrants prefer to seek redress for their grievances through local government. The road to equal access to public and social services is still uncertain. Migrants have a strong desire to integrate into city life, yet they often have a strong sense of being discriminated against (Li, 2006). In fact, the term 'migrant worker', or *'nonmingong'*, represents a stigma and is a distinctive label separating them from other urban residents. Furthermore, they face common problems of identity confusion (whether they should be considered as urban residents or are still peasants) and barriers to integration into city life. In 2012, migrant worker participation in social insurance remained low: only 14 per cent in retirement, 24 per cent in work injury, 17 per cent in health care, 8 per cent in unemployment and 6 per cent in maternity care. They are not entitled to low-cost housing or the housing provident fund (CNC, 9 June 2013). Migrant workers are reluctant to sign labour contracts because they are then obliged to make social insurance contributions – which means a deduction from their income.

Similar national surveys by the NBS in 2005 (Wong, 2011, p. 872), the State Population and Family Planning Commission in 2011 (CNC, 6 February 2013) and the CASS in 2006 and 2008 (Li and Li, 2013, p. 4) confirmed the plight of migrant workers and their difficulties and their vulnerability to a variety of abuses, discrimination and rights violations. Based on a 2002 national household survey, a study indicated that, because of their high aspirations in relation to achievement, influenced by their new reference groups (Knight and Gunatilaka, 2010), urban migrants were on average less happy than rural peasants. Overall, the CASS study indicated that 'the treatment of migrant workers has improved to a certain extent, but still has a long way to go compared with that of urban workers' (Li and Li, 2013, p. 5).

As well as working in factories and the informal economy, many migrants are self-employed in entrepreneurial activities. Often they live together in the same neighbourhoods, called 'urban villages'. These social networks in the cities can facilitate access to business information, financial capital and recruitment of labour. Urban villages, often on the outskirts or in downtown areas of cities, are characterized by poor and debilitating conditions, overcrowding, low government regulation and ambiguous land rights. They can, however, provide migrants with entrepreneurial and employment opportunities, low-cost accommodation, mutual help and social support (Liu et al., 2010). As such, they form a special feature of Chinese urbanization and migration.

With *Time* magazine's selection of the Chinese migrant worker as 'person of the year' 2009 (Ramzy, 2009), the publication of books on the plight of female migrant factory workers (Pun, 2005; Chang, 2009) and the 'massive suicides' among workers of the Foxconn company in 2011 (Chan and Pun, 2010), the low pay and harsh working conditions they endure received international attention. In the last decade, coastal provinces, such as Guangdong and Shanghai, have experienced the unprecedented phenomenon of a shortage of migrant workers. This is not only because of the decline in the size of the working population but also on account of the increase in the number of employment opportunities offering a decent salary in the inner provinces. More rural peasants have chosen to stay in their home provinces as the income gap between inner and coastal provinces narrows.

A number of local reforms have been instituted to counter national and international criticisms of the *hukou* system and the need to integrate migrant workers and their families into city life (Chan and Zhang, 2009). To speed up the arrangements for migrant workers to obtain *hukou* in cities, some provinces, such as Guangdong and Shanghai, introduced a 'points system'. If a migrant worker can accumulate a prescribed number of points, he or she, together with his or her family members, can be awarded local urban household registration status. Point-earning criteria include residence and work permits and contributions to social insurance schemes, as well as volunteering and blood donation. According to the survey by the Tsinghua University, the proportion of the national population with non-agricultural *hukou* remained at around 27.6 per cent in 2012. Throughout the last two decades, the proportion has increased by only 7.7 per cent (CNC, 28 October 2013). Other changes involve the merging of local rural and urban *hukou*, which would have little impact on migrants coming from outside the local area (Koen et al., 2013, p. 37). Rural areas becoming non-agricultural *hukou* has implications for land-use rights in migrants' place of origin and, possibly, the loss of permission to have a second child. The new generation of migrants, however, seems to have no interest in farming; they aspire to an urban lifestyle.

To strengthen the management of migrant workers in the community, in January 2012 the Ministry of Civil Affairs (MCA) announced the *Opinion Concerning the Promotion of Integration of Migrant Workers into the Urban Community*. The *Opinion* prescribed the need to promote the integration of migrant workers into city life through provisions in employment, social security, education, health care, culture, legal assistance, family planning, housing, social assistance, etc. Integration is considered paramount in maintaining social stability. Social unrest involving migrant workers has increased significantly in recent years (Gallagher et al., 2013).

According to estimates by the State Council's Development Research Centre, if the target of an urbanization rate of 70 per cent is to be achieved by 2030, it will cost the government 50 trillion yuan (CNC, 27 June 2013). According to the estimates of the World Bank and the

DRC (2014, p. 184), the additional costs of providing social services cover to current migrant workers and their families would amount to 3.14 per cent of the 2012 GDP, increasing to 4.53 per cent in 2015 and 4.78 per cent in 2020. Therefore, the speed at which *hukou* are abolished and migrants' 'citizenization' is achieved will depend largely on the financial capacity of local governments and possibly subsidies from central government to substantially improve public and social services. As argued by the World Bank and DRC (2014, ch. 3), the integration of migrants into city life should be considered not as a burden to local and central government but as an investment in human capital.

According to the *New National Urbanization Framework* by the State Council (CNC, 16 March 2014) on the situation of urbanization, the major government policy will allow the full integration of migrant workers in small and medium cities first, while the conditions for integration in large cities will be relaxed gradually. In small and medium cities, a stable job and permanent place of residence are essential; in large cities, higher educational qualifications are preferred. In other words, the government strategy is to prioritize wealthy, skilled and educated migrants, followed by the informally employed and low skilled. Over the years, government policy has moved from 'never leave land and home', to 'leave land, but not home' and, finally, to 'leave land and home'. Rural–urban migration has contributed significantly to the economic development of cities but has created thorny issues of integration and the 'hollowing' of the villages. How to 'urbanize' or 'citizenize' migrants has become the foremost challenge for the Chinese government. Urbanization remains incomplete as migrants have not been able to integrate fully into city life.

LEFT-BEHIND CHILDREN

The greatest social impact of the massive rural–urban migration on rural life is the appearance of three main 'left-behind' groups – the older people, children and women. Of these groups, the problems of the left-behind children are more critical. Many of the migrants have left their young children in villages to be cared for by their grandparents or relatives. The report published by the All-China Women's Federation in 2013, based on the 2010 census data, estimated that there were more than 61 million children left behind in rural areas, accounting for 38 per cent of all rural children. This number had increased by 4 per cent, or 2.4 million children, since the census of 2005. Some 44 per cent of the left-behind children were found in five provinces: Sichuan, Henan, Anhui, Guangdong and Hunan. In Sichuan and Henan, which accounted for the highest proportion, some 11 per cent of the local children barely saw their parents (*China Daily*, 13 May 2013). Data indicated that numbers of children of pre-school age were on the increase, whereas those of both primary- and secondary-school children were on the decline. The trend indicates that there is a tendency for migrant parents to take their older children to cities for schooling.

About one-third of the left-behind children lived with their grandparents, and 3.4 per cent, or 2 million, lived alone (*China Daily*, 13 May 2013). Without proper care, left-behind children are vulnerable to poor physical and mental health development. Under loose supervision, they are at risk of injury and accident through carrying out domestic chores, as well as of abuse and kidnap. Long separation from their parents can lead to psychological, emotional, adjustment and behavioural problems, often described as 'left-behind syndrome' (Ye and Lu, 2011). Left-behind groups are often left to engage in agricultural and household work.

There are 36 million children in cities without local *hukou*; some 80 per cent of them have only rural *hukou*. In Guangdong there are 4.34 million such 'mobile children', accounting for 12 per cent of the national total. In Shanghai and Beijing, four and three in every ten children, respectively, are mobile children (CNC, 10 May 2013b).

These children also suffer discrimination in education, health care and social welfare services (Fong and Li, 2013). They have to pay higher school fees and must return to their home province for university entrance examinations. The solution to left-behind children is obviously not to prevent their parents from migrating, but to remove the barriers so that their children can live and study in the cities.

INCOME INEQUALITY

Following the market-oriented reforms, rising incomes have dramatically raised per capita household income in both urban and rural areas and lifted millions of people out of poverty. Yet economic prosperity has not been shared fairly. In fact, rapid market-oriented economic reforms have led to widening income gaps, particularly across regions (coastal and inland) and between rural and urban areas. Inequalities are limited not only to income but also to accessibility to social security and social welfare benefits. In other words, there is inequity in health outcomes and educational attainment too. Government expenditure is much higher in urban and wealthy areas than in rural and poor regions (Li et al., 2013). Accordingly, hospitals, schools and welfare services are concentrated in urban areas and wealthy provinces.

Even though income inequalities have become a prominent issue in China, there is still a lack of empirical evidence based on national representative surveys and reliable statistical methodologies to portray the trends (OECD, 2010a, p. 110). The Gini coefficient can be compiled from two types of survey – the annual national household income and expenditure surveys of the NBS and the periodic national household surveys of the China Household Income Project. These two sources use different definitions of income, and the periodic surveys have included migrants since 2002 (Knight, 2013). China began to release the official figures on the Gini coefficient only in recent years.

All measurements indicate that income inequalities have been widening. Within less than three decades, China has gone from being a relatively egalitarian country to one with high inequality. It was reported that the Gini coefficient in the late 1970s and early 1980s was below 0.3. In 1988, the urban figure was 0.24, the rural figure 0.33, and the national figure 0.38. By the early 1990s the ratio had increased to over 0.4 (OECD, 2004, p. 20), in 2003 it was 0.479, and in 2008 it reached a height of 0.491 (see table 3.2). According to the findings of the China Household Income Project, which surveyed household income in 1988, 1995, 2002 and 2007, income inequality had seemed to stabilize in the late 1990s. However, inequality was on the rise in the 2002 to 2007 period, even though the central government had already made increased redistributive transfers through new social programmes. Rising inequality during this period is attributed to the emergence of asset income as a result of the privatization of housing and the

Table 3.2 China's Gini coefficient as compiled by the NBS

YEAR	GINI COEFFICIENT
2003	0.479
2004	0.473
2005	0.485
2006	0.487
2007	0.484
2008	0.491
2009	0.490
2010	0.481
2011	0.477
2012	0.474
2013	0.473

Source: CNC (20 January 2014b).

expansion of the stock market (Li et al., 2013, p. 37). Finally, the ratio dropped slightly to 0.473 in 2013 (CNC, 20 January 2014b). As the national Gini coefficients are higher than those relating specifically to urban and rural areas, the implication is that income inequalities between rural and urban areas are substantial (OECD, 2010b, p. 111).

China's Gini coefficient according to the OECD is still high by international and Asian standards. Among the emerging economies, its figure is higher than those of India, Chile, Mexico and Turkey, as well as the OECD average, but lower than those of Brazil and South Africa. With a Gini coefficient of 0.479 in 2009, China ranked 36th among 135 countries. One per cent of the Chinese population holds 41 per cent of the wealth. In 2012, the average annual income of the top 20 per cent (43,797.5 yuan) was twenty times that of the bottom 20 per cent (1,587.7 yuan) (CNC, 27 December 2013a).

Income inequalities were prominent between rural and urban areas, between regions, and between industrial sectors. Rising inequalities are attributed to a variety of interrelated and complex factors, including the opening up to foreign investment and the rapid industrialization of the coastal provinces and economic zones, the continuation of the dual urban–rural economic structures, and the special privileges of governmental and SOE employees.

Rural–urban income

Rural and urban per capita incomes are based on different measures. Urban disposable income refers to net income after taxation, whereas the net income of rural residents refers to income after deducting expenses for production and taxes. Income differences were significant even under the socialist economy. In the early 1980s, the rural reform that disbanded the collective commune system and replaced it with the household responsibility system had incentivised peasants. With the emergence of surplus labour, the peasant economy diversified to take in cash crops, animal husbandry, fisheries and sideline production. Following the relaxation of restrictions to labour migration, peasants were allowed to move into towns to become employees in the thriving township industries. As a result, rural–urban inequalities were reduced to a record low for a short period. Thereafter, the ratios began to widen. Only since 2009 have they shown a moderate decline, indicating that rural incomes have risen more sharply than those in urban areas (see table 3.3). Rural incomes are rising as a result of increased wages for 42.5 per cent of rural residents, more government investment, good harvests, and high prices for agricultural products (NBS, 30 January 2012). In 2014, China published for the first time the national annual

Table 3.3 Annual urban per capita disposable income and rural per capita net income (in yuan)

YEAR	URBAN PER CAPITA DISPOSABLE INCOME	RURAL PER CAPITA NET INCOME	RATIO
1980	343	132	2.57
1985	739	398	1.86
1990	1,510	686	2.20
1995	4,283	1,578	2.71
2000	6,280	2,253	2.79
2005	10,493	3,255	3.22
2006	11,759	3,587	3.28
2007	13,786	4,140	3.33
2008	15,781	4,761	3.23
2009	17,175	5,153	3.33
2010	19,109	5,919	3.23
2011	21,810	6,977	3.13
2012	24,565	7,917	3.10
2013	26,955	8,896	3.03

Source: NBS (2014); OECD (2004, p. 18).

disposable per capita income, which was 19,311 yuan, implying the move to soften the rural–urban disparities (CNC, 24 February 2014).

On top of income inequalities, there is a significant gap in social benefits (social security incomes) between rural and urban areas. In 2007, social benefits made up 20 per cent of household final income for urban residents, while that share was only about 2 per cent for rural residents (Luo and Sicular, 2013, p. 750). Simply put, social benefits have been progressive for urban residents but regressive for those in the countryside.

Regional income disparity

China's per capita GDP varies significantly across provinces. At the high end, the per capita GDP (PPP) of Shanghai in 2011 was equivalent to that of Saudi Arabia, Jiangsu to that of Belarus, and Guangdong to that of Kazakhstan. At the low end, Guizhou was equivalent to that of India, Gansu to that of Iraq and Yunnan to that of Vanuatu (*The Economist*, 24 February 2011). According to the OECD (2010b), the proportions of GDP of eastern, central and western provinces in 1980 was 50 per cent, 30 per cent and 20 per cent, respectively. These proportions changed in 2008 to 60 per cent, 21 per cent and 19 per cent, respectively, reflecting the relatively high growth of the coastal provinces versus the low growth of the central provinces. The GDP per capita in 2011 in eastern, central, and western provinces was 53,350 yuan, 29,229 yuan and 27,731 yuan respectively. The central and western provinces were below the national average of 35,097 yuan, but they have experienced higher economic growth in recent years than the eastern provinces. The 2008 Human Development Index varied widely across different regions of China. The highest ranking, Shanghai, was 44 per cent higher than the lowest ranking, Tibet. The level of human development in Beijing, Shanghai and other regions was on a par with that of the Czech Republic and Portugal, while the low level of Guizhou and the western region was similar to that of the Democratic Republic of Congo and Namibia (UNDP, 2010, p.13).

Overall, income inequalities may have been reduced as a result of the inner provinces achieving higher growth rates than coastal provinces, as more manufacturing industries are moving into the hinterland to avoid high wages. Migrant workers' wages have increased significantly, particularly after the emergence of shortages of migrant labour. The central government has also increased investment in rural social services, including pensions, education, social assistance and health care. Another perspective, the study of income mobility, indicates the opportunities for low-income households to move upwards. Studies based on household income surveys have shown that rural income inequality increased in the early 1990s but was accompanied by a level of mobility comparable to that of other developing countries. Income mobility was higher among urban households. In the early 2000s, while inequalities had increased further, mobility in both urban and rural areas had decreased – particularly in urban households, indicating that more people were finding themselves stuck with low income. In urban areas, upward mobility is associated with higher levels of education, being female, being a member of an ethnic minority, and CPC membership. In rural areas, the factors are household size and Party membership (Khor and Pencavel, 2010).

Based on a national survey on attitudes to inequality and distributive justice undertaken in 2004, Whyte (2010b) found that more than two-thirds of respondents perceived national income inequalities to be excessive. However, with regards to their own work units and in the neighbourhoods in which they lived (reference groups), only one-third claimed that income differences were excessive. The Chinese, on the whole, have high expectations of the government to shoulder the major responsibility for providing social services. In particular, disadvantaged groups, including rural residents, did not seem to favour a strong redistributive strategy to create a more egalitarian society. However, after almost ten years of rapid development and the intensification of income inequalities, people may now show greater dissatisfaction and expect a more equal society.

High and rising income inequality are common phenomena in both developing and developed countries. It has been asked whether strong economic growth can coexist with high income inequalities, or whether income inequalities before China's reforms were underestimated or post-reform inequalities overestimated (OECD, 2010a, p. 111). Presumably, the Chinese government is expected to set a base line to evaluate the impact of public efforts to address the issue of income distribution. Among recent efforts are more investment in rural areas, raising minimum wages and pension benefits, and readjusting personal tax rates. However, the accurate calculation of the Gini coefficient has been handicapped by the difficulties of obtaining reliable income figures through national household surveys. Grey or hidden incomes are particularly widespread among high-income households.

POVERTY

Based on basic calorie intake per day, it was estimated that at least 40 to 50 per cent of the Chinese population were living at subsistence level during the Cultural Revolution period (Wang, 2012, p. 476). The decline in poverty, both on overall numbers and rate, was dramatic in the early 1980s, mainly because of rural reform in the household responsibility system, the increase in procurement prices, and the establishment of TVEs. Before the market-oriented reforms, it was estimated that around 250 million people, representing 31 per cent of the rural population, were living in absolute poverty. Using the World Bank's earlier poverty threshold of US$1 a day, 652 million people were living in poverty in 1981 (World Bank, 2009, p. 4).

In the early days, China's extreme poverty line was formulated on a minimum food energy intake in calories and the expenditures involved.

Based on Engel's coefficient of 60 per cent as the minimum proportion of the overall household budget spent on food, the first poverty line of 206 yuan per person each year was established in 1985. By working backwards, the poverty lines for the years before 1985 were established and the size of the poverty-stricken population calculated. Accordingly, 250 million people, mainly in rural areas, were identified as living in extreme poverty. The poverty line was adjusted each year according to the Consumer Price Index (NBS, 2004).

After some dramatic improvements in the early 1980s, China's poverty alleviation efforts slowed down in the 1990s, demonstrating that further reduction is becoming increasingly difficult, as poverty is now more dispersed and less responsive to overall economic growth (see table 3.4). To demonstrate priority placed on rural poverty alleviation by the government, China published the *Seven-Year Priority Poverty Reduction Programme (1994–2000)* in 1994; *Decisions on Further Resolving the Problem of Food Adequacy in Poverty-Stricken Rural Areas* in 1996; *Decisions on Further Strengthening the Development of Poverty Alleviation* in 1999; the White Paper *The Development-Oriented Poverty Reduction Programme for Rural China* in 2001; and the White Paper *New Progress in Development-Oriented Poverty Reduction Programme for Rural China* and the *New Ten Year Rural Poverty Reduction and Development Framework* in 2011. The *Opinion on Reforming the Work of Poverty Reduction in Rural Areas* appeared in January 2014. Since 1996, partnerships have been made between eleven poverty-stricken provinces and fifteen wealthy coastal provinces. Besides financial assistance, rich provinces can provide human resources training and assist in industrial development. Early poverty alleviation efforts were focused mainly on regional development, notably western provinces, including Tibet, Yunnan, Gansu and Ningxia. The extent of rural poverty, and the rate of the decrease, was related to the level of economic development (CDRF, 2009, p. 12).

Poverty is no longer concentrated in the western, ethnic minority, and mountainous areas; nearly half the number of poor people are found in the rest of China. For example, using the $2 per day poverty line, a World Bank study indicated that, in 2007, 10 per cent of the rural residents in the most prosperous province, Guangdong, lived in income poverty and 19 per cent in consumption poverty. In urban areas, residents whose income or consumption in 2007 fell below $2 per day accounted for over 1 per cent of the population (World Bank, 2011, p.4). The previous area-based poverty alleviation strategy may have to shift to a household-based targeting approach (World Bank, 2009, p. vi).

China's success in poverty alleviation can be attributed to the incentives for farmers to retain profits, an input of investment and technology, infrastructure building, improving health, and education. The initial poverty alleviation strategy was focused on supporting the counties and regions defined as poor. Now, as poverty becomes less concentrated, individual households have been added, and development efforts include investment in education, health care and training, as well as tax exemption.

However, critics have claimed that the size of the poverty-stricken population has been underestimated and the alleviation achievements have been overestimated, largely on account of the exceedingly low official poverty line and the measurement bias of the international poverty line based on outdated purchasing power surveys (Riskin, 1994, 2004; Chen and Ravallion, 2008). According to World Bank estimates, China's official poverty line was the lowest in the world – 19 per cent lower than the one used in the Lao People's Democratic Republic, 20 per cent lower than in Vietnam, and 55 per cent lower than in Mongolia (Ravallion et al., 2008). Continuous high economic growth, the elimination of rural taxes and fees between 2003 and 2006, and the introduction of rural social assistance programmes in 2007 also contributed to the improvements in peasant incomes. A study showed that remittances helped to increase rural household incomes. But the overall impact on poverty is modest because most poor people do not migrate (Du et al., 2005).

In 2011, the government formulated a new poverty line of 2,300 yuan per person per year, representing an increase of 92 per cent on the 2010 line. Accordingly, the number in poverty jumped from 27 million (3 per cent of the rural population) in 2010 to 128 million (13.4 per cent) in 2011. In 2013, this figure was reduced to 82.5 million, 6 per cent of the national population (see table 3.4). If calculated on the basis of purchasing power, China's new poverty line is US$1.5, slightly higher than that of the World Bank. Children under twelve accounted for 18 per cent of the poor, and there were 52.9 million rural people living on welfare in 2011 (*China Daily*, 25 June 2012).

Corruption can also be found in poverty alleviation programmes. In 2013, the Audit Department carried out a financial audit in nineteen priority counties, seventeen of which were found to involve the misuse of alleviation funds, amounting to 234 million yuan (CNC, 29 December 2013). Between 1986 and 2012, the number of central government priority counties for poverty alleviation increased from 273 to 592. In 2012, only 38 counties had been lifted out of this list. The central government fund for poverty alleviation in 2010 amounted to 161.8 billion yuan, and in 2011 to 227.2 billion yuan. Ironically, poor counties strive hard to remain on the poverty list, as central government subsidies and preferential benefits have been substantial (CNC, 7 January 2014). The 2014 *Opinion* calls for reforming the mechanism on performance assessment, financial management, fund allocation, cadre training and information management (CNC, 27 January 2014). There is a need for more objective criteria to define poverty-stricken areas which require continuous assistance. Overall, China's poverty alleviation achievements have outperformed those of other emerging economies, including Brazil, India and South Africa. China is on course to meet most of the United Nations Millennium Development Goals by 2015 and has been recognized by international organizations as a learning example for poverty alleviation.

In contrast to rural areas, there is no national poverty line for urban areas and there have been no overall national surveys to measure poverty in cities. It is estimated that less than 1 per cent of urban poverty in 2007 was extreme poverty (World Bank, 2009, p. iv). An OECD study estimated that the number of urban poor declined from 12.1 million in 1981 to 2.7 million in 2009 (OECD, 2010b). Another study put the size of the urban poor population within the range of 15 and 51 million, representing 4 to 8 per cent of the total (Wu et al., 2010, p. 8). Introduced to all cities in 1999, the urban social assistance provided support to 21 million people in 2013 (MCA, 2013b). It is noteworthy that the urban social assistance scheme covers only those with local urban *hukou*. As the migrant population is not counted, the size of urban poverty is grossly underestimated. The emergence of the 'new urban poor', comprising the unemployed, those who have been laid off, low-income workers, retirees and rural migrants, has become more prominent.

Poverty reduction has shifted from tackling the survival and subsistence needs of extreme poverty to higher levels of developmental needs, such as child development, affordable education and employment opportunities. To prevent poverty shock, the development of affordable, effective and sustainable social security programmes is essential.

SUMMARY

The social issues discussed in this chapter are cross-cutting and interrelated. They are attributed partly to social and economic changes and partly to a segmented and inadequate social welfare system. Indisputably, the issue of widening income inequality is the major challenge in China's bid to become a high-income economy. Inequality is not reflected in income alone but has many other aspects. One thing that has been underscored is the emergence of a number of vulnerable people who require reformed and targeted social policies and

Table 3.4 Poverty line, numbers in poverty and headcount rate, 1978–2013

YEAR	POVERTY LINE (YUAN/PERSON/YEAR)	NUMBERS IN POVERTY (MILLION)	HEADCOUNT RATE (%)
1978	100	250	31
1984	200	128	15
1985	206	125	15
1986	213	131	16
1987	227	122	14
1988	236	96	11
1989	259	102	12
1990	300	85	9
1992	317	80	9
1994	450	70	8
1995	530	65	7
1997	640	50	5
1998	635	42	5
1999	625	34	4
2000	625	32	3
2001	630	29	3
2002	627	28	3
2003	637	29	3
2005	683	24	3
2007	785	15	2
2009	1,196	40	4
2010	1,274	27	3
2011	2,300	128	13
2012	2,300	99	–
2013	2,300	83	6

Source: OECD (2010b, p. 122); CNC (24 February 2014).

programmes to improve their quality of life. The latter include income support and social care for older people; the integration of migrant workers and their family members as urban residents; income support for poverty-stricken people in urban and rural areas; social programmes targeting special groups, among them drug addicts, young offenders, AIDS patients, the physically disabled, the mentally ill and the homeless; the care of those left behind, particularly children and older people, in rural areas; and emergency relief and recovery support for victims of natural disasters.

4   Urban Social Protection

The current social security system for the urban population in China has two aspects: social insurance and social assistance. Social insurance programmes cover retirement, medical care, work injury and maternity. Combined with the housing provident fund programme, they are often referred to as 'five insurances and one fund' and serve as the standard provision for employees in the formal sector. Social assistance comprises the Minimum Living Standard Guarantee System (*dibao*), which provides means-tested cash assistance to families living in poverty and subsidies for medical services (Medical Assistance), children's education (Educational Assistance), housing (Housing Assistance), and emergency relief (Temporary Assistance). China's reforms of the urban social security system started with reforms of its economic system, in particular state-owned enterprises. Reforms of the social security system were part of efforts to liberate SOEs from social welfare responsibilities and enhance their competitiveness in the market. The overall strategy is to turn the work unit and employment-based labour insurance system under the centrally planned economy into a social insurance system based on employer and employee contributions and fund management by the government. This chapter describes the major social protection programmes currently operating in urban China, providing an account of the process and contexts that gave shape to the current situation. This is followed by a broad assessment of the main issues regarding their performance.

THE OLD-AGE PENSION SYSTEM

There are a number of international reviews of the evolution and issues of the urban old-age pension system (Chow and Xu, 2001; Leung, 2003; Beland and Yu, 2004; Sin, 2005; Salditt et al., 2007; Frazier, 2010; Herd, Hu and Koen, 2010b; Zhang and Xu, 2012; CDRF, 2012, ch. 5; Dorfman et al., 2013). The current urban old-age pension system consists of two basic parts. The first part is the Employee Old-Age Pension System (EOAPS), which covers employees in enterprises, government organizations and public institutions, as well as migrant workers. In 2012 it covered 304.27 million people, of whom 230 million were employees and 74.5 million retirees. The other is the Residents' Old-Age Pension System (ROAPS), which is designed both for urban residents who are either unemployed or engaged in informal jobs and for residents with agricultural *hukou*. In 2012 this system insured 483.7 million rural and urban residents and provided benefits for 131 million pensioners (MOHRSS, 2013). These schemes operate with different funding mechanisms and benefit structures.

The Employee Old-Age Pension System (EOAPS)

Within the EOAPS, there are three separate schemes for employees in different sectors. One is for enterprise employees, which in 2012 covered 282.72 million urban employees in China. The second scheme is for employees in government organizations and public institutions, which in 2011 covered 21.8 million participants, of whom 5.13 million were retirees. The third scheme was implemented in 2009 for urban migrant workers. In 2012 it covered 45.43 million people (MOHRSS, 2013).

Under the centrally planned economy, China had two separate pension schemes, one for employees in government organizations and public institutions and another for those working in enterprises. The two schemes operated on pay-as-you-go and defined benefits. One main difference between them was that the former was funded with central revenue and administered by individual departments and the latter was financed and administered by individual enterprises.

In the 1980s, rapid increases in the number of retirees in SOEs resulted in huge pension burdens, leading to a 'pension crisis' in many old enterprises. To enhance their competitiveness, social pooling was first piloted in a few cities with the purpose of sharing the SOEs' pension burdens. Participating enterprises paid into local government-administered funds, which would then pay out the pension benefits to the retirees directly. Annual contributions were determined by the total amount of pension payments required in that year. As such, there were no accumulated pension funds. Because pooling was limited mostly to the state sector, it was unable to reduce the pension burden on SOEs. In addition, a wide diversity in burdens, benefits and contribution rates often led to disincentives for well-off and young enterprises to contribute to the pools, while poor enterprises were unable to do so (Chow and Xu, 2001; Leung, 2003).

In 1991, the *Resolution on Reform of the Pension System for Enterprises* called for the establishment of a provincially unified social pooling system covering all types of enterprises and workers. In 1995, the *Notice on Deepening Reform of the Pension System for Enterprises* demanded the transformation of the pay-as-you-go system into a dual system of contributions: social pooling plus an individually funded account. Influenced by World Bank consultants, the Chinese government was convinced that a funded approach with individual accounts would be more sustainable in the long term (Chow and Xu, 2002).

Social pooling and individual accounts can be combined with different emphases according to the local situation. This led to wide variations in contribution rates and the size of the individual account and benefits across the nation. To remedy these problems, in 1997 the State Council issued the *Decisions on Establishing a Unified Basic Pension*

System for Enterprise Employees, which proposed to make three 'unifications' in the system in the following years. First, the pooled contribution rates were set at 20 per cent of the wage for enterprises and 8 per cent for each individual employee. Second, the contribution towards the individual account was set at 11 per cent of a worker's wage, of which employees paid 8 per cent and enterprises 3 per cent. Third, pension benefits consisted of a basic pension and an individual account pension. A worker who reached retirement age after contributing for at least fifteen years was to receive a monthly basic pension equivalent to 20 per cent of the local average wage in the year before retirement, plus a monthly individual account pension equal to the funds accumulated in the individual account divided by 120 (based on a life expectancy of 70 years, a retiree would live on average for ten years, or 120 months).

Because the social pooling funds were increasingly unable to pay the basic pensions of a rising number of retirees, local governments often had to tap into individual accounts for the amounts. There was a need to increase enterprise contributions to the social pooling funds and separate the individual accounts administratively from the social pooling funds. In 2000, the State Council made three major changes to the pension scheme. First, the individual account was made up of contributions from employees only, and was reduced to 8 per cent of the wage. Second, funds in individual accounts were to be managed separately from social pooling funds, so as to prevent social pooling from borrowing funds from individual accounts. Third, to encourage further contributions beyond the minimum requirement of fifteen years, the basic pension benefits would be adjusted according to additional years of contribution. Now, a retiree would receive a monthly basic pension equivalent to 20 per cent of the local average local wage plus, if they have contributed for more than fifteen years, another benefit for each additional year of contribution, up to a total of 30 per cent of the local average wage.

After several years of experimentation with the revisions in three provinces in the northeast region of China, where pension burdens were particularly high, in 2005 the State Council issued *Decisions on Perfecting the Pension System for Employees in Enterprises*, which confirmed the changes and required nationwide adoption of the revised system starting from 2006. The basic pension was to take into account the average and individual wage before retirement and the number of years of individual contribution. That is, apart from a monthly basic pension from the pooling fund equivalent to 20 per cent of the local average wage, a retiree also receives a monthly payment of 1 per cent of the average wage plus an indexed individual wage for each year of individual contribution. The individual account pension is to be established by a government-determined annuity factor, with reference to the national life expectancy and individual retirement age. A worker retiring at the age of 60 is to receive a monthly payment based on the accumulated balance in the individual account divided by 139.

The Pensions for Employees in Government Organizations and Public Institutions is a government-funded, non-contributory programme, which originated in the 1955 Labour Insurance Regulation and has evolved into the present almost intact. Upon retirement, an individual is paid different levels of benefits based on their current wage and the number of years of employment. For instance, a retiree from a government organization usually receives 90 per cent of the basic wage if they have worked for 30 years, but pensions for retirees from public institutions may vary markedly across institutions. Generally, pension benefits for retirees in government organizations are higher than for those in public institutions.

Urban migrant workers were included in the EOAPS only very recently. Local pilots in some cities, such as those in Guangdong, Shenzhen, Beijing and Shanghai, where urban migrant workers were concentrated, started around the turn of the 1990s following the passing of the Labour Law in 1994 and the State Council's 1999

Temporary Regulations on the Collection of Social Insurance Premiums. The Labour Law stipulated that all workers, including those on a contract or self-employed, should participate in pension schemes, whereas the Regulations provided specific methods for the inclusion of migrant workers in the EOAPS. In subsequent years, a number of policy guidelines were provided by the central government to guide the efforts of local schemes, which varied markedly across cities.

In 2009, the Ministry of Human Resources and Social Security issued *Methods of Migrant Workers Participating in the Basic Old-Age Pension System*, which provided a nationally unified policy framework with regard to funding and benefits. Enterprises were to contribute 12 per cent and individuals between 4 and 8 per cent of their wage. Similar to the structure in the EOAPS, benefits would consist of a basic pension and an individual account pension. If a migrant worker has contributed for fifteen years or more, they are eligible to receive a monthly payment of both basic pension and individual account pension. For those who have contributed for less than fifteen years, two methods will apply. If they are enrolled in the New Rural Pension Old-Age Pension System (NROAPS), their account is to be transferred to that fund; if not, they will be paid all the money accumulated in their individual account. Similarly, local governments are allowed to determine the structure and levels of both individual contributions and benefits according to the local context.

The Residents' Old-Age Pension System (ROAPS)

The ROAPS began in 2009 with local trials in several cities, including Beijing, Chongqing, Xi'an and Kunming, and was adopted nationwide in 2012. As a voluntary programme for urban residents outside the formal workplace, it was implemented in response to the situation in which large numbers of urban residents were unemployed and lost their associated social security benefits during the 1990s when SOEs were undergoing reforms. They were ineligible for coverage by the EOAPS. According to the State Council's 2011 *Guidelines for Establishing Urban ROAPS*, all urban residents aged sixteen or above not currently in education are eligible to participate in the system.

The scheme is funded by government subsidies plus individual contributions. Ten rate levels were set from which participants could select the amount of their contributions, ranging from an annual amount of from 100 to 1,000 yuan. Benefits comprise two tiers – a basic pension and individual account pension. The basic pension is funded by subsidies from the central government and matching funds from local governments, which are usually determined on an annual basis. In 2011, the central government bore full funding for the basic tier for cities in the central and western provinces and 50 per cent for those in the eastern provinces. Local governments were required to contribute at least 30 yuan for each participant. Both individual contributions and local government subsidies went into individual accounts. A participant reaching the age of 60 after contributing for fifteen years receives a monthly minimum of 55 yuan from the basic pension plus a monthly sum equal to 1/139 of the total funds accumulated in their individual account. For people already aged 60 and above, the basic pension is given as a universal benefit unrelated to individual contribution. Again, local governments are allowed to determine the structure and level of both individual contributions and benefits according to the local context. In 2013, the number of participants in the urban ROAPS reached 24 million, from which around 10 million older people were receiving monthly benefits (Central People's Government, 2014).

The performance of the old-age pension system

In the development of China's old-age pension system, 'wide coverage and low benefit levels' has been the guiding principle. As of September

2013, the old-age pension system covered around 800 million urban and rural people (325 million participants in EOAPS and 498 million participants in urban and rural ROAPS), accounting for 80 per cent of the 1 billion people estimated to be eligible for coverage. The government expects to achieve 95 per cent coverage by 2020 (Hu, 2013; Central People's Government, 2014). While the attainment of coverage is remarkable, further expansion involves mostly those in the private sector and informal and urban migrant workers. Extension of coverage to urban migrant workers will be particularly challenging. In 2012, 45.43 million of them participated in pension plans, accounting for about 17 per cent of the 262.61 million involved (MOHRSS, 2013). Another source has shown that in 2012 only 14.3 per cent of employers made contributions for migrant workers in pension plans (NBS, 2014).

Because the pension programmes were first established for the formal sector in the 1990s and expanded through several patchworks to the informal and rural sectors almost two decades later, the system has become highly fragmented, differing widely in terms of benefit levels. In 2011, the monthly pension payments averaged 1,528 yuan for retirees from enterprises, 2,105 yuan for those from public institutions, and 2,241 yuan for those from government organizations (NBS and MOHRSS, 2012).

According to OECD estimates, the replacement rate of China's pension benefits in 2012 was around 60 per cent, above the OECD average of 54 per cent (OECD, 2013c, p. 10). However, according to estimates by the CASS, China's replacement rate in 2011 was only 50 per cent, down from 73 per cent in 2002 and 58 per cent in 2005 (CNC, 11 September 2013). This drop is attributed mainly to the rapid increases in employees' wages in recent years. Replacement rates of those in government offices and institutional organizations can be maintained at a level of 80 to 90 per cent (CNC, 1 November 2013). According to the CASS data, the amount of pension a retiree received in August 2011 ranged from 200 yuan to 10,000 yuan; over 75 per cent of retirees had pensions below 2,000 yuan, while 77.3 per cent were below the average amount of 2,615 yuan (*People's Daily*, 25 February 2013). In 2012, the EOAPS system spent a total of 1,556.2 billion yuan for 74.46 million pensioners, averaging a monthly pension of over 1,700 yuan. In contrast, the average monthly payment of the ROAPS was only 73 yuan (total expenditure of 115 billion yuan for 130.75 million pensioners) (MOHRSS, 2013).

In 2013, there were fifteen provinces which had established a unified urban–rural ROAPS. The average pension payment amounted to 81 yuan each month. As compared with the average *dibao* standards of 362 yuan per person per month in cities and 189 yuan in the rural areas, the pension is evidently too low (CNC, 27 December 2013b). This phenomenon is often referred to as the 'dual-track system', which has been one focus in the pension system reforms. In other words, the pension system has been regressive and exacerbated inequalities across different employment groups. It tends to protect and reward the privileged rather than the disadvantaged.

Financial sustainability is another major issue. Individual accounts became 'notional' or 'empty', resulting from the transformation of the pension system from pay-as-you-go into one that is partially funded. Pension deficits have been increasing since the mid-1990s. In 2011 the individual accounts should have held 2,500 billion yuan, but the actual amount available was only 270 billion yuan (*Economic Daily*, 5 September 2013). Since the mid-1990s, the government has been providing increasing funding to the pension system. According to the annual report on pension funds by the CASS, fourteen provinces experienced deficits in 2011, amounting to 76.7 billion yuan. The report also shows that the amount provided by the government increased from 33.8 billion yuan in 2000 to 227.2 billion yuan in 2011, totalling 1,252.6 billion yuan in the past decade (CASS, 2012a).

As in other developed countries, raising the retirement age and promoting private pensions are key strategies for developing a sustainable system in China. By international standards, the Chinese retirement ages of 60 for men and 55 for women are too low (OECD, 2013c, p. 10). However, opinion surveys have indicated that the majority of the Chinese people are against the postponement of retirement (CNC, 27 December 2013c). To tackle the dual-track system, public institutions and their employees are expected to join the EOAPS for enterprise employees with contributions to the social security funds and individual accounts. In recent years, an old-age allowance has been introduced in eighteen provinces for people aged over 80 on low incomes; financial subsidies have been introduced for social services in 22 provinces, and social care subsidies in three provinces (CNC, 5 December 2013b). Overall, public contributions to pensions in China is around only 3 per cent of GDP, which is lower than the OECD average of 7 to 8 per cent (OECD, 2013c, pp. 46–7).

UNEMPLOYMENT INSURANCE

The term 'unemployment' was not used officially in China until 1994. From the early 1990s, unemployment began to increase rapidly along with the restructuring of SOEs, which introduced a series of measures in order to make profits and increase efficiency. SOEs were encouraged to restructure their labour force through such methods as 'optimizing and regrouping' and 'assignment of posts through merit', which were synonymous with reducing the number of employees. With the removal of government guaranteed jobs, many workers were unemployed as a result of dismissal, bankruptcy or termination of contract (Chow and Xu, 2002; Leung, 1995, 2003; Vodopivec and Tong, 2008).

As such, unemployment emerged in China in three forms at different times. In the earlier years of the economic reforms in the 1980s, unemployed workers were referred to as surplus employees. The term 'surplus' implied a temporary status of being out of work, and enterprises continued to provide for these workers and were responsible for assigning them to suitable jobs. Dismissal was still an unfamiliar and unacceptable measure for both enterprises and employees; SOEs were expected to keep as many workers as possible.

The first unemployment insurance programme came in 1986 following the State Council's *Temporary Regulations on Establishment of Insurance for Employees in SOEs Waiting for Job Assignment*. According to the *Regulations*, only a few categories of unemployed workers from SOEs were eligible for coverage: those from enterprises declaring bankruptcy, those being laid off by insolvent enterprises, and those who were dismissed or had had their labour contracts terminated by enterprises. The *Regulations* required local government to set up unemployment insurance pools across SOEs, in which the participating enterprises contributed 1 per cent of the standard wage. Benefits consisted of a regular payment, medical care fees, death compensation and funeral expenses, and survivors' compensation. The funds were also available to pay the pensions for retirees of enterprises declaring bankruptcy and to provide training programmes and financial assistance for unemployed workers to become self-employed. Both the duration and the level of benefits were related to length of service and the standard wage. The maximum period was 24 months if the individual had worked for more than five years and 12 months if they had worked less than five years. With wage-related benefits, the unemployed could receive 60 to 75 per cent of their previous wage during the first 12 months of unemployment and 50 per cent for the remaining 12 months.

With the deepening of reforms in the early 1990s, SOEs were relieved of the obligation to contain their 'surplus workers'. This gave rise to the phenomenon of 'laid-off employees' (*xiagang*), which increased rapidly throughout the 1990s and 2000s. Coverage of unemployment benefits was first extended in 1993 to all workers in SOEs and further in 1999, following the State Council's *Regulations on Unemployment Insurance*, to all types of enterprises. During this period, however, SOEs continued to take care of employees who had been laid off through a temporary programme jointly funded by SOEs, local governments and unemployment insurance funds. The programme provided cash assistance to maintain basic living standards for a maximum period of three years. Only if they failed to find a job during this period would an individual be treated as unemployed and become eligible for unemployment benefits. In 2003, this scheme was merged into the unemployment insurance scheme, and laid-off employees began to be treated as unemployed. In 2011 the Social Insurance Law came into effect, which reiterated the requirement that all types of employees, including those in government organizations, participate in unemployment insurance.

The operation of the unemployment insurance scheme is governed by the State Council's Regulations on Unemployment Insurance (1999) and the Social Insurance Law (2011). All workers, with the exception of civil servants, are required to participate in unemployment insurance. Funding is shared, enterprises contributing 2 per cent and employees 1 per cent of their wage. A one-year fully covered service is the qualifying criterion for eligibility for benefits. Individuals can apply for benefits after three months of unemployment. The maximum period for an unemployed worker to live on benefits is 24 months if they have over ten years of covered services, 18 months if they have contributed for five to ten years, and 12 months if their service was covered for less than five years. If a re-employed person loses their job again, the number of contribution years will be recalculated starting from the most recent period of unemployment, but the maximum period of entitlement would include the previous years of receiving benefits. Since the programme is decentralized, benefit rates are to be determined by local governments, provided that they are below the minimum wage and above the social assistance threshold – that is, benefits from the *dibao*. Apart from cash benefits, the unemployed are also covered for medical care expenses, funeral expenses and survivors' compensation, subsidies for job training services, job introduction, and other related expenses. The 1999 Regulations delinked unemployment benefits from previous wages, implying a much lower level of benefits.

The operation of unemployment insurance has faced a number of issues. Among them is the narrow and limited coverage relative to the number of urban employees. As a 'compulsory' programme designed to cover all types of employees and work units, expansion has been limited. Between 2001 and 2012, the number of urban employees increased from 241.23 million to 371.20 million, but the number of participants in unemployment insurance grew only from 103.55 million to 152.25 million (including 27 million urban migrant workers). Overall coverage declined from 43 per cent of urban employees in 1994 to 41 per cent in 2012 (MOHRSS, 2013). In other words, the majority of the migrant workers are still not included.

Second, the programme is characterized by limited eligibility, low benefit levels, and a large amount of surplus funds. The number of registered unemployed ranged from 8.30 million in 2007 to 9.17 million in 2012, representing a relatively low rate of 4 to 4.3 per cent, but the number of beneficiaries declined steadily, from 3.27 million to 2.04 million, representing slightly more than one-fifth of the registered unemployed. In contrast, the unemployment insurance funds have accumulated a substantial surplus, which grew from 51.1 billion yuan in 2005 to 292.9 billion yuan in 2012 (MOHRSS, 2013). Due to the large number of participants with limited eligibility for benefits, it is expected that surplus funds will continue to grow in the future. Contributions from public institutions where unemployment rarely occurs have been the major source of increases in the surplus funds.

THE MEDICAL INSURANCE SYSTEM

Currently, China has three medical care systems operating in the cities. One is for employees in enterprises (Basic Medical Insurance System for Urban Employees [BMISFUE]), the second is for those in government organizations and public institutions (Public Medical Insurance System [PMIS]) and the third is for urban residents outside of the formal workplace (Medical Insurance System for Urban Residents [MISFUR]). In the past decade, an increasing number of employees and retirees from the PMIS have been merged into the same pool for employees in enterprises. In the future, there will be only two medical insurance systems operating in urban China: one for urban employees and another for economically inactive residents. In 2006, migrant workers were given coverage by the medical care system, allowing them to participate in the BMISFUE, the MISFUR or the rural NCMS. Reviews on the process and critical issues of health-care reforms include those by the World Bank (1984, 1997), Gu (2001, 2010), Duckett (2001, 2011a), Bloom and Tang (2004), Blumenthal and Hsiao (2005), Gu and Zhang (2006), Hu et al. (2008), Yip and Hsiao (2009), Herd, Hu and Koen (2010a), and Liang and Langenbrunner (2013).

The Medical Insurance System for Urban Employees (MISFUE)

Under the centrally planned economy, the Medical Insurance System for Urban Employees (MISFUE) in enterprises was funded by individual enterprises as part of the labour insurance package, while the PMIS for employees in government organizations and public institutions was funded by government revenues at different levels. Both schemes covered in-patient and out-patient care free of charge for employees and at 50 per cent of the costs for their dependants. Since the early 1990s, reforms of the medical care system have been moving in two directions: one is to turn the work-unit-based system for employees in enterprises into social pooling plus individual accounts, and the other is to merge the different systems for employees in government organizations and those in public institutions into one system.

Reform in the medical insurance system started as early as the early 1980s, when medical care costs became an unaffordable burden largely because of the widespread phenomenon of excessive use of medical services. The early reforms were focused mainly on containing costs by requiring individuals to pay a certain proportion. In the latter half of the 1980s, a number of small cities piloted social pooling for medical expenses. In 1991, Hainan took the lead in the establishment of a provincial-level medical care insurance scheme for employees in all enterprises based on contributions made by both enterprises and individuals. In the mid-1990s the reform strategies were further turned into social pooling plus individual accounts, which were first piloted in 1994 in two cities, Zhenjiang in Jiangsu and Jiujiang in Jiangxi, and expanded in 1997 to other cities. This was followed by nationwide adoption of the reform policies with the implementation of the State Council's 1998 *Decisions on Establishing the BMISFUE*.

The *Decisions* laid down the basic principles for the establishment of the medical insurance system for urban employees. In brief, all types of employers and employees, including enterprises, government organizations, public institutions and social organizations, are required to participate in the BMISFUE, which is unified using either the city or the county as the pooling unit. The funding of the schemes is based on social pooling plus individual accounts, to which employers contribute 6 per cent and employees 2 per cent of their wage. Individual accounts are funded by individual contributions plus 30 per cent of the contributions made by enterprises, while the rest of the enterprise contributions go into social pooling. Social pooling and individual accounts are managed separately for different expenditures.

A floor of 10 per cent of the local average wage was set as the threshold above which an individual would be eligible for reimbursement for different proportions of the medical costs from the social pooling, up to a ceiling of 400 per cent of the average wage in the previous year. Medical costs below the floor can be covered either by the individual accounts or paid by the individual out of their own pocket. Funds from individual accounts can also be used to pay out-patient costs. Participants are encouraged to enrol in private medical insurance schemes to cover expenses above the ceiling. Local governments had discretion to determine the exact rates for the floor and the ceiling, as well as the percentages for reimbursement, based on the principle of balancing revenues with expenditures. Across the nation, two payment methods were used. According to the first, a person became eligible for social pooling only after the individual account was depleted; the second method dictated that social pooling and individual accounts covered different services, usually in-patient care by funds from social pooling and out-patient care or purchase of medicine from stores by individual accounts.

The Medical Insurance System for Residents (MISFUR)

The MISFUR was piloted first in some cities under the State Council's 2007 *Decisions on the Pilot MISFUR*. The system was adopted nationwide in 2010. All residents, including children, students attending school below college level, and other informally employed residents were eligible to join. Participation is household-based and voluntary. The system is funded by contributions from participating households and government subsidies. The *Decisions* required local governments in the pilot cities to provide each participant in 2007 with a minimum annual subsidy of 40 yuan, and the central government started to provide 20 yuan of subsidies for each participant in the central and western provinces. Social assistance recipients, older people from low-income families, and people with serious disabilities should each be subsidized for a minimum of 60 yuan a year to participate in the schemes. And the central government would also bear half of the subsidies for governments in the central and western provinces. Benefits covered mainly major illnesses or the receipt of in-patient medical services. The floors, ceilings and reimbursement rates were to be set by local governments.

In 2010, the *Notice on Doing a Good Job in the MISFUR* proposed to cover between 80 and 90 per cent of urban residents in the near future; it also expanded eligibility for coverage to college students, workers engaged in informal employment and migrant workers. Informal and migrant workers were allowed to choose between the BMISFUE and the MISFUR. In addition the *Notice* required local governments to raise their annual subsidies for each participant from 60 to 120 yuan. Accordingly, subsidies from the central government for the central and western provinces increased from 20 to 60 yuan per participant. The *Notice* raised benefits by lifting the ceiling from 400 per cent to 600 per cent of the disposable income of urban residents and setting the reimbursement rates from social pooling at 60 to 70 per cent of the medical costs of in-patient care services. Local governments were also encouraged to set up social pooling to cover outpatient care.

The performance of the urban medical insurance system

In 2012, the medical insurance system (including the rural NCMS) covered 1.34 billion participants. Among them, the system for urban employees covered 264.86 million people, including 198.61 million employees, 66.24 million retirees, and 50 million rural migrant workers, while the residents' system covered 271.56 million urban people (MOHRSS, 2013). China's medical insurance system has attained almost full coverage of the national population.

All along, there were major setbacks in the health-care system, among them high levels of out-of-pocket payments, widespread inefficiencies in health facilities, uneven quality, extensive inequity, and perverse incentives for hospitals and doctors (Hu et al., 2008, p. 1846). One major issue is the merging of the PMIS into the BMISFUE. Since reforms started in the late 1990s, the goal of the government has been to create a unified and insurance-based medical care system for all employees in cities. By 2010, most employees in the formal sector were given coverage, with financial support from the central government for those laid off by bankrupt SOEs. The transfer of employees and retirees from government organizations and public institutions into the unified system, however, has been slow. At the end of 2012, the 'two-track' systems were still in operation in seven provinces, one for employees in enterprises and another for those in government organizations and public institutions. It is expected that the two systems will be completely merged by the end of 2014.

SOCIAL ASSISTANCE

Current social assistance programmes in China emerged in the mid-1990s in response to urban poverty caused by large numbers of workers being laid off from SOEs. Over the years, a variety of social assistance schemes were developed, including *dibao*, Medical Assistance, Educational Assistance, Housing Assistance and Temporary Assistance. All of these programmes are government funded and available to both urban and rural residents. As with other social policies in China, they were first piloted locally and then adopted nationwide. A means-tested programme, *dibao* provides cash assistance to poverty-stricken households with the aim of helping them to live at a subsistence level. *Dibao* also serves as the qualifying entry point for people to access other social benefits. Other programmes were introduced in the 2000s in response to the multidimensional nature of poverty and made available mainly to *dibao* recipients. Medical Assistance was established in 2005. Its benefits are paid out in two ways: one is to provide a premium for the recipients to participate in medical care insurance, and the other is to reimburse some of their costs after they are paid by the insurance scheme in which they are enrolled. Educational Assistance was introduced in 2007 and assists households to cover the costs of their children's schooling. Housing Assistance was introduced around the turn of the 2000s to provide subsidized housing. Reviews on the development and issues of *dibao* include Leung and Wong (1999), Chen et al. (2006), Leung (2006), Solinger (2008), Leung and Xu (2009), Chan (2010), Gustafsson and Deng (2011), Solinger and Hu (2012), and Wong et al. (2014).

The development of dibao

During the centrally planned economy period, China had a social relief programme from the early 1950s. It provided cash and/or help in kind to childless old people outside a work unit. Because most people had a work unit to take care of their needs, few were in need of this support, thus making it a negligible element in the social welfare system. Until the mid-1990s, the scheme, which was limited to the 'three nos' households, continued to operate as the only government-funded benefit programme in the cities.

The early 1990s began to see increasing numbers of urban residents falling into poverty. The causes of poverty of this 'new urban poor' involved many factors. First, the restructuring of SOEs led to rapid increases in the number of workers who became unemployed or were laid off. Second, the generally poor economic performance of most SOEs affected the incomes of current employees and retirees; many enterprises had difficulties in paying pensions and wages at all. In 1999, the then Ministry of Labour and Social Security issued a special document requiring SOEs and local governments to guarantee the prompt and efficient delivery of both pensions and financial assistance to those who had been laid off. In the following years, these 'two guarantees' became a top issue on the agenda of the central government. However, the effectiveness of these 'guarantees' in addressing the plight of those who had been laid off was in doubt (Solinger, 2002; Tang et al., 2007). Third, as increasing numbers of the urban labour force were shifting from the state to the non-state sector, where social protection programmes were virtually absent, many were at risk of falling into poverty. Finally, as a result of the increased marketization of many basic social services from the early 1990s, urban families were faced with huge financial burdens, leading to the phenomenon of 'poverty due to high medical or educational expenses'.

In the early years of the economic reforms, China's social policy was guided by two main beliefs: that economic growth would be the ultimate solution to poverty, as expressed in the slogan 'development is the hard theory', and that social insurance was the most efficient form of social security for China. The emergence of large-scale urban poverty, however, indicated that social insurance schemes had failed to function as expected. Many of the deprived people had no access to social insurance protection. Thus, towards the end of the twentieth century, the attention of the central government was drawn to social assistance as a tool to deal with urban poverty. In the following years, the emphasis of social security reform shifted from social insurance to social assistance. The means-tested social assistance scheme known as *dibao* was first piloted in Shanghai in 1993 and was followed by similar projects in a number of wealthier cities in the mid-1990s. In many of the pilot cities, the design of the programme was an attempt by the local governments to expand the traditional social relief programme while expecting SOEs to continue to perform their social responsibilities.

In many cities, eligibility was limited to four main types of resident: workers who had either become unemployed or been laid off by enterprises; current employees earning insufficient income because of the poor economic performance of SOEs; and the 'three nos' households, who were the traditional social relief targets of the government. The operation of the programmes was referred to as the 'take home your own child' approach, by which the government determined the benefit levels and enterprises were required to provide the cash. Specifically, benefits for the first two eligible groups were to be paid either by an enterprise or by a government department in charge of the enterprise; only those unable to obtain support from such organizations would be provided for by the government. As such, the receipt of *dibao* benefits for many poor households again depended on the financial ability of their employers.

During the experimental period, a variety of locally designed schemes emerged, with funding, eligibility and benefit levels differing widely across localities. In 1999 the State Council issued *Regulations on the Guarantee of the Dibao for Urban Residents*, which provided a nationally unified basic structure for the programme. The *Regulations* expanded eligibility to all urban households whose income fell below the poverty line; however, the principle remained that funding was primarily the responsibility of local government, and that funds from the central government would be available only to localities with financial difficulties. The *Regulations* provided an important directive for local governments to set up *dibao* programmes, though the practice of welfare decentralization proved to be a constraining factor. Local governments tended to decide on programme coverage based on the amount of resources they could afford to devote to the task, which was usually not among the local priorities. A breakthrough in local responsibility for the welfare policy occurred in 1999, when the central government allocated 400 million yuan to subsidize local governments' establishment of *dibao* and promised to increase central transfers in subsequent years until it reach 50 per cent of the total funds. Central government funding has been allocated mainly to western and central provinces. Between 1999 and 2001, the amount of central transfers soared from 400 million to 2.3 billion yuan, while the number of recipients also grew rapidly, from 2.66 to 11.71 million (Leung, 2006).

It seemed that more money from the central government would result in more people eligible for benefits. Baffled by the figures, in early 2002 the Ministry of Civil Affairs set up a nationwide investigation into poverty-stricken households. The investigation identified 19.38 million poor people eligible for assistance. It also became clear that local government funding alone was not reliable, particularly in the less developed regions, a major reason for the previously narrow coverage. Since then, central government transfers have increased substantially. By 2013, the proportion of central transfer had reached 72 per cent. The recipient population declined slightly between 2009 and 2013, dropping from a high of 23.5 million to 20.6 million. Table 4.1 provides information on the funding and coverage of *dibao* between 1998 and 2013.

Dibao provides cash assistance to households whose income falls below the social assistance line, which was determined mostly through budget standards methods. It is intended to cover such items as food, clothing and a few daily necessities, such as fuel, electricity and water, as specified in the State Council's 1999 *Regulations*. An eligible household receives cash up to the assistance line. Although local governments have discretion to develop their own policies, over the years the programmes, through a series of centrally published regulations, have converged in both design and implementation. As such, nationally, the operation of *dibao* can be described as 'one system with different levels of benefits', largely reflecting the levels of economic development across localities. For instance, in September 2013, the average assistance line nationally was 362 yuan per person per month. The standard ranged from 277 yuan in Ningxia to 640 yuan in Shanghai; four localities had a standard over 500 yuan, four between 400 and 500 yuan and three below 300 yuan, with the rest falling between 300 and 400 yuan

Table 4.1 Funding and coverage of *dibao*, 1998–2013

YEAR	FUNDING (IN BILLION YUAN)			RECIPIENTS (IN MILLION)
	TOTAL	CENTRAL TRANSFERS	CENTRAL TRANSFERS (%)	
1998	1.20	0	0	1.84
1999	1.97	0.4	20.3	2.66
2000	2.72	0.8	29.4	4.03
2001	4.27	2.3	53.9	11.71
2002	10.81	4.6	42.5	20.65
2003	15.05	9.2	61.1	22.47
2004	17.28	10.2	59.0	22.05
2005	19.19	11.2	58.4	22.34
2006	22.42	13.6	60.7	22.40
2007	27.74	N/A	N/A	22.72
2008	39.34	N/A	N/A	23.35
2009	48.21	35.91	74.5	23.46
2010	52.47	36.56	69.7	23.11
2011	65.99	50.20	76.1	22.77
2012	67.43	43.91	65.1	21.44
2013	75.67	54.56	72.1	20.64

Source: MCA (various years).

(MCA, 2013b). Table 4.2 provides information on the average standards and the average actual benefits paid to recipients between 2006 and 2013.

In most cities, the determination of the assistance line also takes into consideration levels of other social protection benefits, such as the minimum wage, pensions and unemployment benefits. In the earlier years there were only two requirements for eligibility: that the per capita income of the household was below the assistance line and that the household had the local *hukou*. Eligibility was subject to annual

Table 4.2 Average thresholds and payments of *dibao*, 2006–2013

YEAR	AVERAGE ASSISTANCE LINE STANDARD (YUAN)	AVERAGE ACTUAL PAYMENTS (YUAN)
2006	169.6	83.6
2007	182.4	102.7
2008	205.3	143.7
2009	227.6	172.0
2010	251.2	189.0
2011	287.6	240.3
2012	330.1	239.1
2013	373.0	264.0

Source: MCA (various years).

review: at least one member of the household had to have a local *hukou* and fulfil the means-test requirements. Members of the household without local *hukou* (spouses coming from other localities) would be excluded from the calculation of benefits yet their working incomes would be included. The means test covered all sources of income, and from 2012 onwards household assets were also taken into account – bank savings, securities, vehicles and housing. Again, where assets were concerned, local governments were given discretion to set their own conditions.

In September 2012, the State Council produced the *Opinion on Further Strengthening the Work of the Dibao*, which reiterated the need for local governments to set up and readjust the local assistance line scientifically, make thorough investigations of the assets and incomes of applicants, formulate the processing procedures, and confirm the need for public monitoring. Local governments are encouraged to adopt mixed methods, among them actual basic living expenses requirements, Engel's coefficient, and consideration of the local situation, such as the local minimum wage and local financial capacity.

As a landmark of social assistance development, in February 2014 the State Council issued the *Temporary Method on Social Assistance*, which unifies the operation of the *dibao* system in both urban and rural areas, and specifies assistance targets, the types of assistance actually provided (education, health care, housing, employment, emergencies and disaster relief) and the need to facilitate and mobilize society's resources to provide complementary assistance. The *Method* has not only focused on *dibao* but has incorporated all of the laws and regulations relating to relief work in natural disasters and the Five Guarantees' Scheme (see chapter 2, p. 19), as well as a variety of assistance. Finally, there should be an effective management system for monitoring performance. In essence, social assistance is no longer perceived simply as meeting survival needs but should include support for developmental needs in health, education and employment.

Major issues

Social assistance in China is widely regarded as having played a vital role in facilitating economic reforms and maintaining social stability through offering protection to the unemployed and to laid-off employees. However, along with programme expansion, the operation of *dibao* has been plagued by a number of issues. First, as it is a means-tested programme, assessment of income has been a persistent problem in its administration. In the past, local governments relied mainly upon two methods to target poor households: means-testing and community monitoring. Community monitoring involves publicizing the names of recipients locally, and neighbours are encouraged to report suspected fraud to the street offices (extension administrative units of the district government). Verification of incomes, however, has proved to be extremely difficult for programme administrators. Household incomes are easily subject to fraud, and hidden incomes from informal employment are widespread (Leung, 2006; Leung and Xu, 2009;

Wong et al., 2014). The common practice is to use proxy-means criteria, such as the possession of expensive home accoutrements or leading a luxurious lifestyle, to determine eligibility. So far, fraud and abuse of social security benefits have not been treated as criminal offences. In recent years, an increasing number of cities have established a special department responsible for verifying the incomes and assets of households applying for or receiving social assistance. The creation of such a department, through cooperation with relevant and cross-regional government authorities such as banks and government departments in charge of housing and transportation, is expected to provide a major remedy to the difficulties in checking out the incomes of *dibao* recipients.

Second, along with the rapid expansion in both expenditure and coverage of *dibao*, a rising concern is that a high proportion of the recipients are able-bodied – according to the official data, around 60 per cent (Leung and Xu, 2009). It is generally recognized that recipients rarely exit the programme through re-employment. This has led to general public disapproval of *dibao* for 'encouraging people to become lazy' or 'creating welfare dependency or a welfare trap'. In fact, the moving of able-bodied recipients into paid employment has been a major concern of both central and local governments in China.

Since 2004, many provinces and cities have experimented with some sort of combined measure of workfare, involving the use of 'sticks and carrots' to encourage able-bodied recipients to take paid jobs. Among such measures are compulsory community work; job training, referral and placement services; allowing recipients to retain part of their income from employment without deductions); gradual reduction of benefits after employment; subsidies for enrolment in social insurance schemes; tax incentives for employers; bonuses for finding jobs; and the provision of loans for those engaging in self-employment or other forms of entrepreneurship. These services are usually provided by the Department of Human Resources and Social Security. In most places, more stringent measures are attached to the conditions of benefit receipt for those able to work. For instance, they would lose their assistance if they refused two or three times to take up jobs offered by employment agencies. Despite these efforts to monitor eligibility and promote employment among recipients, low-income and poor households across the country remain reluctant to leave the *dibao* programme. If they lose the *dibao* benefit, they automatically lose all supplementary benefits, such as Medical Assistance, Educational Assistance and Housing Assistance. Low-income families consider these benefits more important than standard *dibao* cash benefits. More importantly, the difficulty of checking informal employment has encouraged recipients to remain in the scheme and combine the benefits of *dibao* and income from employment (Leung and Xu, 2009; Wong et al., 2014).

Third, poverty among the elderly and children has become a significant phenomenon. In 2010, around 3.4 million urban old people lived on *dibao* benefits (MCA, 2012a). In fact, the proportion of older people covered by *dibao* underestimates the magnitude of old-age poverty. In most places, older people have tended to be systematically excluded from *dibao* as a result of the inclusion of family obligations in the eligibility assessment. Based on the household as the receiving unit for benefit, the general practice is to take account of the incomes of adult children, either living separately or under the same roof. The elderly are eligible for *dibao* only if their children are proven to be unable to support them financially. There are also cases where adult children are reluctant both to be means-tested and to meet their filial obligations, leading to the denial of social assistance to the elderly.

One prominent feature of the *dibao* recipient profile in urban areas in 2012 was that around 25 per cent were children (including students) (MCA, 2013b). It is recognized that the risks of children falling into poverty and being deprived of basic rights to education and health care have increased dramatically in China over recent decades. However, child poverty has been a nationally neglected phenomenon in government social policies, including the government social assistance scheme. This is partly because policy-makers tend to perceive the family as traditionally bearing primary responsibility for providing care and support to its members and to believe that any government intervention would erode family welfare obligations.

AN ASSESSMENT

Incremental policy-making and implementation in China exemplifies the Chinese approach to designing and delivering social protection programmes. In the early decades, the development of the social security system was intended mainly to reduce the financial burden of SOEs and to facilitate their restructuring to enhance competitiveness. Later, as the issues of massive layoffs, rising medical costs and inadequate retirement protection emerged, the government was urged to make reforms to tackle the destabilizing factors of social security reforms. With the recent shift of China's developmental priorities from economic growth to social development, the central government has taken greater responsibility for funding social programmes through central transfers, such as subsidies to pension funds, new pension and health-care schemes for urban residents, and social assistance. This has played an important role in incentivising local government spending, redistributing resources, and enabling the less developed areas to set up social programmes.

Although the establishment of a sustainable, affordable and effective urban social protection system has long been on the agenda of the central government, since the mid-1980s, because of the practice of fiscal and welfare decentralization, most of the responsibility for financing social programmes was transferred to local governments – a factor which contributes significantly to the lack of a unified system across China. Indeed, over-reliance on local governments for the financing of social protection measures has not only left vast needs unmet in poor cities but has increased regional disparity in social and economic development.

In the course of policy implementation, the role of central government has been limited to establishing broad guiding principles, while local governments are encouraged to experiment with different solutions or models based on local circumstances and financial capacity. As a result, the highly decentralized delivery approach has led to policy innovations and discrepancies. On the other hand, mutual learning among localities and learning from international practices has contributed greatly to policy improvements.

It has to be recognized that social protection policies in China are faced with both equity and efficiency problems. In the course of reforms in the economic and welfare systems since the early 1980s, people have fared differently not only in incomes and wealth but also in access to social programmes. While the government has taken control of the benefits and policy agenda regarding when and what programmes should be available for different segments of the population, this has led to high fragmentation and inequality in social insurance benefits. Harmonized national social protection is important in integrating different social insurance systems. Both central and local governments must commit sufficient financial resources to ensure sustainability. But there is also an urgent need to ensure coverage for migrant workers and the informally employed. Pooling of social insurance funds must be conducted at the provincial level to ensure better portability.

The total contribution rate of the five urban social insurance systems is exceedingly high by international standards, accounting for about 43 per cent of the wage bill (32 per cent from the employers). As a consequence, employers may attempt to shift the cost by lowering wages or recruiting workers informally without labour contracts. Incentives for non-compliance remain high, particularly for migrant and informally employed workers. In the long run, unification or harmonization of social protection in urban and rural areas, as well as across different sectors, will be required. The development of the private market for social security fund investments, retirement protection and health care through tax exemption is urgent. The development of the urban social assistance programmes has, to a great extent, filled the welfare gaps left by the shortcomings of the social insurance programmes. The programmes should include migrant workers, and the assistance level should be standardized according to actual needs rather than the financial capacity of local governments.

Overall, social protection reforms are often controversial because they require long-term planning in terms of financial sustainability and face short-term pressures in terms of rising demand and adequacy of benefits. Reform priority in the last decade has been on extending social security coverage, so that there are now more employers and employees contributing to the social security funding pools, which, in turn, can become more sustainable. Adequacy of benefits and harmonization of different social insurance programmes will be of foremost concern in the coming years. China still has a long way to go to set up an integrated and coordinated urban social protection system; it will require long-term planning and financial sustainability to ensure viability and effectiveness.

5 Rural Social Protection

Within three decades of the market-oriented reforms, rapid urbanization and large-scale migration of people from the countryside to the cities have transformed the landscape of rural China. Rural development is marked by diversity and heterogeneity both across and within provinces. On top of the wide income disparities, rural areas have been far below the urban areas in social development, in terms of life expectancy, infant mortality and per capita health-care expenditure, as well as educational outcomes, such as years of education and literacy rate (OECD, 2009, pp. 21–2). Overall, rural development has been limited in terms of access and quality of the social protection system and social welfare services.

China's rural social protection policies embrace social insurance and social assistance programmes. Social insurance includes the Residents' Old-Age Pension System (ROAPS) and New Cooperative Medical System (NCMS). Within social assistance there are five programmes: the 'Five Guarantees' programme (*wubao*), the Minimum Living Standards Guarantee System (*dibao*), Medical Assistance, Educational Assistance and Temporary Assistance. In principle, rural residents are eligible for and mainly covered by the social insurance programmes, while social assistance programmes are means-tested, providing cash and/or in-kind support to people in need.

Among examples of international reviews on rural social protection system are those on rural development (OECD, 2009; Xu and Zhang, 2010), health care (Hillier and Zheng, 1994; Han and Luo, 2005;

Wagstaff et al., 2007, 2009; Brown et al., 2009; Duckett, 2011b) and old age support (Shi, 2006; Giles et al., 2010; Shen and Williamson, 2010; Cai et al., 2012; Dorfman et al., 2013). This chapter first presents the major social protection programmes currently operating in rural areas with an account of their development and analysis on the main issues involved. It ends with an overall appraisal of the strengths and weaknesses of the current rural social protection system.

BACKGROUND

Under the centrally planned economy, the communes in the rural areas had two major collectively funded and administered welfare programmes. One was the *wubao* and the other was the Cooperative Medical System (CMS). *Wubao* provided income support and care services to older people and orphans without family, those unable to work, and those lacking sources of income – 'the three nos' – while CMS provided rural people with access to basic medical care. Apart from these, there were several government-funded categorical social relief schemes, such as for victims of natural disasters, people with disabilities, families of martyrs and servicemen, and veterans. Decollectivization reforms in the rural economic system in the early 1980s had led to the abrupt collapse of the community-based welfare programmes in most parts of rural China, particularly in the less developed inland regions. In many places, even the support for those eligible for *wubao* and the most needy was not guaranteed (Tian and Lue, 1991). This is because collective capacity for mutual help in the countryside was generally weakened because of the removal of collective funding and the institutional arrangements.

The rebuilding of the rural social protection system has taken a long and winding road, and substantial progress has been made only since the early 2000s. For decades, rural people were expected to rely primarily on the land and their family for their needs. In the 1980s, government efforts focused mainly on reducing poverty. Overall, other welfare programmes were largely neglected by local governments preoccupied with the economic reforms (Leung, 1990a). Initial concern to rebuild the rural social protection system came to the attention of the government in the mid-1980s. With the 7th Five-Year Plan (1986–90), the government proposed to establish 'a socialist social security system with Chinese characteristics'. Population ageing and the anticipated erosion of the capacity of families to care for the elderly following the implementation of the one-child policy were among the widely acknowledged imperatives for rebuilding the rural social protection system. Without an effective pension system, peasants could not afford to retire. Many of them had to rely on their children, in particular sons, for support in old age, and more sons meant better protection. Since the early 1990s, three major programmes have been piloted for the rural population, including old-age pensions, cooperative medical schemes and social assistance (*dibao*), all of which have undergone a period of retrenchment as a result of economic constraints on local governments. They were resumed in the mid-2000s following substantial subsidies from the central government.

OLD-AGE PENSIONS

The mid-1980s saw an increasing number of locally initiated rural old-age pension schemes in the wealthier localities, where rural labour was increasingly shifting to non-agricultural production in the mushrooming TVEs. These pension schemes differed widely in terms of funding, levels of pooling and benefit structures. In 1987, the Ministry of Civil Affairs was given the mandate to explore and set up a rural social security system. After several years of experimentation, the MCA promoted the establishment of a unified county-based rural old-age pension system and required all the former village- or township-based schemes to merge into county-based ones.

These schemes are often referred to as the Rural Old-Age Pension System.

The funding of the county-based schemes was based on the principle of shared responsibility among individuals, collectives and local governments. These schemes were run on a voluntary basis. All farmers aged between 20 to 59 were eligible, and they could decide both the rates of individual contributions (a monthly sum ranging from 2 to 20 yuan) and the method of contributing (monthly, annually or in lump sum). Collective economic enterprises were required to subsidize the scheme, with a maximum limit of 50 per cent of the individual contribution. Local governments provided preferential taxation policies on the collective subsidies. Funds had to be invested in government bonds. A special unit was set up within the county civil affairs bureaus to manage the schemes and was allowed to use 3 per cent of the funds to cover administrative costs.

Enthusiastically promoted by the MCA, the county-based Rural Old-Age Pension System was rolled out rapidly. By the end of 1997 over 90 per cent of the counties had implemented the schemes, covering 74.5 million peasants (MCA, 1998). The number of participants actually represented only 21 per cent of the total peasant population at this time. In 1998 the management of the schemes was handed over to the newly established Ministry of Labour and Social Security, which was given the mandate to design and manage social insurance schemes for both urban and rural areas. The number of counties implementing the schemes began to decline, however, following the 1998 Asian financial crisis. Most of the schemes, particularly in the less developed regions, came to a halt. By the end of 2006 the number of participants had declined to 53.74 million (NBS, 2006).

The resumption of the rural pension schemes began cautiously in the early 2000s. When rural issues became more prominent, the 16th CPC Congress in 2002 encouraged only those localities with sound economic conditions to explore the establishment of rural old-age pensions, medical insurance and *dibao*. In 2007, a number of cities and provinces took the lead in setting up a new type of rural pension scheme subsidized by government funds. Nationwide experimentation with this new model began in 2008 following the 17th CPC Congress, which encouraged all local governments to experiment with government-subsidized rural old-age pensions. The experiments finally led to the launch of the New Rural Old-Age Pension System (NROAPS) in 2009, replacing the old and defunct system established in the 1990s.

According to the State Council's 2009 *Guidelines for Experimenting with the NROAPS*, the new system operates based on a partially funded approach – a pay-as-you-go benefit funded by the government, plus fully funded individual accounts. Participation is also voluntary. All rural residents aged sixteen or above, other than current students, who are not covered by the urban employee pension schemes are eligible. Five levels of individual annual contributions were set, ranging from 100 to 500 yuan. Participants are allowed to select a level for individual contributions. Both central and local governments provide subsidies for the schemes. The central government bears responsibility for full funding of the basic tier for counties in the central and western regions and 50 per cent for those in the eastern regions. In 2009, local governments were required to provide subsidies of at least 30 yuan per year for each participant. There are two levels of benefits – a basic pension and an individual account pension. A participant reaching the age of 60 after contributing for fifteen years receives a monthly minimum of 55 yuan from the basic pension plus a monthly sum equal to 1/139 of the total funds accumulated in the individual account. Those currently aged 60 years and above receive only the basic pension. Local governments were allowed to determine the structure and levels of both individual contributions and benefits according to the local context.

In 2013, the NROAPS covered a total of 363.5 million participants, with 128 million retirees receiving monthly benefits (Central People's

Government, 2014). In February 2014, the NROAPS was formally unified with the urban ROAPS under the *Opinion on Establishing a Unified Urban and Rural Pension System* and the policy standard and management were unified to facilitate rural–urban mobility. The new unified scheme has twelve monthly contributory levels (100 to 2,000 yuan).

POVERTY AND SOCIAL ASSISTANCE

The poverty alleviation projects

As described in chapter 3, the market-oriented economic reforms in the 1980s substantially reduced the size of China's rural poor population. All along, the Chinese government interpreted poverty as associated with adverse natural conditions and a low level of economic development. Under the State Council Leading Group of Poverty Alleviation and Development, projects were set up in the mid-1980s as a major approach to address rural poverty. In the earlier years, liberalized economic reforms had contributed enormously to raising the living standards of the general population in China and were regarded as the most effective measure in reducing development-related poverty (CDRF, 2009; Wang, 2012). Through a geographical targeting method, poor counties were selected by the national and local governments for poverty reduction. It is noteworthy that old revolutionary and ethnic minority areas were given higher priority for assistance. This strategy has involved a series of measures, such as building infrastructure, supporting agricultural production, providing employment through public works or TVEs, and organizing the migration of people from poor to well-off areas. Natural conditions, such as disasters or scarcity of resources, had been the prominent cause of poverty in rural areas, which provided the rationale for the development-based poverty alleviation approach.

Since the second half of the 1990s, however, poverty reduction has slowed down. Besides hostile natural conditions, poverty can be caused by disabilities or illness rather than the lack of opportunities to work. Now, lack of labour, medical costs arising from major illness, and children's education were found to be the major factors pulling rural households into poverty. In other words, rural poverty became related more to the characteristics of individual households than to natural or economic conditions. The remaining poverty-stricken areas were geographically scattered, not only in mountainous and ethnic minority areas but also in rich areas, with the aged, the sick and the disabled becoming the major components of the rural poor population (Riskin, 1994; World Bank, 2009). In the early 2000s, therefore, the government began to give increasing attention to the restructuring and establishment of social assistance programmes targeting individual households, significant among them *dibao*, *wubao* and Medical Assistance. With the adjustment of the poverty line (2,300 yuan per person per year) closer to the international level, the number of poverty-stricken people was reduced to 82.5 million in 2013 (World Bank, 2013).

Dibao

The start of rural *dibao* was mainly a response in the mid-1990s to the alleged inefficiency of the development-based poverty alleviation projects in tackling the hard-core poor households. Meanwhile, the widely acknowledged success of urban *dibao* provided an 'encouraging example' (see chapter 4) for the Ministry of Civil Affairs to replicate the programme in the countryside. In fact, alongside the pilots of urban *dibao* in the mid-1990s, experiments with rural *dibao* began in some economically developed provinces. Later promoted by the MCA, it was adopted rapidly in many counties in less developed regions. Due to economic constraints, however, most dropped out of the pilot projects and moved to a Temporary Assistance scheme named Assistance for the Extremely Poor Households (AFEPH), which provided temporary relief to rural households impoverished by major illness or loss of family labour. Subject to the financial capacity of local governments, this programme provided small, short-term and discretionary cash benefits based on the nationally defined poverty line.

In the early years, funding responsibility and assistance levels were defined exclusively within local governments and rural communities. The proportion of funding each party shared differed across areas, and the local civil affairs department was put in charge of managing the schemes. By 2001, over 80 per cent of the counties reported having set up such schemes. Following the implementation of fee-to-taxation policy in 2002 and the abolition of agriculture taxation in 2006, many townships and villages were no longer able to provide their portion of funding. As a result, most of the counties which had relied on townships or villages for finance abandoned the scheme and only a small number in the economically well-off regions were able to afford the costs and continue. In response to this, between 2003 and 2005 the State Council and the MCA issued a number of policy directives to advise local governments not to rush to set up the schemes without first ensuring the appropriate financial conditions. In particular, the central government encouraged pilot projects only in places where local economic conditions would allow, whereas it advised economically underdeveloped regions to continue with the AFEPH as an alternative.

Further to address the issue of rural poverty, the attitude of the central government towards the establishment of rural *dibao* changed markedly in the Sixth Plenum of the 17th Party Congress in 2006. The central government encouraged all counties to establish the scheme. This was announced again in 2007 by the State Council in the *Notice on Setting up Rural Dibao Nationally*, which proposed to set up rural *dibao* throughout the country by the end of the year. One major incentive for the rapid expansion was the availability of central transfers. In 2007, the central government allocated 3 billion yuan to subsidize local government establishment of rural *dibao*. In the following years the subsidies increased substantially, mostly going to provincial governments in the central and western regions. Along with the increased central government transfers, the number of recipients grew rapidly and by 2013 had reached 54 million; central government transfer accounted for 71 per cent of the total expenditures. Table 5.1 shows the rising proportion of central transfers and the number of rural *dibao* recipients between 2007 and 2013.

The design of rural *dibao* is a modified version of urban *dibao*, its objective to guarantee a basic living for poor households. According to the State Council 2007 *Notice*, the assistance line for rural *dibao* should be determined by governments at or above the county level in accordance with the costs required for local residents to maintain a basic living – namely, food, clothing, water, electricity and other expenses. It also required that the line should be adjusted along with changes in

Table 5.1 Coverage and funding of rural *dibao*, 2007–2013

YEAR	NUMBER OF RECIPIENTS (IN MILLION PERSONS)	TOTAL EXPENDITURE (IN BILLION YUAN)	CENTRAL TRANSFERS (%)
2007	35.66	10.09	N/A
2008	43.05	22.87	N/A
2009	47.60	36.30	70.4
2010	52.14	44.50	60.4
2011	53.06	66.77	75.3
2012	53.45	71.80	60.1
2013	53.88	86.69	70.6

Source: MCA (various years).

the price of basic living necessities. In a subsequent document, *Notice on Strengthening the Management of Rural Dibao Fund*, which was jointly issued by the MCA and the Ministry of Finance in 2008, the central government allowed rural *dibao* benefits to be determined either as the difference between family incomes and the threshold or by grouping eligible households into different categories according to the severity of poverty.

In practice, the determination of benefit rates and eligibility varied markedly across localities. A study of four provinces revealed several features with regard to these aspects (Zhang, Xu et al., 2011). First, in the early years, when central government transfers were not available or very limited, local governments were usually very cautious in the provision of benefits. As most *dibao* schemes, particularly those in the less developed regions, evolved out of the AFEPH, many places either tended to use the same standards for *dibao* or determined the rates with reference to the national poverty line. Since 2009, when central government transfers began to increase markedly, most provinces have shifted to more standardized methods, such as the budget standards method, Engel's coefficient, or the income or consumption-based method, and raised the overall benefit rates. Obviously, central government transfers worked as important incentives for local governments to improve programme design and implementation.

Second, to balance the availability of funds and the adequacy of benefits, most localities have used more than one method to determine the *dibao* income threshold, and the formulation of the assistance line is the result of many factors. The most important is local financial capacity. Discretion is often exercised through a very complicated 'adjustment coefficient', which reflects the local situation. Another is a comparison of standards with those of other localities. In this regard, economic conditions often served as the main reason for local governments to decide whether the benefit rates should be set higher or lower than those in other localities.

Third, the provision of actual benefits to a household is often loosely related to the assistance line. Because the incomes of rural households are difficult to verify, it is an almost impossible task to allocate *dibao* benefits based on the difference between household income and the assistance line. Instead, 'categorical assistance' has been used widely to classify eligible households according to the severity of financial difficulty for different rates of benefits. The categorization is based on various factors, such as household incomes, number of dependents, available labour force and contingent expenditures. Households in the greatest need or without their own incomes are often prioritized for assistance with a higher level of benefits. Those less urgently in need, or with incomes of their own, are often given a discretionary amount of money based on the availability of funds.

The attitudes of local programme administrators towards benefit allocation also affected the actual benefits received. Local administrators tended to have a strong bias against the 'undeserving poor' – those with the ability to work. In contrast, they tended to favour households who faced difficulties as a result of factors beyond their control or those who may not survive without assistance. On the other hand, because the allocation of *dibao* benefits to the able-bodied is less acceptable to villagers, households with healthy members were usually given much less in order to avoid 'welfare dependency'. In addition, the categorical scale was often designed with a considerable degree of detail. Apart from the need to differentiate households by degree of poverty, it was also necessary to ensure fairness of benefit allocation and convenience for village committees to process claimants and determine benefits.

As such, there are substantial disparities across localities in the levels of *dibao* benefits. In 2013, the national average assistance standard for rural *dibao* was 203 yuan per person per month, though it ranged from less than 100 yuan to more than 300 yuan, reflecting differences in local financial capacity. Table 5.2 provides the average assistance standards and actual payments of rural *dibao* between 2007 and 2013.

Table 5.2 Average assistance standard and actual payment of rural *dibao* (yuan per person per month)

YEAR	ASSISTANCE STANDARD	ACTUAL PAYMENT
2007	70	39
2008	82	50
2009	101	68
2010	117	74
2011	143	106
2012	172	104
2013	203	116

Source: MCA (various years).

The study by Zhang, Xu et al. (2011) showed that poverty targeting has been a major problem since the inception of *dibao* and remained an unresolved issue. By design, *dibao* is a means-tested programme where the unit being tested is the household. Although all provinces have specified an income threshold below which households are eligible for benefits, in practice means-testing is rarely used because of the difficulties and high administrative costs involved in verifying incomes. Where this method is used, it is often used to estimate the potential income of a household based on its human or productive assets, such as the availability of able-bodied persons, the size of its farmland, and husbandry.

In addition, 'community democratic selection' has been the most common form of poverty targeting in rural *dibao*. Most localities have relied on village committees to determine eligibility through a series of 'democratic procedures' in which key representatives of the village committees are consulted to determine the actual needs of *dibao* applicants. The village committee is a kind of self-governing organization, in principle democratically elected by local residents. Supervised by the township government, the committee manages local resources, delivers social services, and implements family planning policy. In the early years, when rural *dibao* benefits were low and covered only those households in extreme poverty, this practice was widely acknowledged to be an effective method in the allocation of benefits. As benefits and coverage increased, more and more low-income households became eligible. This rendered the democratic community targeting method increasingly difficult, and it was often fraught with problems such as abuse or fraud. For example, a common practice is for village committee members to grant *dibao* to those applicants with whom they have a good relationship and to reject those with whom they have a poor relationship. This is often described as 'relationship *dibao*'.

For this reason, local governments increasingly do not trust the village committees to carry out the task of targeting poor households. In many places, local civil affairs departments have implemented various checks and balances to ensure that the targeting reflects collective decisions. On the part of the government or civil affairs departments, in particular, much of the work in poverty targeting has been to monitor the processes in order to prevent abuse of the system by village representatives. Local civil affairs departments have obviously recognized these problems, but their capacity to improve the application process is limited. Village committees by design are self-governing organizations, and their members are the elected representatives of the residents. Local civil affairs departments do not have the authority to supervise or discipline these elected leaders. For this reason, in many provinces, counties or townships, civil affairs departments have begun to receive and process applications directly, while village committees play only an auxiliary role in facilitating assessments or making household visits. This is a major improvement in the targeting method. However, a major problem with local civil affairs departments is that they usually have limited administrative capacity and resources, including personnel and funds, to manage the schemes directly. If such constraints cannot be dealt with, it is likely that they will have to continue to rely on the village committees for the determination of eligibility and benefits.

The World Bank made a critical assessment of the design and implementation problems of rural *dibao* in Guangdong province, mentioning inadequate programme coverage, very low levels of support, insufficient fiscal inputs, weak programme governance and limited administrative capacity. It raised doubts as to whether the programme could ensure a minimum subsistence level for the poor and eradicate extreme poverty (World Bank, 2011, p. 80). Similarly, the China Household Income Project survey in 2007 indicated that more than 90 per cent of the households in poverty did not receive *dibao* and that more than half of the households in receipt of *dibao* were not poor (Luo and Sicular, 2013, p. 225). Hopefully, the situation has now improved.

Finally, the phenomenon of marginal poverty – households which are disqualified for *dibao* because their incomes are slightly above the income threshold – has recently become a major issue. Local civil affairs departments have different definitions of marginally poor households, based either on incomes or on contingencies. Two basic approaches are used to define and deal with marginally poor households. One is based on household incomes, which defines the marginally poor as those with incomes above the eligibility threshold by a certain percentage. The other defines the marginally poor more broadly as those households who are not *dibao* recipients but are experiencing financial difficulties due to circumstances such as loss of working members of the family (through death, illness or disability), natural disasters, high medical expenditures, or children being enrolled in a fee-paying high school or college.

The concept of marginal poverty highlights the general vulnerability of rural households on account of the absence or limited coverage of social security programmes and services. Faced with natural disasters or illness among their breadwinners, most rural households are vulnerable. They are mostly denied *dibao* benefits because of limited funds available or because their incomes are slightly above the assistance threshold. While they usually have enough money to maintain a basic standard of living in normal circumstances, they may fall into poverty when faced with unexpected demands on their finances, such as medical fees and recovery after natural disasters.

Currently, the locally funded Temporary Assistance scheme is the main policy addressing the needs of the marginally poor. In most places, Medical Assistance and Educational Assistance are also available to those suffering financial difficulties due to high medical or educational fees. These programmes were originally designed only for *dibao* recipients, but later they were extended to marginally poor households in response to their vulnerability in these aspects. In fact, in most places, all households are eligible for these supplementary benefits if they have incurred high medical costs or encounter unexpected contingencies.

All rural households, including the *dibao* recipients, are eligible for some sort of Temporary Assistance from the civil affairs department if their basic standard of living is affected by unforeseen circumstances. One reason is that *dibao* recipients may frequently meet with difficulties even though they are regularly supported by the scheme. Another reason is that non-*dibao* households would often come to civil affairs departments for help whenever they faced difficulties. As the formal application and approval procedures usually take a long time, assistance from *dibao* would not immediately be available to them. As a government organization with the mandate to take care of the poor, the civil affairs department is not in a position to reject such requests, and would therefore often give applicants some temporary relief on a case-by-case basis. In the event that circumstances such as the death or permanent disability of an able-bodied family member could lead the household into long-term poverty, the civil affairs department would usually advise them to apply for *dibao* by going through the formal application procedures. In other cases, such as a household incurring high medical costs or with a child attending college, they would either be advised to apply for *dibao* or be provided with a discretionary amount of cash assistance through the Temporary Assistance scheme. As such, while *dibao* was designed with a strong anti-poverty goal in that it provides assistance to poor households up to the threshold, in practice it is stretched to address the consequences of the lack or inadequacy of other social programmes to address poverty resulting from catastrophic illness, disability or the loss of family breadwinners. As *dibao* needs to provide support to households in emergencies, it serves multiple functions, not only in poverty alleviation but also in helping people to address uncertainties.

The 'Five Guarantees' programme (wubao)

Wubao was established in the mid-1950s as a collective social relief programme catering mainly for rural older people without family caregivers and sources of income, though it also covers a small number of orphans. The communes were responsible for providing the elderly with a minimum level of food, clothing, shelter, medical care and funeral expenses (and educational expenses for orphans). People were cared for either in their own homes in the villages with cash and in-kind benefits or collectively in the homes for the aged administered by the communes. Soon after the disbandment of the commune system in the early 1980s, collective provision for the *wubao* became difficult. In the early years, the central government focused its main efforts on ensuring the continued provision by the village committees and township governments. In practice, there were two funding methods. In places where villages maintained some form of collective economy, the programme would be financed by the collective. In other places, financial support had to come from the income of the township government via village households. After the disbandment of communes, village committees were given the authority to collect fees and levies from the peasants to support public and social services. The collections had to be submitted to the township governments, while the village committees could retain a certain proportion for administrative expenses. In some poor places, those qualifying for *wubao* would be allocated a piece of farmland, which they were obviously unable to manage on their own. There were also villages where there was an old-age 'tax' on each of the households, and the *wubao* recipients had to collect the 'tax', door to door, by themselves (Zhang and Xu, 2012).

This situation continued until 1994, when the State Council issued a major document to reinvigorate this programme, *Regulations on the Work of Rural Five-Guarantees Households*, which laid down the basic principles with regard to eligibility, financing, types and levels of benefits, and methods of providing the service. The programme was still defined as collective welfare, but the township government was put in charge of its administration. Sources of funding included the rural collective economy as well as 'township unified collections and village retainings', whichever was suitable for the local situation.

Eligibility was clarified by including a definition of legitimate caregivers as those persons who bore the legal duty of family support as set by the Marriage Law of 1980. Provisions were divided into five categories: food and fuel, clothing and pocket money, housing with the basic necessities, medical care and nursing care for those unable to perform daily activities, and an adequate funeral. Levels of benefits were left to the discretion of the local government, provided that it was not any lower than the general living standards of local villagers. The *Regulations* encouraged township governments to set up homes for the aged and allowed the homes to engage in income-generating activities and use the profits to improve services (Zhang and Xu, 2012).

The 1994 *Regulations* soon met with new difficulties in financing the scheme. The 'township unified collections and village retainings' were intended to cover the costs of village administration and a limited number of communal welfare services, including care for the needy elderly. However, the policy was soon abused by local governments as an important source of income outside of the budget. Both the services and the amount of money collected grew rapidly in the following years and became an increasingly heavy burden on the farmers as well as a major source of social instability in the countryside. For these reasons, throughout the 1990s the central government took various measures to 'reduce peasants' burdens'. Following the introduction of 'tax-for-fee' policy (2002) and the abolition of the agricultural tax (2006), township governments and villages were no longer able to rely on collections or taxation from farmers as sources of funding for the *wubao* programme. The problem of financing re-emerged once again.

This led to a revision of the 1994 *Regulations* in 2006, which eventually turned *wubao* from a collective- into a government-run programme. Specifically, the central government would allocate a block grant to local governments for the general administration of townships and villages which could be used to support elderly care. The county government was held responsible for funding and managing the homes for the aged. Thereafter, *wubao* was divided into two separate programmes, with the central and local governments sharing financing responsibilities. The revised *Regulations* also redefined the benefit levels for *wubao* recipients as equivalent to the average standards of local residents, which was regarded as progress over the previous vague definition of 'general' standards. It reaffirmed the definition of legitimate caregivers in accordance with the revised Marriage Law of 2001, which specified parents, children and grandparents as those who bore the legal duty of family support. In practice, with the introduction of the *dibao*, the *wubao* has become redundant. In principle, the *dibao* can also cover those who qualify for *wubao*.

In 2013, the *wubao* programme covered 5.37 million older people, of whom 1.8 million were cared for collectively in homes for the aged and 3.5 million in their own homes in villages. The average annual cost of caring for an older person in their own home was 3,499 yuan, while for those cared in the homes for the aged it was 4,685 yuan (MCA, 2014b). The assistance standard is higher than the average *dibao* standard of 203 yuan per person per month.

Medical Assistance

Local experiments with Medical Assistance schemes for the rural population started in Shanghai and Guangdong as early as the early 2000s. The decision of the central government to implement rural Medical Assistance was first announced in 2002, and the Ministry of Civil Affairs was in charge of the programme. In 2003, the *Opinion on the Implementation of Rural MA*, issued jointly by the MCA, the Ministry of Finance and the Ministry of Health, defined the goal of Medical Assistance broadly as protecting rural households against poverty through serious illness. In line with this goal, Medical Assistance provides cash assistance for poor people to cover expenses for in-patient services or treatment of major illnesses. Funds are also used to support poor households' participation in the New Cooperative Medical System and to cover part of their remaining medical expenses after reimbursement by the NCMS.

Financing was shared by central and local governments and drew on a wide range of sources, including transfer payments from the central government, revenues of local governments, incomes from welfare lottery funds administered by civil affairs departments, charity donations, and other funds available to the locality. Again, the central government was responsible for subsidizing local governments in the central and western provinces. Between 2003 and 2007, 22 out of the 31 provinces received subsidies from the central government, the amount of which was based on the number of eligible households reported by the local government. By the end of 2006, most counties had established such schemes.

Faced with many constraints, particularly the lack of decision-making power over government funding sources and the limited control over health service providers, the MCA adopted a learning-from-practice approach to the task. Implementation of the programme was allocated to county authorities, which were given considerable discretion over both policy design and execution, including financing, eligibility, types of illness or services to be covered, and levels of benefits and payment methods – leading to marked variations across localities.

According to the 2003 *Opinion*, the intended beneficiaries of Medical Assistance were primarily *dibao* and *wubao* recipients. However, local governments had been given discretion to include other categories of people for the assistance, such as families of ex-servicemen or martyrs, people with disabilities in government offices, or single-child families. In fact, in most localities, eligibility has been extended to cover all households whose livelihood is severely affected by unexpected high expenditure on medical services, even though they are not currently receiving social assistance. In short, all rural households are potential Medical Assistance beneficiaries.

Direct cash payments from Medical Assistance are made on a reimbursement basis. The amount of money for which an applicant can be reimbursed is usually set as a percentage of the total medical costs between a floor for co-payment and a ceiling of maximum payment, which vary with different categories of eligible households and depending upon the amount of medical expenses. Generally, recipients of *wubao* are subsidized at a higher rate than other poor households and better-off households at a lower rate than the poor ones. Reimbursement rates are usually based on a progressive structure – the higher the medical costs, the larger the proportion to be reimbursed. In addition, most schemes specify a fixed amount to be borne by the applicant, above which the costs are calculated for subsidy.

In the early years, a major problem was that *dibao* recipients tended to be rejected by both the NCMS and Medical Assistance. While all *dibao* recipients were provided with the premium to enable them to enrol in the NCMS, in most localities it was the non-recipients of *dibao* who tended to receive most of the Medical Assistance (Xu and Song, 2006). This phenomenon is due largely to the reimbursement methods, under which potential beneficiaries, including poor households, are generally required to provide evidence of medical expenses when they apply for assistance. That is, they have to pay their medical bills before they can apply for support and get the costs reimbursed. Combined with the fact that Medical Assistance covers only expenses for receipt of in-patient services and that lump sum pre-payment for hospitalization is common practice in most hospitals, poor households usually have to spend a large sum of money before they can qualify for assistance. Those who cannot afford or manage to pay the costs in the first place could find it difficult to receive Medical Assistance support later.

Since early 2007, the failure of the Medical Assistance system to reach the poorest of the poor – because of high fixed costs, low rates of reimbursement and low ceilings – has been increasingly recognized by the government. In many places, changes were made to develop the utilization of funds by poor households. The rules on reimbursement based on evidence of medical expenses were loosened and more flexible measures were used to enable poor households to receive medical services. In most localities, poor households can apply for and receive support either before or during a period of hospitalization. More recently, many localities have improved the reimbursement procedures through direct payments to hospitals by the civil affairs departments, while recipients pay only the compulsory fee after receiving a service (Xu and Zhang, 2010).

In most localities, eligibility for Medical Assistance was expanded to out-patient services. Poor households on *wubao* and *dibao* schemes are each given a medical care account, in which a fixed amount of money is deposited to cover expenses related to out-patient care and the purchase of medicines. This is partly in recognition of the fact that the health of poor people tends to deteriorate because they fail to obtain early treatment. Furthermore, most localities have raised the ceilings and reimbursement rates to varying degrees, and the fixed payment floors have been removed for recipients of *dibao*.

By 2012, a total amount of 13.29 billion yuan had been allocated for Medical Assistance by governments at different levels; 44.9 million poor households were supported to enable them to participate in the NCMS, averaging 57.5 yuan each. In terms of direct assistance, the programme paid out an average of 722 yuan each to cover 15 million treatments. Nationally, in 2010, reimbursement rates ranged from 30 to 50 per cent of the remaining costs after NCMS payment (MCA, 2013b).

THE NEW COOPERATIVE MEDICAL SYSTEM (NCMS)

In 1956, rural cooperatives were required to provide medical assistance to those in need. By the late 1950s, the Cooperative Medical System was being piloted in many communes. During the Cultural Revolution, the CMS was further expanded rapidly to cover most of the rural villages, and in 1976 it was reported that over 90 per cent of the peasants had participated in the system. The brigades (the basic accounting and farm production units under the commune system) were responsible for funding, administering and delivering the schemes. Farmers were required to contribute a small sum as a registration fee in order to receive the service. During the Cultural Revolution, health workers were called 'barefoot doctors'. They were selected by the brigades from among the villagers and were given brief practical training in either the county or commune hospitals. They usually played the role of both farmer and doctor and were paid with work-points in the same way as the rest of the villagers.

In the early 1980s, the rural CMS was dismantled following reforms in the rural economic system. The abolition of the communes not only led to funding difficulties but also removed the organizational basis for collective health care (Hillier and Zheng, 1994). As a result, most of these schemes and facilities were abolished shortly afterwards, and in most places barefoot doctors were replaced by private practitioners. By 1986, only 5.4 per cent of the villages had CMS schemes (MOH, 1987). In other words, most peasants were paying fees for treatment which had become increasingly unaffordable.

Entering the 1990s, the collapse of the rural health-care system was followed by a nationwide trend of privatization or market-oriented reform in China's health system, which further exacerbated problems of access to health care for the rural population. Public hospitals were given increasing autonomy in fee charging, managing resources, and the remuneration of employees. The soaring prices of medicine and medical services contributed to rising rural poverty (Han and Luo, 2005). It was reported that poverty arising from illness increased from 21.6 per cent in 1998 to 33.4 per cent in 2003, that 48.9 per cent of people did not go to see a doctor when falling ill, and that 29.6 per cent did not receive hospitalization when they should (MOH, 2004, p. 15).

Throughout the 1990s, a major concern of the government was to explore new schemes for rural health financing. Beginning in the early 1990s, a number of provinces experimented with community-financed health-care insurance schemes based on voluntary participation. Because of the absence of financial support from the central government, however, these efforts resulted in only limited improvements. By 1997, only a small number of schemes had proved to be successful, mostly in wealthy areas. More importantly, as the schemes were primarily township- or village-based, the pooling of risk was limited. It was not until 2002 that the State Council issued the *Decision of the Central Government to Strengthen Rural Health Work* to confirm the key role of the central government in rebuilding the rural health programme. Further, in early 2003 the State Council endorsed the *Proposal on Establishing NCMS*, which was jointly prepared by the ministries of Health, Finance, and Agriculture. The *Proposals* laid down the basic directions and principles for the implementation of the rural NCMS.

According to the *Proposals*, the focus of the NCMS was covering expenses related to catastrophic illness and in-patient care. It continued to operate based on voluntary participation, but the township- or village-based pooling was replaced by county-based pooling. Funding was shared between the government and individual participants. For the central and western provinces, government funding was shared between the central and local governments; in 2003, both provided a subsidy of 10 yuan annually for each participant, while the latter was required to contribute a minimum of 30 yuan. Since then, subsidies from central and local governments have increased periodically. Again, central transfers had an immediate impact on nationwide adoption of the NCMS.

By 2008 all counties had implemented the programme, and by 2012 NCMS covered over 95 per cent of the rural population. Between 2003 and 2014, government subsidies grew substantially, from 20 yuan to 320 yuan per person per year, while individual contributions also increased, from 10 yuan to 70 yuan. This led to steady growth in both coverage and funding of the programme. Table 5.3 provides information on the situation of the NCMS between 2005 and 2012. The decreasing number of participants but the greater proportion of coverage from 2010 onwards may be a result of the continual decline in the rural population.

The NCMS originally provided coverage primarily for expenses related to in-patient care. Recently, a limited amount of out-patient expenses, particularly in relation to selected chronic diseases, have become reimbursable. Across the country, differences are found mainly in the structure and levels of benefits. In the early years, there were

Table 5.3 Coverage and funding of the NCMS, 2005–2012

YEAR	PARTICIPANTS (IN MILLIONS)	COVERAGE (%)	PER CAPITA FUNDING (YUAN)
2005	179	75.7	42.1
2006	410	80.7	52.1
2007	726	86.2	58.9
2008	815	91.5	96.3
2009	833	94.2	113.4
2010	836	96.0	156.6
2011	832	97.5	246.2
2012	805	98.3	308.5

Source: National Health and Family Planning Commission (2013).

both varying floors for fixed payment above which reimbursement was payable and varying ceilings of maximum payments. Along with general improvement in funding, benefit levels have generally been boosted by reducing the co-payment floors and raising both the ceilings and the rates for reimbursement. In 2013, nationally, benefits were paid ranging from 40 to 80 per cent of the total medical costs, varying with the type of service provider. Higher rates of reimbursement are found for services received in township hospitals than those in the counties or cities.

AN ASSESSMENT

Since the early 2000s, social programmes on retirement, health care and social assistance have been rolled out rapidly in the countryside. These programmes have contributed greatly towards improving the living standards of the rural population. In principle, they are accessible in most of the rural areas. Despite social insurance schemes for retirement and health care remaining voluntary, the number of participants has soared significantly. The success of the introduction of these programmes has been largely owing to the acceptance of financial responsibility by the central government, particularly in western and central provinces, where local governments often lack the financial capacity to shoulder their obligations.

Compared with the old CMS, the NCMS and Medical Assistance focus on supporting in-patient costs rather than promoting public health and preventive services. Even though coverage has been significantly increased, the level of protection remains low. For a current retiree without an individual account, the basic pension is 55 yuan a month. According to one estimate, after contributing at the lowest level to an individual account (100 yuan a year) for fifteen years, a participant can obtain a total of only 73 yuan (55 yuan from the basic pension and 18 yuan from the individual account) a month (CNC, 19 July 2013). The amount is much lower than the national poverty line (2,300 yuan a year/192 yuan a month) and the rural national average *dibao* line (203 yuan a month).

Even with transfers from the central government, the programmes still present significant variations because of differences in administrative capacity and government priorities. The objective role of the village committee in the delivery of *dibao* is questionable, and greater investment and training of local cadres or civil servants in designing and implementing these programmes is required. In the case of the local civil affairs department, there is usually only one worker, often poorly equipped and trained in the county/township, who is responsible for administering all kinds of social assistance programmes, which has seriously affected their efficacy. Without adequate resources for administration, it is impossible to undertake the procedures and attain the objectives of social assistance programmes, such as addressing fraud and misuse, monitoring the eligibility and incomes of recipients, and calculating and avoiding overlapping of benefits.

Furthermore, coordination among different policies has become one of the major issues. Among the current programmes, *dibao*, *wubao* and Medical Assistance are administered by civil affairs departments, the NCMS by departments of health, old-age pensions by departments of human resources and social security, and poverty alleviation policies by the poverty alleviation offices. These programmes were designed to be linked to one another and implemented in a concerted manner – for example, the *wubao* can be integrated into the *dibao* scheme. But at the local level they often lack coordination, creating overlaps and confusion.

6 Social Care for Older People

In recent years, the Chinese government has set out to develop a new social protection system with universal coverage and citizenship-based entitlement, moving towards a welfare state (*The Economist*, 8 September 2012; World Bank, 2013; CDRF, 2012; Shi, 2012). However, the development of professionally based social care services for older people, the disabled, youth offenders, orphans and victims of domestic violence has been limited and unevenly distributed. Social welfare reforms to increase provision, enhance professionalization and design a pluralistic service delivery system are long awaited (Wong and Leung, 2012).

One of the major social challenges faced by China is rapid population ageing. China is now an ageing society, even though it is still regarded as a middle-income economy. Coupled with the market-driven reform of social services and the rapid erosion of family support, the provision of affordable and accessible social care services to older people has already become an urgent issue to be tackled by the government. In fact, residential care and home care have become the major welfare services emerging in China. Looking into the future, the formulation and implementation of sustainable long-term care policy and services will increasingly become the major focus of social policy. Through an analysis of the background and structure of services for older people, this chapter provides a glimpse into the emerging pattern of social care in China.

According to the Ministry of Civil Affairs, social welfare expenditures in 2013 amounted to 428 million yuan, representing 3.1 per cent of the state budget. Financial transfers from central government to local government constituted 50 per cent. There were 46,000 institutions providing 5.27 million beds for the destitute, including 4.9 million beds for the elderly; 45,000 for the mentally disabled; 98,000 for orphans; and 97,000 for the homeless. In terms of child welfare, there were 549,000 orphans, of whom 94,000 were placed in institutional care, while around 455,000 were placed in foster care or were looked after by relatives. The number of adopted children reached 24,460 (86 per cent locally adopted), declining from 50,921 in 2005. Welfare factories provided jobs for 539,000 disabled persons (MCA, 2014b).

ERODING FAMILY SUPPORT

Family support for older people is a long and cherished Chinese tradition. According to *Time* (Powell, 2009), one of the five things that the United States can learn from China is how families look after their older members (the other four are 'be ambitious', 'education matters', 'save more', and 'look over the horizon'). The Criminal Law (1979, 2011), the Marriage Law (1980, 2011), the Inheritance Law (1985), the Law on the Protection of the Rights and Interests of Older People (1996) and the Chinese Constitution (2004) all prescribe that society and the family have a legal responsibility to take care of the elderly. These laws strive to realize the ideals of providing support, medical care, entertainment, education and fulfilment to older people (Leung and Lam, 2000). A revised care law implemented on 1 July 2013 specifies that children who live separately should visit their elderly parents regularly. In fact, more cases involving disputes over the support of older people have to be resolved in court (CNCA, 2010a).

Meanwhile, in 2005, 57 per cent of older people were living with their children, down from 73 per cent in 1982 (Herd, Hu and Koen, 2010b). In the 2010 census, it was estimated that 22 per cent of families had to take care of at least one family member aged over 65. In 2010, the proportion of 'empty-nest' families, in which older people live alone or with their spouses, reached 50 per cent in the cities and 38 per cent in rural areas (CNCA, 2012). Moreover, average family size has been declining, from 4.4 persons in 1982 to only 3.1 in 2010 (NBS, 2014). Because of the one-child policy, families have fewer children and so a lower capacity to provide care for the elderly. The phenomenon of '4-2-1' refers to the burden of the single child taking care of their two young-old parents and four old-old grandparents. Another impact of the one-child policy is the issue of older people losing their only child and carer through accident or sickness. In such cases, family care is not available, and they can hardly have another child in old age. According to the Health and Family Planning Commission, 355,000 parents aged 49 or over had lost their only child in 2012 (*China Daily*, 7 July 2013).

According to the findings of the CHARLS 2008 pilot project, intergenerational transfers between elderly parents and adult children in Zhejiang and Gansu provinces flowed predominantly from children to parents. Those who were married and had a higher educational background, particularly if they were an eldest son, tended to show more commitment to financial support for the elderly. But, with declining numbers of children per family and the growing inadequacy of pensions, the issue of financial support for older people will remain critical (Lei et al., 2012).

According to a national survey of disabilities conducted in 2006, over half of the 83 million disabled persons were aged over 60. Another national survey in 2010 found that, of older people living in cities, around 5 per cent and 9.6 per cent respectively claimed to be either completely or partially unable to take care of themselves. The corresponding figures in the villages were 6.9 and 14.1 per cent, respectively (CNCA, 2011). Another estimate in 2009 put the proportion of the elderly population who are unable to take care of themselves at 19 per cent. This represented 10.4 million completely disabled and 21.2 million semi-disabled older people (CNC, 8 November 2010). The 2013 *National Report on the Development of China's Elderly Business* indicated that the number of older people with functional disabilities and chronic diseases had reached 37.5 million (Wu, 2013). Overall, the number of elderly people in China needing assistance to carry out daily activities is rising. As more of them are living alone, family support is eroding and formal social care services are underdeveloped, a greater number of people face higher risks of being poor and socially excluded.

DEVELOPMENT OF SOCIAL CARE

Immediately after 1949, the responsibility for providing social care and support to people in need rested primarily with the family, whose efforts were supplemented by the work-unit-based social welfare system. The government took responsibility only for the 'three nos'. Such individuals were cared for in welfare institutions operated by local governments. These institutions comprised a mixed group of destitute residents, including the elderly, the disabled and orphans. In the rural areas, communes (now township governments) provided basic support to older people among the 'three nos' under the *wubao* scheme (see chapter 5). In addition, 'honour homes' were established to provide residential care for those who had made significant contributions to the country during the civil war, family members of martyrs and disabled ex-servicemen. Traditionally, a residential service financed, provided and managed by the government was the only formal service catering to the needs of destitute older people. The nature of the services and their targets, financing, and mode of operation were limited. Under the socialist system, demand for social care was limited. In

1978, there were around 7,000 residential homes with only 100,000 residents (Leung and Nann, 1995, p. 118).

After the market-oriented reforms in the 1980s, the MCA adopted the reform directive of 'socialization'. According to the *Opinion Concerning the Implementation of the Socialization of Social Welfare* published in 2000, socialization refers to the goal of a pluralistic service system comprising residential services, community services and home care; diversified funding sources include government allocation, public donations and fee payments. In other words, socialization refers to the extension of welfare responsibilities beyond the government to the wider society, in the form of businesses, the family and charity organizations. The Chinese government has recognized that it cannot take sole responsibility for the provision of social care services.

Under socialization, among specific changes in welfare institutions were the opening up of government-operated homes to those non-'three no' users who could afford to pay the fees; the development of profit-making businesses within the homes to generate income; the development of specialized welfare institutions, including hostels and nursing homes; and the emergence of privately operated homes. In 2009, around 78 per cent of the residents in government-operated homes were from among the 'three nos', and fee-paying residents constituted only 17 per cent of the total. Those homes operated by the private sector are mainly dependent on fees as a major source of revenue (MCA, 2010).

In 1998, the government enacted a regulation to allow civil non-enterprise units (*minbian fei qiye*), including enterprises, NGOs and individuals, to invest in and operate non-profit-making social welfare units. These regulations officially permitted the entry of NGOs into social welfare services. Since the 1990s, the central government has enacted legislation and guidelines to standardize and improve the quality of homes for the aged, in particular service quality and management practices – staffing, premises, the physical environment, and personal care. Among the various laws and regulations are *Rules for the Five Guarantees Work in Rural Areas* (1994), *Law on the Protection of the Rights and Interests of Older People* (1996), *Interim Administrative Measures on Social Welfare Institutions for Older Persons in Rural Areas* (1997), *Interim Administrative Measures on Social Welfare Institutions* (1999), *The Code for Building Design for Older Persons* (1999), *Standards of Social Welfare Institutions for the Elderly* (2001), *Opinion Concerning the Implementation of the Socialization of Social Welfare* (2000) and *Opinion on Supporting the Operation of Social Welfare Institutions by NGOs* (2005). In 2013, the MCA further introduced *Methods of Setting up Homes for the Aged* and *Methods of Managing Homes for the Aged*. The government has recognized the need to diversify social care services for older people through the development of NGOs and the market, as well as the need to establish the required mechanism to regulate and monitor their performance.

In 2002, the Ministry of Labour and Social Security issued the *Professional Standards of Carers for Older Persons*. The document prescribed the detailed knowledge and skill requirements for the daily, medical, rehabilitation and psychological care of older people. In addition, a job classification for different ranks of care workers was proposed. Now that this is a clearly defined occupational category, the recruitment and training of care workers has received a higher priority. In short, a series of laws, guidelines and circulars has been promulgated to regulate and improve the development of homes for the aged. Because there are difficulties in enforcing compliance and monitoring service quality, these regulatory guidelines are, in reality, a wish list.

In a State Council meeting in August 2013, Premier Li Keqiang stressed the need to turn to society, rather than the government, as the major actor and provider in the provision of services for older people; to encourage private investment; and to stimulate the importation of new technology in welfare services. The role of the government should concentrate on those 'three nos' older people with functional disabilities, whereas the role of the market should be increased, targeting those with the ability to pay (CNC, 19 August 2013b). According to the MCA, there is a need to learn by continuous innovation, using pilot or demonstration projects to develop models of good practice, to incorporate social care provision into the agenda and budget of local governments, and to mobilize the collective efforts of society. Local governments are encouraged to contract out or purchase services from NGOs. The overall approach is that the central government will direct and facilitate policy, while local government will experiment with different practice models. Bottom-up good practice examples will be shared nationally (MCA, 2010).

RESIDENTIAL CARE

In contrast to the situation in developed countries, residential care in China is loosely defined. It comprises a variety of settings, ranging from nursing homes to hostels, providing social care for older people who are either destitute or are able to pay the market fees. Services provided in these settings are not standardized, formalized or closely regulated. In many of the homes for the aged in rural areas, in particular, professionally trained staff – nurses, social workers and personal care workers – are difficult to find. For example, it is estimated that only 60 per cent of homes for the aged are equipped with medical treatment rooms and have professional medical staff (CNCA, 2011).

According to the longitudinal study carried out by the CNCA in 2010, only 11.3 per cent of older people in cities and 12.5 per cent in villages intended to live in residential homes. Compared with the percentages in 2000 and 2006, older people seem to show declining desire to seek institutional care. In fact, 76 per cent of those in cities and 71 per cent of those in villages live in houses they own (Xinhua, 2012). According to a national survey by the CNCA, the major reasons for older people to seek institutional care were children unable to provide for them (44 per cent); living in homes for the aged is better than at home (39 per cent); and not to burden children (16 per cent). In choosing homes for the aged, the major criteria were affordable fees (50 per cent), high quality services (24 per cent), good living conditions (18 per cent) and proximity to home (8 per cent) (CNCA, 2010b).

Overall, deeply influenced by traditional values, older people are reluctant to leave home and live in residential care (Zhan et al., 2011). Under market-driven policy, the relatively high fees charged by homes mean that a lot of older people cannot afford to live in residential care anyway. There has been no objective assessment of the need for service support for the elderly. Estimates of this have been based on surveys of expressed demand. More importantly, a national survey indicated that over half of homes for the aged do not accept residents who lack the capacity for self-care (CNCA, 2011).

So far, there is neither a precise definition nor a classification of homes for the aged in China. By the end of 2013, there were 42,475 such homes providing a total of 4,937,000 beds and accommodating 3,074,000 residents. The number of beds has increased dramatically in recent years, from around 1 million in the late 1990s to 1.6 million in 2005, and to 4.9 million in 2013. The institutionalized rate (the number of beds to the elderly population) showed general improvement, increasing from 0.8 per cent in 1994, to 1 per cent in 2000, and 2.4 per cent (1.5 per cent in terms of actual utilization) in 2013. The average utilization or occupancy rate in 2013 was only 62 per cent (see table 6.1). Lower occupancy rates are found in the rural areas and in homes operated by the private sector. At first glance, despite the apparent great demand, beds in homes for the aged have not been fully utilized. Even though 53 per cent of the national population lives in cities, only 18 per cent of the beds were in urban areas (MCA, 2014b).

The annual service statistical reports of the MCA did not regularly show the number of beds operated by the 'society sector' (township

Table 6.1 Provision of beds, number of residents and occupancy rates, 1990–2013

YEAR	TOTAL NUMBER OF BEDS	TOTAL NUMBER OF RESIDENTS	OCCUPANCY RATE (%)	NUMBER OF 'SOCIETY'-OPERATED BEDS
1990	780,000	599,000	77	635,000
1991	828,000	646,000	65	679,000
1992	898,000	696,000	78	742,000
1993	927,000	724,000	78	766,000
1994	955,000	736,000	77	–
1995	976,000	747,000	80	–
1996	1,008,000	769,000	76	–
1997	1,026,000	785,000	77	844,000
1998	1,058,000	800,000	76	–
1999	1,089,000	826,000	76	876,645
2000	1,130,407	854,040	76	908,847
2001	1,246,000	893,000	72	–
2002	1,251,000	926,000	74	–
2003	1,298,097	965,470	75	–
2004	1,468,000	1,109,000	76	–
2005	1,639,000	1,236,000	75	–
2006	1,753,000	1,356,000	77	–
2007	2,513,000	2,000,000	80	–
2008	2,794,000	2,219,000	79	–
2009	2,088,000	1,730,000	83	–
2010	3,149,000	2,426,000	69	–
2011	3,532,000	2,603,000	74	–
2012	4,165,000	2,936,000	71	–
2013	4,937,000	3,074,000	62	–

Note: Before 2008, the figures for the number of beds refer to those in welfare institutions (where the majority of the beds are for older people). After 2008, the number of beds in homes for the aged has been separated from those in welfare institutions.
Source: MCA (various years).

government and street offices, NGOs, and the private sector). In 1990, 81 per cent of the beds were operated by 'society'. Beds provided by the government have always constituted around 20 per cent of the total. Within the 'society' sector, the majority of beds are provided by collectives (township government in the rural areas and street offices in the urban areas), whereas those provided by NGOs and the private sector constitute less than 2 per cent of the total. By 2009, the private or NGO sector owned 4,141 homes, providing 412,000 beds (15 per cent of the total) with 238,000 residents (11 per cent of the total). Private sector-operated homes have lower utilization rates (58 per cent), reflecting lower popularity (MCA, 2013b).

In 2006, ten ministries and commissions jointly issued their *Opinion on Speeding up the Development of Services for Older People*. According to this, the government should encourage a multiple operational mode to facilitate the rapid provision and development of services for the elderly. The government can contract out services, provide subsidies and give support. The foci in the *Opinion* were the following (Wong and Leung, 2012):

- Local government should ensure adequate care support for 'three nos' older people. NGOs should be encouraged to provide residential, educational, and entertainment services for older people. The unemployed and people who have been laid off should be recruited as care workers.
- A variety of home care services, including daily care, home care, counselling, rehabilitation and emergency services should be developed; medical care and hospice services should be explored.
- The quality of care workers should be enhanced through in-service training.
- Funding sources for elderly services should diversify. Local governments have to provide a variety of preferential policies, such as land, premises, utility charges and tax incentives in order to encourage

NGOs and the private sector to operate residential services for older people.

In 2013, the MCA enacted the *Methods on the Setting up of Homes for the Aged* and *Methods on Management of Homes for the Aged*. These two documents indicate the intention of the government to ensure the proper registration of homes and assure the quality of their operation. Government-operated homes should give priority to those with financial difficulties and disabilities. The government should encourage other sectors to operate homes for the aged – meaning that other sectors should focus on those who can afford to pay the market fees.

Methods on the Setting up of Homes for the Aged sets out necessary requirements for establishing a home. All homes with more than ten elderly residents should have the necessary management, professional and service staff, equipment and facilities and meet the prescribed care, safety and health standards. All qualifying homes should be registered with the civil affairs departments. *Methods on Management of Homes for the Aged* sets out the objectives, service content, internal management process, performance monitoring and legal responsibilities. The two *Methods* are intended to facilitate the establishment of more homes by NGO and private sectors. Even foreign investment is welcome.

Current residential care provision comes largely from the collective sector, followed by the government sector and, lastly, an emerging non-state or private sector. Homes operated by this last sector are usually small, hostel-like and informally organized, and cope with a shortage of financial, manpower and professional resources. Despite receiving public subsidies, welfare homes operated by local governments have to rely on fees and other sources of income. With partial support from local governments, these homes are much better served in terms of resources and manpower and can therefore provide a relatively superior service. Homes operated by the non-state sector face uncertain levels of government support and have to rely solely on fees. Their quality is usually poor and occupancy rates tend to be low (Wong and Leung, 2012). More importantly, they have to compete with the homes operated by the government and those run by collectives for fee-paying residents.

In large cities such as Shanghai, Tianjin and Guangzhou, non-state residential homes have developed rapidly. According to Wong and Tang (2008), in practice most are directly or indirectly supervised by the government. According to this survey, over one-third of such homes are in deficit. Of those claiming to have made profits, most had not earned enough to pay off their debts. All looked to the government for assistance in terms of preferential treatment in utility charges, tax exemption and land allocation. The preferential policies that had been promised by the government do not seem to have materialized in practice. With rising costs and low profit margins, private homes often run into deficit. Now all types of residential services take fee-paying residents, and ability to pay rather than need is the basic criterion for admission. Overall, residential institutions are now more open to market competition based on the level of fees and quality (Wong and Tang, 2008; Guan and Zhao, 2012).

Under the direction of socialization, the government will support its policy of increasing the role and responsibility of the NGO sector in the provision of residential care by contracting out services. Specifically, the city governments in Shanghai, Beijing and Guangdong are developing a contracting-out mechanism through which to buy services from the collective and non-state sectors. Under the direction of 'state-owned, society-operated', there are proposals to allow the NGO sector to operate social welfare homes which are currently being run by the government. The role of the state will then become more that of a funder and regulator (see chapter 7).

In summary, there is little differentiation or classification of residential care in China according to residents' needs. Homes are largely a commodity and admission is largely dependent on the ability to pay market fees. The majority of homes are still heavily reliant on local governments for financial support. The emerging homes operated by the private and NGO sectors are still vulnerable, facing uncertainty over income and government support. Despite efforts to raise standards through the publication of regulations on the management and design of homes for the aged, as well as occupational standards for personal care workers, the quality of services for the elderly remains uneven. Many of the privately run homes are poorly equipped in terms of both facilities and professional support.

INTERFACING BETWEEN RESIDENTIAL AND HOME CARE SERVICES

According to a study on the need for home care services in urban China, it was shown that 49 per cent of older people had certain daily needs that required formal assistance. Some 25 per cent were in need of someone to help with domestic chores, 18 per cent with personal care, and 14 per cent with social conversation. It was estimated that current urban home care services can satisfy only 16 per cent of the expressed needs (Wong and Leung, 2012). As such, the need for home care services is tremendous. Because of the lack of social care facilities, a phenomenon of 'refusing to leave the beds' has emerged, in which older people refuse to leave hospital after medical treatment (CNC, 8 November 2010).

The overall policy direction for the development of services for older people has always been 'Home care is the foundation, community care provides the necessary support, and residential care is supplementary' (MCA, 2010). The policy directive was reiterated in the period of the 12th Five-Year Plan (2011–15). It appears that a higher priority has been placed on the development of home-based community care services in recent years. These can provide a range of community support for older people, including home-making and meal delivery, transportation and escort services, rehabilitation care and home spiritual support. Day-care centres have been developed to serve frail older people whose children cannot take care of them during the day.

Community services were initiated in the late 1980s to fill the service gaps created by the erosion of work-unit welfare protection and the marketization of emerging social services (Leung and Wong, 2002; Parris, 2012). *Instruction on Speeding up the Development of Community Service*, published in 1993 by the fourteen relevant ministries, introduced the concept and practice of community-based social services for older people. *Opinion on Strengthening and Improving Community Services* (2006) and *Opinion on Strengthening and Improving the Construction Work of Urban Residents' Committees* (2010) reiterated the role of neighbourhood organizations in providing community services to the needy.

To develop community-based social care services, the MCA implemented the Star Light project in 2001. Financed by welfare lotteries, involving a total investment of 13.4 billion yuan, this project assisted local governments in setting up 32,000 community-based home-care facilities; according to the Chinese government, over 30 million older people benefited from the services (MCA, 2010), which can cover daily life support (meal delivery, house cleaning, bathing, escort services and conversation) and medical and nursing care. In some neighbourhoods, day care, canteens and respite services have also been developed.

To strengthen home care services, in 2008 the government published the policy directive *Opinion on Promoting the Work of Home Care for Older People*, which prescribed the need for local governments to establish home-care services, ensure government funding, management and supervision, develop care standards, and provide for care professions and volunteers. To reiterate the priority for development, in 2009 the CNCA further announced policy directives to promote home care. Overall, the lack of funding and policy support from the central government has led to the uneven and inadequate development of home-care services.

In 2012, the MCA reported that community-based facilities (day care and residential care) had 198,000 beds, an increase from 100,000 in 2001. Home-care services covered 41 per cent and 16 per cent of urban and rural areas, respectively (MCA, 2013b). It is reported that some 80 per cent of the neighbourhoods in Beijing do not have sufficient social care services, such as day care, escort services and meal delivery, for the elderly (CNCA, 2013b). So far, there are no official figures on the scope and number of recipients of home-care services.

Shanghai was the first city in China to become an ageing society, in 1979. In 2012, it was home to 3.8 million older people with local *hukou*, constituting 26 per cent of the total city population. By 2015, the proportion is expected to reach over 30 per cent. In 2010, there were a total of 97,841 beds in homes for the aged, constituting 2.96 per cent of the ageing population with local *hukou*. In 2011, a further 10,843 beds were provided. An additional 5,000 beds were planned in 2013, to reach a total of 125,000 by 2015, with a workforce of 100,000 involved in social care services. To encourage the development of a high-quality workforce, the Shanghai government intended to raise salaries (CNCA, 2013b). Shanghai has 631 homes for the aged, only 5 per cent of which are government-operated; the rest are run by civil non-enterprise units. Around half were built by the government (Shanghai Civil Affairs Bureau, 2011, 2012).

In 2012, around 3.7 per cent of older people did not have the capacity for self-care. There were 233 community-based centres employing 33,000 community care workers and serving a total of 252,000 elderly recipients (7.6 per cent of the city elderly population with local *hukou*). In 2010 there were 303 day care centres, providing services to 9,000 older people, and 404 meal canteens serving 40,000. Community care services were purchased from community-based semi-government NGOs. Policy and regulations were established to regulate, inspect and evaluate the services, as well as to provide training to care workers (Shanghai Civil Affairs Bureau, 2011). In Beijing and Shanghai, older people on low incomes can receive cash vouchers to buy home-care services from their neighbourhood community care service operators, who receive subsidies from the city and district governments for this purpose. In Shanghai, the value of the voucher is based on a needs assessment. In Guangzhou, heavy emphasis is still placed on expanding residential care. In 2012, there were 34,000 beds in homes for the aged, 30 per cent of which were operated by the city and district governments. By 2015, the number of beds will have increased to 56,000, with a ratio of beds to elderly population reaching 4:100 (CNC, 10 September 2013).

Up until now, there have been no national figures on how home-care services are provided. The division of responsibility between home care and residential care has not been clearly defined. Without a national legal and policy framework prescribing required provision and minimum standards, different cities and communities may have different packages of home-care services. More sophisticated services, such as basic nursing care, respite services, environmental risk assessment and home modification, emergency support, and care management, are still not yet available. Their development is hindered by the availability of qualified professionals and care workers. It is estimated that China requires at least 10 million trained elderly care workers; currently, only a small proportion are qualified (CNC, 8 November 2010). The situation is further aggravated by the low wages of the workforce. Many in home-care services have been laid off by other enterprises. High turnover is expected (CNC, 17 February 2010).

It is indisputable that significant progress in the development of services for older people has been made in the last decade. Both residential and community-based home-care services have become mainstreamed in the cities. As reiterated in the policy papers, the government is aware that home care is the most important and preferred mode of delivery. Yet residential homes are still expanding rapidly, while community-based home-care services remain underdeveloped, largely through lack of government investment. Services are generally fragmented and lack coordination, often competing with one another for users. Local governments are locked into a vicious circle of committing resources to the building of new care homes, which makes it difficult to free up funding to develop community care services.

PROSPECTS

According to the 12th Five-Year Plan (2011–2015) for the Development of Social Care Services for Older People, the MCA has pledged to strengthen social care services for the elderly. It aims to reach a ratio of 30 residential care beds per 1,000 people by 2015 (CNC, 8 November 2010). In September 2013, the *Opinion Concerning the Speeding up of the Development of Elderly Services* issued by the State Council reiterated the division of responsibility between state, society and the market. As a milestone for the development of elderly services in China, the *Opinion* outlines the four principles to speed up service development: deepening the structural reforms, providing basic protection, coordinating development, and perfecting the market mechanism. Six major tasks are coordinating the development of urban facilities, perfecting the home-care network, strengthening the construction of residential care organizations, developing rural services for older people, expanding the consumption market for older people, and actively integrating medical and social care.

According to the *Opinion*, local governments should facilitate and strengthen the society sector to share responsibility through relaxing the registration procedures and requirements. Investment from the private and overseas sectors is welcome. There should be more preferential policies on taxation and fees. By 2020, China will have established a pluralistic social care system with home care as the foundation, community-based and organizational support, and full coverage in both rural and urban areas. By then, the number of beds in homes for the aged will reach 35 to 40 per 1,000 people (CNC, 14 September 2013). However, under the current decentralized social care system, which relies heavily on the responsibility of local governments, these policy directives may still represent ideals and will be implemented unevenly. Unless the central government provides financial transfers to support those economically less developed provinces, the current development trends will further accentuate the inequalities across regions and between rural and urban areas.

The *Circular of the MCA on Promoting Pilot Projects on Reforming Government-Operated Residential Institutions for Older People* in December 2013 reiterated that the government-operated homes for the aged should focus mainly on the service needs of those with financial or functional disabilities, the 'old old' (those over 80), and childless older people. Pilot projects can be established to improve service quality and the purchase of services from social organizations, and to encourage some of the government-operated homes to turn into self-financed business operations. Again, it reflects the 'residual' concept of welfare.

In summary, social care services for older people in China are marked by acute shortage, low quality, uneven development between regions and between urban and rural areas, low levels of private and NGO involvement, poorly trained staff, and segmented interfacing between community services, informal care and residential care. Government support to facilitate the development of the social care market has not been effective. Government-provided services are dependent not only on central financial allocation for support but must also charge their residents fees. Under the direction of 'corporatization', public services, such as schools, hospitals and homes for the aged, have to rely on fees for income. There is a tendency for these public service institutions both to overcharge and mischarge users. The widespread use of the market mechanism has in fact widened regional and provider disparities rather than promoting the image of public services being about welfare and justice (Shue and Wong, 2007). It can be seen that services for older people provided by the NGO and private sectors, despite some significant expansion in recent years, still face an uncertain future. It remains for the government to assume overriding responsibility for financing and supervision and for facilitating the development of the NGO and market sectors.

Besides the urgent need to encourage the development of profit-making private and NGO involvement in the provision of social care services, the government must also develop minimum or optimal standards for residential homes for older people in terms of facilities, staffing, space and care. Effectively enforcing the compliance of these standards is critical. Specialized residential and community-based services should be developed to cater for those with special needs, such as the frail elderly and those with mental illness or dementia. The population of older people with dementia was estimated in 2013 to have reached 5 million and is projected to increase by 300,000 each year (CNCA, 2013a).

In modernizing formal social care services, China has to cope with the rising number of older people and the corresponding increase in expectations. More importantly, it has to develop a means of making a more objective and accurate assessment of future social needs and demand. The establishment of an effective, affordable, pluralistic and sustainable system of social care requires the integration of residential care and community-based home care and a balance between publicly and privately financed services. More importantly, social care services should strengthen and promote family support and family caregivers.

7 Innovating Social Governance: The Emergence of Social Work Organizations

INTRODUCTION

Facing new social challenges threatening social stability, the Chinese government understands the need to reform its governance system to be able to mobilize social resources, meet the mounting needs of the people, resolve social problems and mitigate social conflicts. Only through modernizing the public management system, can China deliver affordable, accountable, accessible and appropriate public and social services. In recent decades the country has been active in learning from overseas public management experiences. The concept of 'innovating social management' (*qiangxin shehui guanli*) or 'innovating social governance' (*qiangxin shehui zhili*) has been advocated, which includes the development of professional social work, NGOs and the purchase of services (POS) by the government. Under the directive on the transfer of government functions, one of the major initiatives is for the government to empower social organizations. To allow social work organizations and their workers to play a greater role, local governments have increasingly used POS to fund emerging social welfare services. This chapter describes the background, objectives, policy development and implementation of the government purchase of social welfare services. The pioneering development of Guangdong province is used as a case illustration.

INNOVATING SOCIAL GOVERNANCE

To maintain social stability and mitigate social tensions, the local governance system has to be responsive to people's needs and grievances. The 16th Party Congress in 2002 pointed out the need to 'perfect the government functions in economic adjustment, market monitoring, social management, and public services'. In the Fourth Plenum in 2004, the document *Decisions Regarding the Strengthening of the Construction of the Governing Capacity of the Party* introduced the concept of 'strengthening social construction and management, and promoting the innovation of social management'. The social management framework is summarized by the motto of 'party leadership, government responsibility, society facilitation, and public participation'. The 17th Party Congress in 2007 and the *Opinion Concerning the Deepening of the Administrative System Reform* of the Second Plenum in 2008 advocated administrative and governance reforms to construct a 'service-oriented government'.

In 2011, the Party issued the *Opinion Concerning Strengthening and Innovating Social Management* to direct the development of social management through local pilots, overseas learning and the promotion of good practice. According to Hu Jintao, the former Party General Secretary, the major tasks of social management were to strengthen:

- the leadership function of the Party and government in developing different types of social organizations;
- the mechanism of the Party and government in protecting and coordinating different interests and resolving social conflict;
- the management of mobile populations and special population groups;
- the grassroots system of community management and services;
- public security in food and medicine;

- the social responsibility of non-state economic and social organizations;
- the information management system; and
- ideological and ethical construction.

Under the strengthened Party leadership, the social sector will play an increasingly active role in the governance system. In trying to tackle the rising social conflicts between social strata and social groups, the core objective of social management is to maintain social stability and social cohesion.

The 18th Party Congress in 2012 reiterated the need to strengthen social management in order to maintain social stability and solidarity. The social management framework included an additional dimension of 'rule of law protection'. One of the key directives is to encourage the active participation of social organizations in the delivery of public and social services. The Party Congress emphasized the need to separate government from enterprise, the financial system and social organizations. Properly to manage and rationalize the relationship between government, market and civil society, the government must allow the market and society to assume more responsibility. Government responsibility should be limited rather than omnipotent. Without an open competitive process and society's participation, the development of public and social services has been restrictive. Accordingly, the governance system should move from the previous practice of 'the government allocating meals to the people' to 'allowing the people to make their orders' (People's Network, 2013).

The 12th Five-Year Plan on Developing a Basic Public Service System in 2012 pledged to make progress in public education, employment, social security, social services, health care, population and family planning, housing protection and public culture. In his last 2013 Government Report to the 12th National People's Congress, former Premier Wan Jiabao announced the need to construct a 'service-oriented government' that can satisfy people's expectations and which has scientifically based functions, an optimized structure, and high integrity and effectiveness.

Furthermore, in March 2013, the *Options on Reform and Transfer of Functions of the Organizations of the State Council* recognized that 'transfer of government functions' is the core task of public-sector reform, involving the repositioning of the relationship between government, market and society, as well as between central and local government. To handle properly the relationship between government, society and market, three core words are important: 'transfer' (*zhuan*) the government functions; 'support' (*fu*) social organizations; and 'activate' (*huo*) the market. To achieve the directives of 'small government and big society' or 'strong government and big society', and 'streamlining the administration and delegating power', the administrative relationship between the government and social organizations has to be separated (de-administration) and competition between social organizations encouraged (de-monopolization). To do so, the government pledged to improve the management of social organizations.

Traditionally, before it can formally register, a social organization has to receive the endorsement of two government departments, one responsible for business supervision and the other for administrative supervision (the civil affairs department). In addition, only one type of social organization can be registered within each trade and region. This arrangement is supposed to avoid competition and duplication. In other words, registration of new social organizations has been difficult. Under the new directives in the 2013 *Options*, the registration of social organizations has apparently been relaxed. Four types of social organizations, involving business, science and technology, charity, and community services, can register directly with the local civil affairs departments. By the end of 2012, nineteen provinces had implemented the practice of direct registration of these four types of social organizations (*People's Daily*, 29 March 2013).

In a State Council meeting in August 2013, Premier Li Keqiang reiterated the need to strengthen the construction of basic public services in the cities through purchasing services from the society sector. He claimed that local government had to assess accurately the needs and types of basic services to be purchased; purchase services through delegation, competitive bidding or public procurement under the principles of fairness and openness; strictly manage the financial and audit arrangements; establish vigorous monitoring and evaluation systems; and ensure that the people receive quality services by eliminating ineffective programmes (Xinhua, 2013a). In September 2013, the State Council issued the *Guiding Opinion on Government Purchase of Services from the Social Sector*, clarifying the background, objectives, principles, content, mechanism and financial management of POS. According to the *Opinion*, China will establish a mature POS system by 2020. It is noteworthy that similar policy documents have already been enacted, in Guangdong province in 2009 and in the social welfare sector in 2012.

The Third Plenum of the 18th Party Congress in November 2013 replaced the term 'social management' with 'social governance', signifying a more collaborative and coordinated approach to other social sectors. According to the interpretation of the Minister of Civil Affairs, social governance involves a major change in approach, from government-centred unidirectional social management to collaborative joined governance and from management based on administrative rules and regulatory procedures to the rule of law and protection, as well as multiple and integrative aspects, including ethical education, self-discipline and the coordination of social conflicts (CNC, 5 December 2013b).

To innovate social governance, the communique of the Third Plenum pointed out the need to speed up the transfer of functions, deepening the administrative reforms to enhance credibility and service-oriented government. Through competition, collaboration and delegation, local governments can activate social organizations in terms of their responsibility, self-governance, functions, public service provisions and volunteer development. Under Party leadership and guidance from the central government, public participation is to be promoted and the relationship between the government and social organizations redefined. Innovating social governance through the rule of law is considered as critical in solving social problems, preventing and mitigating social conflicts.

Overall, promoting POS is a key initiative of innovating social governance. It can nurture the development of social organizations, promote the transfer of government functions, construct a service-oriented government, improve public service provision, and enhance the quality of public services. Yet the *People's Daily* (16 October 2013) commented that this is still an exploratory project, lacking a sufficient legal framework and public understanding. Issues remain on how to ensure the system is open and fair in terms of financing, regulating and monitoring. According to *Outlook* (22 October 2013), government funds as a proportion of the total revenue of NGOs ranged from 65 per cent in Germany, 45 per cent in the United Kingdom and 40 per cent in the United States to 36 per cent in India. In China, the figure in 2012 was only 5.2 per cent (640 million yuan).

ACTIVATING THE SOCIAL SECTOR

Traditionally, under the centrally planned economy, the model for society emphasized the idea of 'strong state and weak society'. Under the dominant work-unit system, most social services were provided by the work units themselves, often with the support of Party-sponsored organizations such as the trade unions, the Communist Youth League and the Women's Federation. The revitalization of the urban residents' committees and village committees in the late 1980s provided a strategic platform for the government to implement social services (Leung and Wong, 2002). However, these organizations were often perceived as part of the government or the Party rather than as independent civil society organizations. Economic globalization and marketization have inevitably increased the economic freedom and rights of individual people in terms of property, employment and movement, yet certain civil liberties, including the freedom to organize, are still largely restricted (McMahon, 2012).

Since the late 1990s, three types of social organizations have emerged: societies (membership-based organizations) and civil non-enterprise units (service providers), both in 1998, and charity foundations or funding bodies, in 2004. In 2013 there were 289,000 societies, 14.5 per cent of which involved the provision of social services. Some 14.4 per cent per cent of the 255,000 civil non-enterprise units were involved in social service provision. Around 39 per cent of the 3,569 foundations are permitted to raise funds publicly, and the total of public donations received in 2013 amounted to 30 billion yuan. In 2004, the figures were 153,000 societies, 135,000 civil non-enterprise units and 892 charity foundations. By 2013 the number of social organizations had reached 547,000; they had total assets of 150 billion yuan and employed 6.4 million peopple (MCA, 2014b). As can be seen from table 7.1, the number of social organizations has almost doubled in the last decade.

After the 1989 Tiananmen protest and crackdown, a large number of social organizations were de-registered (their registration has always been tightly regulated) (Saich, 2000; Lin 2011; Shallcross and Huo, 2012; McMahon, 2012). Some social organizations have chosen to register as commercial companies, while others remain subsidiaries of existing social organizations and government business organizations (Saich, 2000; Shieh and Knutson, 2012; Shieh and Brown, 2013). Even when registered as a business, a social organization may face challenges from the Industry and Commerce Bureau over its involvement in non-commercial activities. The government tends to tolerate

Table 7.1 The development of social organizations

YEAR	SOCIETY	CIVIL NON-ENTERPRISE UNITS	FOUNDATIONS	TOTAL
1991	156,000	–	–	156,000
1992	179,000	–	–	179,000
1994	175,000	–	–	175,000
1996	185,000	–	–	185,000
1999	137,000	6,000	–	143,000
2001	129,000	82,000	–	211,000
2003	142,000	124,000	954	266,954
2004	153,000	135,000	892	288,892
2005	171,000	148,000	975	319,975
2006	192,000	161,000	1,144	354,144
2007	212,000	174,000	1,340	387,340
2008	230,000	182,000	1,597	413,597
2009	239,000	190,000	1,843	430,843
2010	245,000	198,000	2,200	445,200
2011	255,000	204,000	2,614	461,614
2012	271,000	225,000	3,029	499,029
2013	289,000	255,000	3,569	547,000

Source: MCA (various years).

the existence of those social organizations not formally registered so long they do not challenge its authority (Ma, 2006; Deng, 2010; Shieh and Knutson, 2012). In 2009, in keeping with the *Interim Measures for Banning Illegal Social Organizations* (Deng, 2010), the Shenzhen government banned two social organizations involved in advocating the rights of migrant workers.

According to the *Methods on Assessing Management of Social Organizations* (2011) and *Methods on Implementing the National Assessment on Social Organizations* (2011), local governments are expected to establish local review committees to facilitate the registration of social organizations and monitor their performance. Local governments are beginning to rate performance based on assessment by a third party, usually a research institute or a professional group. Those with higher ratings are awarded government contracts and even financial grants. In 2012, the MCA reviewed all the national social organizations, which were classified into different grades according to their performance, ranging from the top category of 5A to the lowest of 1A (CNC, 3 January 2014).

Overall, registration as a social organization in China is still strictly controlled in terms of membership and funding requirements, as well as in the registration processes. To be sure, the operation of social organizations has to be heavily dependent on local governments for political and financial patronage (Lin, 2011). As recent public-sector reform has encouraged the development of social organizations as vehicles through which to deliver public services, a new form of state–NGO partnership has emerged (Lu, 2009; Shieh and Schwartz, 2009; Wang, 2011; Jia, 2011; Fisher et al., 2012). NGOs had been largely restricted to working in rural poverty alleviation and relief work (CASS, 2012b).

On the one hand, the government is expected to create a more favourable environment in which social organizations might thrive. On the other, it has to increase its monitoring of the operation of social organizations to ensure their public accountability. Specifically, the policy directive seems to 'de-regulate' and even actively support the development of those social organizations that do not threaten the status quo and can assist the government in providing needed social services. In addition, the use of the 'soft' approach to address social issues, particularly through the use of professional social workers, will be strengthened (Leung et al., 2012). For those organizations that involve advocating and championing human rights, government policy is still restrictive. Even though social organizations in China still lack autonomy, the emerging interdependency between government and social organizations is pointed out by Yu and Guo (2012, p. 6).

THE RE-EMERGENCE OF SOCIAL WORK

The early history of social work education can be traced back to the establishment of social work programmes in the departments of sociology in universities founded by the American missionaries in Shanghai in 1914 and in Beijing in 1922. These programmes served to meet the staff training needs of the NGOs established by American Christian missionaries. Before 1949, only eight universities in China offered social work programmes (Leung, 1990b).

After the establishment of the PRC in 1949, all social work education programmes, and the social sciences in general, were regarded as pseudo-sciences and 'bourgeois disciplines' supporting the capitalist system. Under the socialist system there should be no social problems, including unemployment and poverty. Direct government intervention, administrative procedures, participation in labour production, ideological re-education and political mobilization were adopted as the key approaches to resolving social issues and rehabilitating people with problems. Accordingly, for almost three decades under socialist China, social work education and practice were virtually non-existent.

Following the reinstatement of social science subjects in 1979, social work programmes were re-established in a small number of universities in the late 1980s (China Association of Social Work, 2013). The China Association of Social Work and the China Association for Social Work Education were formed in 1991 and 1994, respectively, to promote the development of professionalism and education in the discipline. As a result of increased international exchanges, particularly with the social welfare sector in Hong Kong, interest in Western-based social work has flourished. However, throughout the 1980s and 1990s endorsement from the government remained hesitant. Social work was still regarded as a Western product promoting human rights and social justice. Both education programmes and positions in social work were limited. In 1994 there were only twenty social work education programmes. With the expansion of university education in the 2000s, restrictions on introducing new programmes into Chinese universities were relaxed (Xiong and Wang, 2007). The number of social work programmes jumped to 90 in 2002, to 172 in 2003, and to 200, turning out 10,000 graduates, in 2006 (China Association of Social Work, 2013).

Rapid urbanization and industrialization, together with an ageing population and eroding family support, has resulted in the emergence of a wide array of social problems. These increasingly require care and treatment from professional social workers with the skills and experience to support victims of domestic violence and natural disasters, frail older people, orphans, the mentally ill, the disabled, drug addicts, youth offenders, the unemployed and the poor (Leung, 2007, 2010). Some of the regulations formulated by the MCA, on the management of residential homes for older people (2001), children's homes (2001), rehabilitation centres for those with disabilities (2001), foster care for orphans (2004) and services for homeless children (2006), prescribed a need to employ professional social workers (China Association of Social Work, 2013). However, because of poor enforcement, the functions, tasks and job descriptions of social workers in these settings have not been clearly outlined or substantiated. Without clear job classifications and ranks, most government departments cannot formally employ social workers or pay them a decent salary. Overall, emerging social welfare services have tended to be staffed by untrained social workers who see their work as administrative rather than professional. Social work graduates have largely been unable to find employment in their field (Leung, 2007, 2010).

In 2004, following the recommendation of the MCA, the Ministry of Labour and Social Security enacted *Regulations on the Occupationalization of Social Workers*, categorizing social workers as technical workers. In 2006, the Ministry of Personnel and the MCA issued jointly *Regulations on the Social Workers Occupational Standard System*. Both sets of regulations envisaged the function of professional social work as implementing policy, mitigating tensions, resolving problems, maintaining social stability, promoting social justice and building a harmonious society. Social work has been variously described as a 'shock absorber', a 'safety valve', a 'social lubricant', a 'firewall' and a 'windshield'. Social workers apply professional knowledge and methods in providing services to individuals, families, groups and the community at large. They can be involved in social welfare services, charity work, social assistance and medical care for people with financial problems. Specifically, they can provide services to older people, people with disabilities or illnesses, veterans, young people and offenders (China Social Worker Association, 2013).

The 2006 *Regulations* also attempted to classify three levels of social workers based on qualifications and work experience, as well as the use of public examinations to establish professional qualifications and implement registration. The first national examination for qualification at the junior or social worker grades was held in June 2008. An individual is granted the title of social worker if they pass the examination, regardless of their educational and training background (Leung, 2010).

In terms of practice involving professionally trained social workers, Shanghai city has been considered a pioneer. Several NGOs were established there in the mid-1990s to provide a community-based welfare service. Pilot social work stations were created in schools, hospitals and neighbourhoods. In 2003, three NGOs were set up by the government to deliver youth crime prevention services in the community. The Shanghai government also began subsidizing or purchasing services directly from these NGOs (Leung, 2007). However, the development of social work jobs was still limited.

The Sixth Plenum of the 16th Party Congress published an official policy document on constructing a harmonious socialist society in October 2006. Under the section on Party construction, the CPC acknowledged the contribution of social work to the promotion of social stability and the need to build a large, well-structured and qualified workforce. It also recognized that the government should put the policy and related mechanisms in place to train, assess, employ and motivate social workers. The communique states that the development of the profession is considered an integral part of the Party's development plans. The task of developing the profession is under the auspices of the Organization Department of the Party, which is responsible for personnel matters.

This has been regarded as a turning point in the development of social work, with the government and Party making pledges to develop long-awaited jobs. Thereafter, the MCA authorized pilot projects in 170 local government districts involving 260 government units. Financed by local governments, these projects served to create social work jobs. Furthermore, in 2010 the State Council issued the *National Development Mid- and Long-Term Framework on Human Capital 2010–2020*. Social work was included as one of the six key professions to be promoted. The *Framework* projected the need for 2 million social workers by 2015 and 3 million by 2020 (State Council, 2010).

In October 2011, the MCA, together with eighteen other ministries, issued a policy on strengthening the workforce. This is considered to be a key policy directive guiding the future development of professional social work in China. It emphasizes the need to integrate the development of a high-quality professional workforce with the development of social work positions (in terms of job design and provision of standards, job responsibility, recruitment, registration, compensation and rewards). More importantly, the cultivation of social work organizations (SWOs) was considered a key strategic element in developing jobs in social work. According to the 12th Five-Year Plan on the Development of Community Services and the Work of Civil Affairs, among new local initiatives are the establishment of integrated community service centres in all neighbourhoods together with incubation and training centres for social workers. Recent developments include the promotion of social work – enterprise social work, youth work and social assistance programmes – in the 'three areas', namely old revolutionary areas, remote poverty stricken areas, and ethnic minority border areas.

In April 2012, the publication of the *Report on the Mid- and Long-Term Development of the Social Work Workforce* marked a new phase in social work development (MCA, 2012b). According to the *Report*, since the implementation of the examinations in 2008–11, a total of 54,176 people – 13,421 social workers and 40,755 assistants – have qualified in China. However, it is also estimated that more than 200,000 people are actually practising as social workers. The *Report* revised its estimates on the requirement for qualified social workers to 0.5 million and 1.5 million by 2015 and 2020, respectively. By 2020, the demand for senior social workers is expected to reach 200,000 and that for top-level social workers to reach 30,000. It seems that no other country in the world has such a comprehensive and long-term plan for the development of its social work profession! The MCA also published ethical guidelines for social workers for the first time in January 2013.

There are plenty of international publications indicating the shortcomings of social work education in China, including the poor quality of educators, curriculum design, fieldwork placements and supervisors, and reference books. Mainly because of the lack of formal social work positions in the government sector and the underdeveloped NGO sector, available jobs are limited and poorly paid. Overall, social work education has developed much faster than the profession itself. In other words, it has become dissociated from field practice (Leung, 2007, 2013).

To train advanced social work practitioners, 33 Master of Social Work programmes were established from 2010 onwards. However, they did not require students to have an undergraduate degree in social work. In 2012, there were around 320 social work education programmes, 60 of which offered the Master of Social Work degrees, and the numbers graduating annually reached 20,000. By 2020, there will be 500 social work schools in China (MCA, 2012b). Though there are currently over 300 schools, there is no overall mechanism for accreditation and curriculum standardization. In the pursuit of quantity rather than quality, significant variations have arisen across programmes. In fact, the field is full of low-quality and ill-equipped programmes.

In short, the government has launched long-term, vigorous and comprehensive plans to introduce and expand social work. There is growing demand for professionally trained social workers to support the thriving social welfare services sector. It is largely uncertain why the CPC has begun to endorse the development of professional social work at this time. On the surface, the need to professionalize the emerging services is important to meet mounting social needs. Politically, the CPC may perceive that the development of social work in NGOs under the close supervision from the government is necessary to resolve social conflicts in the community. As the chairperson of the China Association of Social Work Education, Professor Wang Sibin, said, 'In China, the biggest difference from Western countries is that social workers act as assistants for the Party to provide social work and management' (Leung, 2010). Simply put, social work is accepted as a new governing tool of the CPC. Yet, its development has been hindered by poor pay, uneven development, and the need to professionalize the large existing population of untrained personnel engaged in social work tasks. The issue is how educational institutes can now respond to the thriving demand for competent practitioners at different levels.

THE EMERGENCE OF PURCHASE OF SERVICES AND SOCIAL WORK ORGANIZATIONS

Besides specifying the procedures for public procurement, the Government Procurement Law in 2002 prescribed five major methods of purchase of services, namely open bidding, invited bidding, competitive negotiation, single-source procurement and price enquiry (Jing and Savas, 2009). However, it did not include key public services, such as welfare and education. More importantly, there has been criticism of the fact that most social organizations receiving funding support from the government are 'government-affiliated'. Competition for projects is not open and transparent; supporting policies and laws, such as tax exemption and capacity building, are inadequate (Jing, 2008; Jia and Su, 2009; Jing and Savas, 2009; Shieh, 2011).

In order to provide support to social organizations in recent years, local governments have been active in POS from social organizations in areas ranging from rural development, poverty alleviation and managing homes for the aged to professional legal and research consultation services. Under the directive of welfare socialization, local governments, such as those in Shanghai and Guangdong province, have been establishing pilot projects to subsidize local NGOs' delivery of welfare services since the early 1990s (Jia and Su, 2009; Jing, 2008). On a limited scale, welfare services cover rural poverty alleviation, AIDS prevention and treatment, and services for the elderly, delinquents and the disabled. By gradually changing the role of the government from provider to funder, facilitator and monitoring body, it is generally believed that POS can enhance service efficiency and effectiveness as well as promote the development of social organizations.

The *Opinion on Supporting the Society Efforts in Operating Social Welfare Organizations* (2005) and *Notice Concerning the Promotion of the Development of Non-Governmental SWOs* (2009) enacted by the MCA recognized the urgency and importance of developing SWOs through formulating and improving their registration, monitoring and self-regulation. SWOs are defined as social organizations registered as civil non-enterprise units for the purpose of delivering social work services. Registered social workers sit on their executive boards and must comprise at least one-third of their employees. To promote and cultivate the development of SWOs, local governments are encouraged to purchase services from them and to provide preferential policy supporting their development. The performance of SWOs should be assessed by a third party.

In recent years, there have been a number of policy documents encouraging government POS for different target populations. The *Opinion Concerning the Promotion of the Business for Disabled People* (2008), the *Report on the Development of Social Work in China* (2013), the *Opinion Concerning Speeding up the Development of Services for the Older People* (2013) and the *Opinion Concerning Improving the Government Purchase of Pilot Service for the Disabled* (2014) all point out the need to promote government POS. In 2012, the MCA and the Ministry of Finance enacted the *Guiding Opinion on the Government Purchase of Social Work Services*. The *Opinion* comprises five parts: recognizing the urgency and importance of the purchase of social work services; the guiding ideology, principles and objectives; the purchase process of budgeting, purchasing, signing agreements and guiding implementation; the establishment of a monitoring structure comprising purchaser, service users and a third party; and strengthening government leadership in constructing the guiding and operational system. To expand the development of SWOs, in April 2014 the MCA issued the *Opinion on Further Promoting the Development of Non-Governmental SWOs*, which specifies the need both to strengthen the governance system and capacity of SWOs and to increase support from the government. By 2020, there will be 80,000 SWOs (MCA, 2014a).

According to a national survey report of the MCA in 2013, the development of social work services and positions has been extremely uneven. Only a handful of provinces, such as Guangdong and Shanghai, have established high-level leading groups, social work departments and social work associations and formulated relevant policies to promote the development of social work services and positions. Nationally, in early 2013, there were 84,126 qualified social workers, 72,086 social work positions had been created, and 1,247 SWOs were in operation. They were concentrated mainly in the coastal provinces, such as Guangdong, Shanghai, Zhejiang, Jiangsu and Beijing. There were 11,723 registered social workers in Beijing, but only seven in Tibet and 184 in Ningxia. There were 300 SWOs in Guangdong, but only one each in Hainan and Shanxi. Of the 1.25 billion yuan committed by all the local governments to the development of social work services, 46 per cent, or 570 million yuan, was invested in Guangdong (MCA, 2013a).

A survey was carried out among SWOs by the Beijing Normal University and the University of Hong Kong in January 2013. Questionnaires were sent out through the MCA to provincial civil affairs departments, which then distributed them to all the SWOs within their provinces. By March 2013, a total of 560 completed questionnaires had been received. Initial findings showed that most of the SWOs were from the eastern provinces (67 per cent), followed by the western provinces (25 per cent) and the central provinces (8 per cent). Some 73 per cent were independently registered, while the rest operated under local government departments; 78 per cent were new, registered after 2006. In general, they were small, with an average annual budget of around 1 million yuan and employing seventeen social workers (44 per cent of whom were qualified). Their salary was low, on average 2,000 yuan a month. Relatively high turnover was expected.

Major social issues addressed by SWOs were poverty (23 per cent), mental health (17 per cent), family (12 per cent), education (9 per cent), employment (8 per cent), marriage (6 per cent), legal issues (6 per cent) and drug abuse (2 per cent). Major targets were the elderly and the disabled (Leung and Xu, 2013). Overall, the majority of the SWOs are small and young, and their development is uneven.

DEVELOPMENT OF PURCHASE OF SERVICES IN GUANGDONG

As a leader in China's economic growth and a pioneer for three decades of the reform and opening-up agenda, Guangdong province is perceived as a leading example for other provinces to learn from. Guangdong and Shenzhen were recognized by the MCA in July 2009 as the key pilot locations for the development of SWOs and social work. The Shanghai government signed a similar agreement with the MCA in 2011.

In 2011 the Committee for Social Affairs of Guangdong Province was formed, headed by a deputy Party secretary of the Provincial Party Committee, comprising key government department heads. The committee is responsible for overseeing and implementing the innovation of social management in the province. Social affairs committees have also been set up under the city and district Party committees. In the same year, the committee published a major policy paper on social construction and seven other policy documents, on POS, nurturing social organizations, managing floating population, constructing the social work workforce, strengthening the information management on social construction, and restructuring the urban residents' committees and the village committees. Similar sets of policy documents have been enacted in Shenzhen (2007), Dongguan (2009) and Guangzhou (2011) (Committee for Social Affairs of Guangdong Province, 2014).

To support the establishment of social organizations, including SWOs, the registration procedures and tax exemption requirements have been simplified and relaxed. By 2012, Guangdong had a total of 28,509 registered social organizations: 13,058 societies, 15,249 civil non-enterprise units and 202 charity foundations. The ratio of the number of social organizations to the population is 3.35:100,000. The facilitation of the registration of social organizations in Guangdong has been regarded as a shining achievement of the provincial government. In 2012, there were 4,200 newly registered social organizations, representing an increase of 14 per cent over the previous year (CNC, 10 April 2013). According to government estimates, by 2015 the ratio of social organizations to population will become 5:100,000. Currently, only 15 per cent of social organizations are capable of delivering public services for the government, and around 9 per cent are funded by the government, but it is intended that the percentage of capable social organizations will increase to 80 per cent by 2015. According to the description of the Guangdong government,'the golden period' of social organizations has arrived (*Guangming Daily*, 16 October 2013).

As early as 2008, the Guangdong government enacted the *Opinion Concerning the Development and Regulation of Social Organizations*, requiring local governments to initiate the transfer of government functions to social organizations. The 2009 *Opinion on Piloting the Government POS from Social Organizations* specified 130 tasks to be transferred to social organizations. The 2012 *Temporary Methods on Government POS from Social Organizations* indicated that POS can involve public services, community affairs and social welfare services, whereas those tasks involving state security, legal jurisdiction, administration assessment, confidential issues and mandatory implementation should be exempted. All those social organizations with a good track record and qualified by an annual inspection are eligible to apply.

In 2012, the government published three catalogues listing services to be contracted out, services to be purchased from social organizations, and social organizations eligible to apply. There were 262 projects in the 2012 catalogue, covering basic public services, social affairs services, management of occupations, technical services and supplementary services. In 2011, the amount of funds involved in POS reached 104 billion yuan, constituting one-tenth of the total nationally (*Nanfang Daily News*, 15 August 2013). Through the introduction of government POS by competitive bidding, SWOs have been provided with full resources and support to assist the government in the delivery of welfare services. To ensure good-quality working conditions for employees, policy provisions include local household registration for social workers from other provinces, standardized salary schemes for social workers with different qualifications, and staff development programmes.

In late 2012, Guangdong province had a total of 300 SWOs, compared with only 170 in 2011; the number was set to increase to 400 by 2013 and to 500 by 2015. Currently, SWOs employ over 3,000 social workers (*Shenzhen Business News Network*, 2012). In Guangzhou, SWOs can be divided into five types: those set up by the street offices; those transferring from previous social organizations involving specialized social welfare services; those established by the social work departments of universities; social welfare agencies from Hong Kong and Singapore; and social organizations outside Guangzhou. Most of the social work schools in China have set up SWOs and deliver social welfare services through government POS. For example, the Department of Social Work in Sun Yat Sen University, Guangzhou, operates three SWOs.

The funds for POS in social welfare services amounted to 570 million yuan in 2012. Around 80 per cent of the fund comes from the government, while the rest is from welfare lotteries (Zhang and Shang, 2013). Through government subsidies, their primary aim is to deliver a wide array of welfare services to older people, families, the disabled, drug addicts and delinquents. Support available to SWOs can involve special one-off grants, POS through delegation or competitive bidding, tax exemption, premises and utilities expenses, and relaxation on fee charging. The performance of SWOs in receipt of subsidies is assessed by a third party. Among areas of assessment are governance, service effectiveness, financial management and community relations. Such assessment can include reviewing reports, interviews, random checks and observations. SWOs given a rating of distinction in these assessments can receive appropriate rewards, such as special grants from welfare lotteries. Those that fail cannot bid for new government contracts for two years (Guangzhou Civil Affairs Bureau, 2010). In Guangzhou, the assessment is carried out by the Social Work Association of the Guangzhou Civil Affairs Bureau and other independent social organizations, and in Shenzhen and Dongguan by a social organization formed by a university from Shanghai.

According to the policy document *Constructing the Social Work Workforce*, the Guangdong government has pledged to improve the quality of social workers by strengthening social work education in the province. One initiative to be in place by 2015 is the establishment of key training centres at different levels (four provincial-level training and 50 city-level practice centres). The plan also involves the recruitment of 30 high-level specialists from outside the province, or even outside China itself, to engage in education, training and research. In addition, there will be various training initiatives: 30 selected young social work teachers and 100 NGO administrators will study outside China and also go on study tours, 100 social welfare administrators will attend university, 500 social work supervisors will also be trained, and continuous professional education will be made widely available (Committee for Social Affairs of Guangdong Province, 2014). By 2015, the number of registered social workers will reach 50,000. In the service units of the civil affairs departments and mass organizations, no less than 20 per cent of welfare service jobs will employ social workers (Guangdong Social Workers' Association, 2012).

Before 2007, social work development in Shenzhen was almost non-existent. In 2007 the city government enacted the *Opinion on Promoting the Development of Social Work and Social Work Workforce* and seven supplementary policy guidelines on assessing the occupational standards, promoting training, setting up social work positions, formulating salary scales, developing social organizations, providing financial support, and implementing the integration of social work and volunteers (Shenzhen Civil Affairs, 2007). Between 2007 and 2012, the city government allocated a total of 350 million yuan, mainly from welfare lotteries, for the development of POS. Social workers are recruited nationally. Over 150 experienced social workers had been recruited from Hong Kong to provide supervision, and by the end of 2012 there were over 2,000 practising social workers in Shenzhen. There were 87 SWOs, of which five employed more than 100 social workers. Services have been introduced into fourteen areas to help the aged, the disabled, drug addicts, young people, school students, hospital patients, community residents, the army, petitioners, ethnic minorities, etc. One major future service development is the establishment of over 700 community centres by 2015 (Shang and Ye, 2013).

In 2010 Guangzhou enacted a set of documents comprising the *Opinion on Promoting the Development of Social Work and Social Work Workforce* and five other supplementary policy guidelines, on managing the registration of social workers, promoting the development of SWOs, establishing social work positions and their salary scales, the financial support of social work development, and assessment methods for government POS (Social Work Information Network, 2010). In 2008, Guangzhou had devoted only 5.22 million yuan for POS; this increased in 2012 to 260 million yuan and in 2013 to 320 million yuan. Major welfare services involved establishing 132 integrated family service centres, one in each street office administered district. Each centre costs on average 2 million yuan each year. As such, Guangzhou will need at least 8,000 to 10,000 social workers, whereas currently only 2,500 are registered (Guangzhou University, 2013). In 2008, Guangzhou had only eight SWOs; in 2013 it had more than 200 (Zhang and Shang, 2013).

It is clear that Guangdong is a pioneer nationally in encouraging the development of social organizations, developing professional social work, setting up SWOs and implementing POS. Reflecting the strong commitment of the provincial government, related policy documents and POS procedures and regulations were formulated. Financial support has been secured. New welfare services have been emerging, particularly in creating integrated community centres or family service centres in each neighbourhood. The development of social work services in schools, hospitals, drug abuse centres and rehabilitation centres has been recognized. These achievements were made with the significant contribution of experienced social workers from Hong Kong employed in the region since 2007 to provide supervision to frontline social workers and consultation to SWOs in Shenzhen, Dongguan and Guangzhou. The achievements of Guangdong in formulating supporting policy, ensuring financial support, expanding new pilot projects, developing special services and creating new SWOs have been praised by the Minister of Civil Affairs (*China Philanthropy Times*, 2 April 2013).

EMERGING ISSUES

National development has been uneven. The development of Guangdong is exceptional, and it is still not clear to what extent its experiences are relevant to other provinces, particularly those that are less wealthy. Even in Guangdong, development is uneven, having been concentrated in the Pearl River Delta. Some 98 per cent of POS expenditure, 97 per cent of the SWOs and 91 per cent of the registered social workers are in this area (Zhang and Shang, 2013).

SWOs are characterized by their heavy dependency on government funding. According to the *Guangdong Regulations on Promoting the Development of Public Benefit Organizations* (2009), they can neither raise funds publicly nor charge fees (Xu and Li, 2013). In Guangzhou, however, SWOs are allowed to raise funds publicly. Without other sources of income, SWOs tend to rely primarily on government funding and so function more as government subsidiaries. They largely lack resources for capacity building, innovating new services, and developing their own methods according to their visions and missions (Law, 2013). In the case of family service centres in Guangzhou, because the street offices have been involved in their selection as service providers, SWOs tend to be treated as a subsidiary of the street office, being 'supervised' directly by local governments rather than operating independently as service partners (Guangzhou University, 2013). According to a report by the *Economic Reference Daily*, POS has created opportunity for corruption. 'Kick back', a form of negotiated bribery, is common in the POS process, involving 20 to 40 per cent of the project fund. The market for competitive bidding is neither transparent nor open, often with poor performance management and programme evaluation (CNC, 3 July 2014).

The majority of the SWOs have been created in recent years under government encouragement. Under the 'de-administration' principle, government officials should refrain from participating in their management as office bearers. In the case of Guangdong, however, government officials, particularly retired officials, are still widely involved in SWOs created by local government and street offices (Jia, 2011; *Nanfang Daily News*, 4 June 2013). It is also common practice for the chairperson of the executive committee of the organization to receive a salary or to act as the chief executive officer. In some cases, not only do executive board members receive a salary but family relations can join the board (Zhao, 2011). Corporate governance needs to be improved to prevent role conflicts.

Despite the provision of tax exemption for public benefit organizations (taxes are complicated, including levies on income, business operations, value added tax, real estate tax, etc.), most social organizations, except those under government control and those enjoying a good relationship with the government, do not enjoy full tax exemption. According to the Enterprise Income Tax Law and Public Welfare Donation Law, all income of social organizations, including fees, donations and government allocations, are liable to income tax. Tax exemption is subject to tight assessment (Jia, 2011).

Further to the Procurement Law (2002), there is a lack of specific regulations guiding the government purchase of services. Only a handful of provinces and cities have begun to enact regulations in this respect. Even with the regulations provided, an open and fair competitive bidding process on deciding service providers is not fully in place. Particularly in Guangzhou, where POS on social welfare services is determined largely by the district governments and street offices, there is a tendency for the bidding process to favour those SWOs with strong government connections (X. F. Zhao, 2013; Xu and Li, 2013; Zhang and Shang, 2013).

Social work education in Guangdong has been largely underdeveloped in comparison with the situation in other coastal provinces in the north. Many of the social workers have to be brought in from elsewhere, mainly from the western and central provinces, where social work positions are largely not available. Because they face a less than satisfactory working environment and earn a relatively poor salary, the turnover rate among social workers is high. In Shenzhen, the turnover rate increased from 8.2 per cent in 2008 to 18.1 per cent in 2012 (*People's Daily*, 27 February 2013). With the rapid development of job opportunities in the Pearl River Delta, experienced social workers in Shenzhen have become key targets for recruitment. Around 30 per cent of turnover can be attributed to active enrolment by neighbouring cities (*Nanfang Daily News*, 21 August 2012).

At first glance, the relaxation of the registration of selected types of social organizations and the introduction of government POS have led to dramatic increases in the number of SWOs in Guangdong. The trend may appear politically welcome. However, the creation within a short period of a large number of SWOs, chiefly dependent on government funding, inevitably raises the concern that many of them lack the capacity of self-government and sustainability. All of them have to rely on the government for service contracts. As newly established social organizations, most would inevitably face the challenges of capacity building in nurturing new leadership, promoting the brand name and public trust, securing financial stability, and developing staff competency. Social organizations are still under-resourced, lacking in prominent leadership, and poorly managed.

PROSPECTS

Market-oriented reforms have led to a more pluralistic and diversified society in which the government cannot assume sole responsibility for welfare. It requires the support of society. Accordingly, SWOs have been receiving encouragement in the registration process and through government funding. Under the directive of 'party leadership, government responsibility, society facilitation, public participation, and the rule of law protection', the CPC will continue to lead the development of social organizations. The general public will be engaged to take a more active role in supporting the development of a 'civil society with Chinese characteristics'. Attempts have been made through public-sector reforms to separate the government from the emerging social organization sector to allow social organizations to be registered more easily and present a more 'non-governmental' image. The employment of professional social workers is an attempt to handle social conflict through a softer and more indirect approach.

Nevertheless, the government, through POS, has striven to set up a new system of indirect monitoring and control under the rubric of enhancing accountability. As such, a new form of relationship between the government and thriving social organizations has emerged and become redefined. This relationship has changed from one intermingling connections of ideological control and direct command to a more formal contractual association based on specified terms of provision, incentives, coordination of interests and performance evaluation. Government control has changed shape, and social organizations are under more indirect and implicit forms of authority. Despite all these reforms, the function of social organizations has been largely passive, dependent on government funding, serving primarily the interests of the government, and struggling to secure government contracts. In other words, independent social organizations are still difficult to find. We are still a long way from seeing the emergence of a genuine and egalitarian partnership between the government and social organizations.

8 The Third Turning Point

BECOMING A WELFARE STATE

According to estimates by international organizations (World Bank, 2013; OECD, 2013d, 2014), China will soon become a high-income economy. However, this is not simply a matter of increasing GDP income: there is an urgent need to step up to support much needed social reforms in the areas of education, social welfare, employment, pensions and health. In view of the marked disparities in social services between urban and rural residents, across regions, and among different social groups, there have been increasing calls for more equitable provision (OECD, 2006, 2010a, 2010b, 2012, 2013a, 2013d, 2014; UNDP, 2008, 2013b; CDRF, 2012). According to the OECD (2013d), China's development is at a crossroads. Social reform is urgently required to ensure inclusive, broad, sustainable and equitable growth in the years to come.

- Further progress is needed to unify the fragmented system of welfare assistance, pensions and health care. Responsibility for social protection should ultimately be transferred from cities to the national level to ensure better integration, efficiency and solidarity.
- The registration system and restrictions on migrant workers' access to social services create obstacles to labour mobility and should be relaxed.

* Health-care reforms must be pursued to ensure that provision at a local level is improved, that hospitals are run more efficiently, and that the different insurance systems are eventually merged.

China has learned that a high-income economy must be accompanied by a stable political system and a high quality of life for all citizens. Its emerging social welfare system is modelled on those in Western countries, with social insurance programmes as the basic protection, supplemented by social assistance as the last resort. In the last decade, profound reforms have been made to establish new social insurance programmes in pensions and health care for rural residents, urban migrants and the economically inactive in urban areas. The implementation of these schemes has to be enforced, particularly for the informally employed and migrant workers. Key directives are needed in social protection to integrate or harmonize the segmented system, across regions, between rural and urban areas, and between different occupations, as well as enhancing portability. Other inevitable reforms are the raising of the retirement age and the promotion of the private market for social welfare protection in health care, social insurance and care for the aged. The safety net of *dibao* requires restructuring to ensure that it is targeting the poor and providing sufficient employment service support. In the coming years, social policy reforms will centre on whether China can effectively enhance the social welfare of migrants and peasants.

According to the 2013 *Views on Deepening the Reforms on Income Distribution System*, the proportion of SOEs' profits submitted to the central government will be increased by 5 per cent. The increased revenue will be used to finance social security and social expenditures. The policy directive is to 'raise the bottom, expand the middle, and adjust the top'. 'Adjust the top' implies the introduction of new and higher taxes. The concern is how to 'raise the bottom' in order to close the widening income gap. Greater social spending is expected to facilitate improvements in social security benefits, including pensions, the minimum wage and social assistance. 'Expand the middle' refers to the reduction of the tax burden and increased spending on social services. The future social structure of Chinese society should be 'olive' shaped (CNC, 26 October 2013).

Following the introduction of a number of new social welfare programmes in both urban and rural areas, China has made significant improvements to reverse the previous pro-economic growth policy in the last decade. The successful implementation of these programmes, particularly in the western and central provinces, hinges on financial transfers from the central government. Significant subnational variations and diversity of the social welfare system imply that the policy of the central government has not been strictly followed (Carrillo and Duckett, 2011; Brixi et al., 2011). In essence, in redressing regional and urban–rural disparities and programme implementation failure, it is pivotal that the central government takes on a more centralizing role in financial support and policy directives.

The foremost and central development strategy of China is rapid urbanization. Urbanization is expected to increase from 53 per cent in 2012, to 60 per cent in 2020, and then to over 75 per cent by 2030, and will involve 300 million people having to leave the countryside and move into cities (CNC, 16 March 2014). One of the recommendations by the World Bank and the Development Research Centre on this strategy is to reform the *hukou* system to create a mobile and versatile labour force with equal access to a common standard of public services. To support the increased investment in urban infrastructure, public and social services, local government fiscal revenue and central government transfer have to be strengthened (World Bank and DRC, 2014, p. xxv). By blurring the distinction between urban and rural *hukou*, the social service and welfare systems can be unified. In short, *hukou* reform is an integral part of the grand urbanization strategy. It should be noted that the way to reduce inequalities effectively is not to improve further the situation in urban areas and absorb more rural people into cities, but to improve significantly the quality of life in rural areas. The crux of effective social transformation is also determined by what happens in rural areas.

At the same time, modernized and professional social welfare programmes for people in need, such as frail older people, the disabled, youth offenders, drug users, victims of domestic violence, etc., are emerging. In view of the substantial regional differences in social welfare programme accessibility, 'equalizing', and 'unifying' these programmes based on citizenship and entitlement will be a profound challenge. For the Chinese government, a sustainable welfare state is important in maintaining social stability and cohesion and supporting continuous economic growth. Promoting social cohesion, economic growth and greater equality are not mutually exclusive developmental goals.

The strong role of the state is still decisive in welfare and social policy development. Rather than retrenching, retreating or withdrawing, the state will maintain a pivotal role in shaping future social policy development. At issue is what kind of welfare system China will develop. In the short and medium term, the Chinese government will inevitably assume more responsibility for protecting the deprived. But China will not become a fully fledged welfare state with universal coverage and entitlements. Even though inequalities may be moderated through increased government transfers, they will remain a significant and intractable issue in the near future. China will create a largely residual welfare state to make sure that no one is left behind, but it will certainly not pursue a radical redistributive policy to reduce inequalities drastically.

INCREASED SOCIAL SPENDING

When facing a mounting fiscal crisis with escalating debts and deficits, most Western governments have to cut social spending. Yet an ageing population and rising expectations have trapped most governments in a quagmire. In contrast, China's financial situation is, on the whole, healthy. It is capable of increasing its social spending to achieve social reforms. Indeed, the proportion of total GDP represented by China's public spending targeted at meeting basic social needs is well below that of developed countries and most comparable developing countries, whereas its private spending in these areas is among the highest in the world (OECD, 2006, 2013d, 2014; CDRF, 2012). In 2011, total social spending constituted only 9.6 per cent of total GDP (higher than in Mexico and India, but much lower than the OECD average of 21.8 per cent), including 3.4 per cent in health care, 3.1 per cent in education, and 2.8 per cent in pensions. In health care, the OECD average was 9.3 per cent. Health expenditure per capita in China was only US$432 (calculated based on PPP) compared with an OECD average of US$3,339. Public spending accounted for only 56 per cent of the total, as compared to the OECD average of 72 per cent (OECD, 2013a, p. 7; 2013d, p. 13).

Market-oriented reforms have created a decentralized administration with greater regional autonomy. As regions are allowed to pursue their own strategies and reap the benefits of economic development, wide variations of economic and social development become inevitable. The fiscal relation between central and local governments is marked by a high but uneven degree of decentralization. Spending decisions are more decentralized than tax revenues. In 2011, local governments accounted for 85 per cent of all spending despite receiving only 51 per cent of government revenues (OECD, 2013a, p. 247). There is a discrepancy between local governments' expenditure mandates and the funds allocated to them by central government. Responsibilities are often delegated to local governments without the corresponding resources. This explains why the latter often resort to off-budget funds and illicit borrowing. Despite the increasing transfers from the central government to help deprived localities, there remains wide variation in public spending across the country. As such, deprived local governments may struggle to finance social service responsibilities. It is becoming vitally important that the transfer system to central and western regions be further strengthened.

There is a marked difference in local government expenditures on social services. Sharp differences in social spending produce staggering inequalities in educational and health outcomes. More importantly, local government finance remains complicated and is not transparent, and the high debts are worrying (Xinhua, 2013b). According to the National Audit Office, liabilities of local governments in 2013 may have doubled, to 20 trillion yuan, since 2010. Debt burdens will constrain not only economic investment but also the financing of public and social services (*South China Morning Post*, 23 September 2013, p. B1).

Extra-budgetary and off-budget expenses have posed risks to accountability and transparency. China needs to follow the recommendations of the OECD and conduct a needs assessment using international standards as a guideline to review and determine levels of expenditure in the priority areas of education, health care and social security. Such an assessment could help the central government channel funds more effectively to meet its development goals (OECD, 2013a, p. 254). The Third Plenum of the 18th Party Congress has promised to streamline the division of revenue between central and local governments through a modernized fiscal system (Xinhua, 2013c). In a nutshell, the central government will have to make larger transfer payments and allow local governments to increase their revenue.

A circular on improving the work evaluation of local party and government leadership and officials stressed that economic growth rates should not be the only index for the evaluation of local officials' achievements. More distinctive indicators should include people's livelihood, social harmony and ecological protection (CNC, 9 December 2013). A slowdown of economic growth in the coming years is foreseeable and inevitable. How to share the financial responsibilities of growing social welfare expenditures between central and local governments remains a very sensitive and profound challenge.

BUILDING A MIXED ECONOMY OF WELFARE

China can now be described as a mixed economy, in which the private or market and state sectors both have key roles to play. Alongside SOEs and the government in its regulatory function, the market is expected to play a more decisive role. Up until now, social welfare in China has often been synonymous with state and employment-based provisions. The part played by charities and civil society has not yet been fully recognized. However, we cannot expect the government to continue to take care of everything. The term 'mixed economy of welfare' or 'welfare pluralism' refers to the integration of different sectors in the provision of welfare – the private, the voluntary and the informal sectors (Powell, 2007). Under welfare pluralism, the role of the state is that of an enabler, shifting or sharing welfare responsibilities with other sectors of society (Gilbert, 2002).

As pointed out at the Third Plenum of the 18th Party Congress, China is attempting to rebalance responsibility between public, private, non-profit and informal sectors. The boundaries between these sectors must be redefined, with the market and civil sectors playing a greater role. However, increasing the responsibility of the market and civil sectors does not mean the retrenchment of the influence and responsibility of the state. As regards the development of the civil charity sector, the traditional Confucian principles prescribe that people relate differentially to others, according to their distance from the family centre. People are obliged to provide assistance to those within their social network, not to unrelated strangers. Thus, an individual can be compassionate and kind to those within their personal family network yet inconsiderate and even cruel-hearted to strangers. It is in this context that Chinese people have at times been described as selfish, individualistic, lacking unity, lacking public morality and being 'spectators' to accidents (Leung and Nann, 1995, p. 3). With their family-centred culture, they seemingly feel no impulse to support charity programmes. Political campaigns under Mao Zedong further discouraged social trust. According to the World Giving Index, China ranked overall 131st out of 135 countries; in terms of charity donation it ranked 115th, of volunteering 13st, and of helping strangers 120th (Charity Aid Foundation, 2013). There have been incidences in which passers-by fail to offer help to victims of accidents. This phenomenon may indicate a lack of civic virtue or moral decline, or a high level of social mistrust.

Because of historical restrictions on the growth of NGOs and the underdevelopment of a charitable, giving culture, the financial and administrative capacity of NGOs in China has been extremely limited. The majority are not transparent about their financial situation. Following a number of recent fund mismanagement scandals, public trust in NGOs has been poor. These scandals have partly accounted for the decline of public charity donations, from 84.5 billion yuan in 2011 to only 70 billion yuan in 2012. Charity donations in 2011 accounted for only 0.18 per cent of national GDP, as compared with 2.2 per cent in the United States (CNC, 29 June 2012). Recent natural disasters, however, including the earthquakes in Sichuan in 2008 and in Qinghai in 2010, have invigorated the charity movement, particularly in terms of private donations and volunteer participation. The government has been active in promoting charity through giving public recognition and awards to business philanthropists. Despite rapid development in recent years, charity donations are often limited to relief work in natural disasters and poverty alleviation (China Charity Donation Information Centre, 2012; CASS, 2012b). According to the

2013 Report on the Transparency of Charity Organizations in China, only 30 per cent of 1,000 charity organizations surveyed were qualified in 2012 (20 per cent in 2011) (CNC, 23 September 2013). A study in 2011 on charity foundations in China showed their underdevelopment. They were concentrated largely in coastal provinces. Each foundation had on average only 3.6 employees, assets of 33 million yuan, and income amounting to 29 billion yuan (90 per cent of which came from individual donations); 97 per cent of their expenditure was for charity (Yang, 2013).

China also performs poorly in terms of other civic virtues, such as organ and blood donation. The ratio of patients waiting for organ donations to the number of organ donors is 150 to one in China, versus five to one in the United States and three to one in the United Kingdom. Organs are often harvested from the bodies of dead prisoners (CNC, 23 March 2013). As voluntary blood donation is still limited, local governments have assigned donation quotas to universities and work units. Even though the number of blood donors has increased, from only 50,000 in 1998 to 12.78 million in 2013, in the latter year China registered only 9.4 blood donations per 1,000 people. This is below the minimum ratio of the 10 to 30 donations proposed by the World Health Organization to meet a country's clinical demand (Xinhua, 2014). According to a study by *Fortune* on corporate social responsibility (CSR), the concept was still little understood within the Chinese business community. In 2006, the number of Chinese companies issuing CSR reports stood at just eighteen. By 2010, over 600 companies in China issued CSR reports (Lee, 2011). Yet, in a study in 2011, about 68 per cent of the large enterprises were merely 'spectators', not actively promoting CSR (CNC, 8 June 2012).

A high-income economy needs to move towards a welfare society in which people share a culture of helping others through donations of time and money, as well as a willingness to assist strangers. Civic engagement is fundamental in providing effective channels by which to receive dissenting voices and political feedback from all stakeholders, as well as gaining policy legitimacy and support (OECD, 2011).

LESSONS TO LEARN

This book has tried to show that China has made three turning points in developmental strategies since 1949. Each turning point involved a significant shift in economic and social policy. The first transformed China into a socialist country based on central planning and political mobilization. As a result, the country was inward-looking and economically backward. Even though it was claimed that Chinese society was egalitarian and guaranteed security of livelihood, people lacked basic civil liberties. At the second turning point, in 1978, the economy was gradually liberalized and social security and social service provisions were marketized. This successfully moved China towards a globalized and high-growth economy. Yet decentralization and marketization caused rising inequalities across regions and between rural and urban areas. Recognizing the need to address the rising inequalities, which threaten social stability and the CPC's legitimacy to govern China, the government pledged in 2006 to develop a harmonious society with more balanced growth. Social programmes have been rolled out with the aim of building up a universal welfare state with an affordable, pluralistic and effective social welfare system.

China is at a critical juncture, in terms not only of economic transition but also of social welfare development. The Third Plenum of the 18th Party Congress in 2013 said that, 'At present, our country's development has entered a new phase, and reform has entered a period of storming fortifications and an area of deep water' (Pallotta, 2013). New social challenges and risks include an ageing population, the erosion of demographic dividends, rapid urbanization, an increasingly mobile population, widening income and social inequalities, the need to integrate the segmented social welfare system, and a more divided society whose members are increasingly aware of their human rights and thus have greater expectations for their lives.

If China can successfully navigate the third turning point, it will be able to make the transition to a high-income economy, a *xiaokang* society, as it is called by the Chinese, with shared prosperity. However, if it fails to tackle these formidable social issues through decisive and effective social reforms and so achieve the desired impacts, Chinese society will reach a 'tipping point'. It will be trapped as a middle-income economy and become more divided and unstable. Without complementary social development, the economic development of China cannot be sustainable. The Third Plenum of the 18th Party Congress in 2013 indicated a market-oriented development in the economy but a more conservative political orientation of maintaining overall Party control. In short, it can be described as economically to the left and politically to the right. In social policy, the communique has limited coverage. Some of the key terms, such as fairness, competition, equality and justice, are used repeatedly. The term 'fairness' appears ten times. These would seem to have become the core values of the CPC. However, the history of Chinese reform is filled with vague ideals and wish lists whose full implementation presents difficulties. There are goals and principles, but they lack specific action plans and timelines.

In a loose sense, the Chinese model has been relying on a strong and authoritarian state, a pro-growth economic policy, pragmatic and incremental reforms, and decentralized and residual welfare. Looking into the future, China will continue to pursue a hybrid model, combining a market-oriented approach to the economy with a socialist, authoritarian political framework. So far, the CPC seems to have enjoyed a high degree of public trust. The OECD has indicated that two-thirds of China's citizens trust their government, versus the OECD average of only 40 per cent (OECD, 2013e, p. 26). To the

Chinese people, a 'high level of trust' does not imply that they support and respect the CPC – rather, that they have both high expectations and a level of dependency on the government to deliver them a better livelihood. The popularity of the use of petitions to redress grievances in China reflects the belief of the people that the benevolent higher government authorities can still promise them justice. The people's trust is considered critical for a government to carry out reforms. The emerging system of governance will be more pluralistic, diversified and modern, and policy-making will be guided more by public engagement and opinion. Within limitations, the role of civil society will be more empowered, and a civic culture based on charity will be promoted.

Growing rights consciousness has led to more labour and civil disputes in the form of industrial action, such as strikes, petitions, insurgency, large gatherings and disturbance. According to the *Report on the Rule of Law*, published by the Chinese Academy of Social Sciences, there were 871 protest actions involving over 100 people between 2000 and 2013. Some 92 per cent of these took place after 2008. A total of 2.2 million people were involved. Protests were fuelled by labour disputes, land appropriation, forced demolition, pollution, traffic accidents and ethnic relations. Some 31 per cent of the protests happened in Guangdong (CASS, 2014). Labour and civil insurgency is typically short-lived, issue-based, directed at the firm in question or at local government, and does not escalate into class movement or cross-boundary struggle (So, 2007).

China does not have a clear-cut model from which other developing countries might learn, but its agriculture-led poverty reduction experiences have been recommended for African countries (Ravallion, 2009; Li, 2013; Wan, 2014). Its development experiences have been unique and cannot be duplicated easily elsewhere (Naughton, 2010). China has been trying to integrate overseas learning with the local context pragmatically. Millions of Chinese students and civil servants have studied in the West. Even though many of these students have not returned, China has benefited from its openness to adopting modern technology and knowledge (Yang and Tan, 2010; Wan, 2014). In a sense, the critical success factor of the Chinese model has been its pragmatism through active learning and adaption.

As the nation faces the destabilizing issue of widening income disparities, there is evidently a strong need for the government to intervene and manage income redistribution. Improvements in employment, the wage system, social protection and taxation are required. The building of a harmonious society necessitates the active redistribution of resources through the continuous improvement of public and social services, targeting the vulnerable populations. The previous pro-economic growth model, which focused on decentralization, incrementalism and flexibility and has been so successful in the past 30 years, is not sustainable; a more balanced, centralized, systemic, inclusive and unified approach with effective implementation is required. If its government is not prepared to achieve substantial and long-term social reforms through a new developmental strategy in the face of new social challenges and risks, China will be caught in the middle-income trap and fail to become a high-income economy. Even worse, if the CPC fails to fulfil its promises of social transformation, it will inevitably face rising political instability.

References

Adam, J. (ed.) (1991) *Economic Reforms and Welfare Systems in the USSR, Poland and Hungary: Social Contract in Transformation.* London: Macmillan.

ADB (Asian Development Bank) (2011) *Asian Development Outlook 2011 Update: Preparing for Demographic Transition.* Manila: ADB.

— (2013) *The Social Protection Index: Assessing Results for Asia and the Pacific.* June, Manila: ADB.

Aspalter, C. (2005) The welfare state in East Asia: an ideal-typical welfare regime, *Journal of Societal and Social Policy* 4(1), pp. 1–20.

— (2006) The East Asian welfare model, *International Journal of Social Welfare* 5, pp. 290–301.

Banister, J., Bloom, D., and Rosenberg, L. (2012) Population aging and economic growth in China, in M. Aoki and J. Wu (eds), *The Chinese Economy: A New Transition.* Basingstoke: Palgrave Macmillan, pp. 114–49.

Beland, D., and Yu, K. M. (2004) A long financial march: pension reform in China, *Journal of Social Policy* 33(2), pp. 267–88.

Besharov, D., and Baehler, K. (2013) *Chinese Social Policy in a Time of Transition.* Oxford: Oxford University Press.

Bloom, G., and Tang, J. (eds) (2004) *Health Care Transition in Urban China.* Aldershot: Ashgate.

Blumenthal, D., and Hsiao, W. (2005) Privatization and its discontents – the evolving Chinese health care system, *New England Journal of Medicine* 353, pp. 1165–70.

Brandt, L., and Rawski, T. (eds) (2008) *China's Great Economic Transformation.* New York: Cambridge University Press.

Brixi, H., Mu, Y., Targa, B., and Hipgrave, D. (2011) *Equity and Public Governance in Health System Reform: Challenges and Opportunities for China.* Policy Research Working Paper 5530, January. Washington, DC: World Bank.

Brown, P. H., de Brauw, A., and Du, Y. (2009) Understanding variation in the design of China's New Cooperative Medical System, *China Quarterly* 198, pp. 304–29.

Cai, F., and Zhao, W. (2012) When demographic dividend disappears: growth sustainability of China, in M. Aoki and J. Wu (eds), *The Chinese Economy: A New Transition*. Basingstoke: Palgrave Macmillan, pp. 75–92.

Cai, F., Giles, J., O'Keefe, P., and Wang, D. (2012) *The Elderly and Old Age Support in Rural China: Challenges and Prospects*. Washington, DC: World Bank.

Cai, Y. S. (2006) *State and Laid-off Workers in Reform China: The Silence and Collective Action of the Retrenched*. London: Routledge.

Caijing (2013) Former World Bank economist Lin sees China as high-income country by 2020, http://finance.chinanews.com/cj/2013/09-08/5259049.shtml [in Chinese].

Cameron, L., Erkal, N., Gangadharan, L., and Meng, X. (2013) Little emperors: behavioral impact of China's one-child policy, *Science*, 11 January; www.sciencemag.org/content/339/6122/953.

Carrillo, B., and Duckett, J. (eds) (2011) *China's Changing Welfare Mix: Local Perspective*. New York: Routledge.

CDRF (China Development Research Foundation) (2009) *Eliminating Poverty through Development in China*. London: Routledge.

— (ed.) (2012) *Constructing a Social Welfare System for All in China*. London: Routledge.

Central People's Government (2014) Questions and answers on the urban and rural residents' pension system, 28 February, http://big5.gov.cn/gate/big5/www.gov.cn/gzdt/2014-02/28/content_2625751.htm [in Chinese].

Chan, C. K. (2010) Rethinking the incrementalist thesis in China: a reflection on the development of the minimum standard of living scheme in urban and rural areas, *Journal of Social Policy* 39(4), pp. 627–45.

Chan, C. K., Ngok, K. L., and Phillips, D. (2008) *Social Policy in China: Development and Well-Being*. London: Routledge.

Chan, J., and Pun, N. (2010) Suicide as protest for the new generation of Chinese migrant workers: Foxconn, global capital, and the state, *Asia-Pacific Journal* 37(2); http://japanfocus.org/-jenny-chan/3408.

Chan, K. W., and Zhang, L. (2009) The *hukou* system and rural–urban migration in China: processes and changes, *China Quarterly* 160(6), pp. 818–55.

Chang, L. T. (2009) *Factory Girls: From Village to City in a Changing China*. New York: Spiegel & Grau.

Charity Aid Foundation (2013) *World Giving Index*, https://www.cafonline.org/publications/2013-publications/world-giving-index-2013.aspx.

CHARLS (2014) *China Health and Retirement Longitudinal Study*, http://charls.ccer.edu.cn/en.

Chen, J. Y., Lucas, H., and Gong, Y. L. (2004) Urban health reform in China: the impact on vulnerable groups, in G. Bloom and S. Tang (eds), *Health Care Transition in Urban China*. Aldershot: Ashgate, pp. 96–110.

Chen, S. H., and Ravallion, M. (2008) *China Is Poorer than We Thought, But No Less Successful in the Fight against Poverty*, Policy Research Working Paper 4621, May. Washington, DC: World Bank.

Chen, S. H., Ravallion, M., and Wang, Y. J. (2006) *Di Bao: A Guaranteed Minimum Income in China's Cities?* Policy Research Working Paper 3805. Washington, DC: World Bank.

China Association of Social Work (2013) *Report on the Development of Social Work in China, 2012*. Beijing: Social Science Academic Publishers [in Chinese].

China Charity Donation Information Centre, MCA (2012) *China Charity Development Report 2012*. Beijing: Social Sciences Academic Publishers [in Chinese].

China Daily (29 September 2007) Harmonious society, http://english.people.com.cn/90002/92169/92211/6274603.html.

— (25 June 2012) New poverty line poses new challenges, www.chinadaily.com.cn/china/2012-06/25/content_15522162.htm.

— (13 May 2013) Number of left-behind children surpasses 60 million, www.china.org.cn/china/2013-05/13/content_28806092.htm.

— (7 July 2013) 355,000 parents have lost their only children, http://usa.chinadaily.com.cn/china/2013-06/07/content_16580615.htm.

— (11 July 2014) Second-child policy having limited effect, www.china.org.cn/china/2014-07/11/content_32919208.htm.

— (24 August 2013) Sex ratio may cause marriage squeeze, www.china.org.cn/china/2013-08/24/content_29813872.htm.

China Philanthropy Times (2 April 2013) Ten important events in social work in 2012, www.gongyishibao.com/html/yaowen/2684.html [in Chinese].

Chinese Academy of Social Sciences (CASS) (2012a) *Report on the Development of Pension Funds in China in 2012*, http://finance.chinanews.com/cj/2012/12-17/4412886.shtml [in Chinese].

— (2012b) *Blue Book on Charity in China 2012*. Beijing: Social Science Academic Publishers [in Chinese].

— (2014) *2014 Report on Rule of Law in China*. Beijing: Social Science Academic Publishers [in Chinese].

Chow, N., and Xu, Y. B. (2001) *Socialist Welfare in a Market Economy: Social Security Reforms in Guangzhou, China*. Aldershot: Ashgate.

— (2002) Pension reforms in China, in C. J. Finer (ed.), *Social Policy Reforms in China: Views from Home and Abroad*. Aldershot: Ashgate, pp. 129–42.

Chowdhury, D. (2013) Bare branches, bitter fruit, *South China Morning Post*, 29 January, p. 4.
CNC (China News Centre) (27 July 2005). State Council DRC's assessment and recommendations on medical care reform, www.china.com.cn/chinese/health/927874.htm [in Chinese].
— (17 February 2010) The number of service workers in homes for the aged is critically insufficient, www.china.com.cn/policy/txt/2010-02/17/content_19 431191.htm [in Chinese].
— (8 November 2010) 70% of older people in the large cities in China are empty-nested, http://newschina.com.cn/txt/2010-11/08/content_ 21294042.htm [in Chinese].
— (30 May 2011) Review and prospects of China's population policy, http:// guoqing.china.com.cn/node_7140203.htm [in Chinese].
— (8 June 2012) Foundations less than charitable with disclosure, www.china. org.cn/china/2012-12/27/content_27526785.htm
— (29 June 2012) Charity donations decline by over 20%, http://china.cnr.cn/ NewsFeeds/201309/t20130921_513648183.shtml [in Chinese].
— (7 August 2012) State Population Planning Commission announced the 2012 report of mobile population, www.china.com.cn/renkou/2012-08/07/ content_26155072.htm [in Chinese].
— (6 November 2012) Opinion poll shows that people are worrying most about the division between the rich and the poor, http://news.china.com.cn/2012 -11/06/content_27012992.htm [in Chinese].
— (28 January 2013) China's working age population has declined for the first time, http://news.china.com.cn/2013-01/28/content_27808859.htm [in Chinese].
— (6 February 2013) China is experiencing the largest scale of population migration, http://news.china.com.cn/2013-02/06/content_27902254.htm [in Chinese].
— (23 March 2013) China pledges not to rely on dead prisoners for organ donations, http://news.163.com/12/1122/06/8GT70G7A0001124J.html [in Chinese].
— (10 April 2013) Guangdong lowers its requirements, 4,200 social organizations were formed, www.gdshjs.org/s/2013-04/10/content_66746488.htm [in Chinese].
— (12 April 2013) Survey by the MOHRSS showed that more than half of the migrant workers want to become urban residents, http://news.china.com. cn/2013-04/12/content_28521383.htm [in Chinese].
— (10 May 2013a) Bluebook on India: India's total population exceeds 1.2 billion, http://news.china.com.cn/txt/2013-05/10/content_28785062.htm [in Chinese].

REFERENCES

— (10 May 2013b) Report shows that in every 10 children, four are mobile children, http://news.china.com.cn/txt/2013-05/10/content_28781597.htm [in Chinese].
— (9 June 2013) City life is not easy for migrant workers, http://finance.china.com.cn/news/special/czh/20130609/1542520.shtml [in Chinese].
— (27 June 2013) Five big barriers for China's urbanization, migrant workers have no citizenship treatment, http://finance.china.com.cn/news/special/czh/20130627/1587160.shtml [in Chinese].
— (19 July 2013) Residents' pension has not been raised in four years, http://news.china.com.cn/2013-07/19/content_29467264.htm [in Chinese].
— (19 August 2013a) China's population aged over 60 to reach 400 million by 2025, http://news.china.com.cn/txt/2013-08/19/content_29763950.htm [in Chinese].
— (19 August 2013b) Government can no longer be fully responsible, http://news.china.com.cn/2013-08/19/content_29755149.htm [in Chinese].
— (10 September 2013) Relieving the shortage of beds in homes for the aged, http://finance.china.com.cn/roll/20130910/1801756.shtml [in Chinese].
— (11 September 2013) Figures on declining incomes of retirees indicate serious pension gaps, http://finance.china.com.cn/news/gnjj/20130911/1803604.shtml [in Chinese].
— (14 September 2013) Reverse mortgage on trial next year, http://finance.china.com.cn/roll/20130914/1813906.shtml [in Chinese].
— (23 September 2013) China's charity transparency report, http://news.china.com.cn/2013-09/23/content_30099834.htm [in Chinese].
— (8 October 2013) WB cuts growth forecast for China, East Asia, www.china.org.cn/business/2013-10/08/content_30223332.htm [in English].
— (26 October 2013) Reform on the distribution of income will proceed after the Third Plenary, http://finance.china.com.cn/news/gnjj/20131028/1914674.shtml [in Chinese].
— (28 October 2013) China: less than 30% of the people have urban *hukou*, http://news.china.com.cn/2013-10/28/content_30426293.htm [in Chinese].
— (1 November 2013) China's pension benefits as a proportion of the wage continue to fall for nine years, http://china.com.cn/2013-11/01/content_30468147.htm [in Chinese].
— (5 November 2013) China specifies urbanization paths for different types of cities, http://finance.eastmoney.com/news/1377,20131105334909090.html [in Chinese].
— (12 November 2013) Family planning has prevented 400 million births in the last 40 years, http://news.163.com/13/1117/04/9DRSSL4B00014AED.html [in Chinese].

- (18 November 2013) Relaxing the one-child policy, http://news.china.com.cn/2013-11/18/content_30628501.htm [in Chinese].
- (5 December 2013a) Maintenance fees of 20 provinces amounted to 20 billion yuan, http://news.china.com.cn/2013-12/05/content_30801085.htm [in Chinese].
- (5 December 2013b) State News Office press conference on the deepening the development and innovation of civil affairs work, www.china.com.cn/zhibo/2013-12/05/content_30783752.htm [in Chinese].
- (9 December 2013) China shifts away from economy-obsessed assessments, http://english.people.com.cn/business/8479191.html [in English].
- (27 December 2013a) CASS reported that low income families have higher income growth rates, http://news.china.com.cn/2013-12/26/content_31008788.htm [in Chinese].
- (27 December 2013b) Average basic resident pension benefit is only 81 yuan, http://news.china.com.cn/2013-12/27/content_31017992.htm [in Chinese].
- (27 December 2013c) CASS recommends gradual extension of retirement age by 2016, http://finance.china.com.cn/news/dcbg/20131227/2079790.shtml [in Chinese].
- (29 December 2013) 17 among 19 priority poverty alleviation counties involved in the cheating of over 21.5 million yuan, http://news.xinhuanet.com/politics/2013-12/29/c_118749861.htm [in Chinese].
- (3 January 2014) The blue book: 664 national social organizations were assessed, http://news.china.com.cn/txt/2014-01/03/content_31084988.htm [in Chinese].
- (7 January 2014) China's strange poverty phenomenon, http://news.china.com.cn/2014-01/07/content_31114423.htm [in Chinese].
- (20 January 2014a) Disposable income of urban residents in 2013 amounted to 26,955 yuan, http://finance.china.com.cn/news/special/jjsj2013-12/20140120/2135957.shtml [in Chinese].
- (20 January 2014b) China's rich–poor gap eases in 2013, www.china.org.cn/china/2014-01/20/content_31251413.htm [in English].
- (27 January 2014) China reduces 660 million poverty stricken population, http://news.china.com.cn/2014-01/27/content_31318277.htm [in Chinese]
- (24 February 2014) China for the first time published the overall urban–rural incomes, http://finance.china.com.cn/news/special/jjsj2014-1/20140224/2208950.shtml [in Chinese].
- (16 March 2014) *New National Urbanization Framework*, http://news.china.com.cn/2014-03/16/content_31803504.htm [in Chinese].

REFERENCES | 191

— (3 July 2014) Government POS has become a new corruption disaster area, http://news.xinhuanet.com/yuqing/2014-07/03/c_126705965.htm [in Chinese].

CNCA (China National Committee on Ageing) (2010a) Reasons and policy responses for the rise of disputes concerning elderly support, 12 January; www.cncaprc.gov.cn/yanjiu/4175.jhtml [in Chinese].

— (2010b) 44% of the older people entered homes for the aged because of the lack of care from children, 19 February, http://finance.ifeng.com/news/special/laolinghua/20100218/1835366.shtml [in Chinese].

— (2011) Development of services for the older people during the 12th Five Year Plan, www.cncaprc.gov.cn/zhengce/22312.jhtml [in Chinese].

— (2012) The 6th National Census: empty-nest families reached 31.77%, 20 December, www.china.com.cn/news/2012-12/18/content_27445809.htm [in Chinese].

— (2013a) China has annual increase of 300,000 dementia older people, 22 September, www.cncaprc.gov.cn/news/36514.jhtml [in Chinese].

— (2013b) Beijing elderly population exceeds 20%, 25 September, www.cncaprc.gov.cn/news/36751.jhtml [in Chinese].

Committee for Social Affairs of Guangdong Province (2014) website, www.gdshjs.org/ [in Chinese].

Deacon, B., and Szalai, J. (eds) (1990) *Social Policy in New Eastern Europe*. Aldershot: Avebury.

Deeming, C. (2013) Addressing the social determinants of subjective well-being: the latest challenge for social policy, *Journal of Social Policy* 42(3), pp. 541–65.

Deng, G. S. (2010) The hidden rules governing China's unregistered NGOs: management and consequences, *China Review* 10(1), pp. 183–98.

Dorfman, M., Holzmann, R., O'Keefe, P., Wang, D., Sin, Y., and Hinz, R. (2013) *China's Pension System: A Vision*. Washington, DC: World Bank.

Du, Y., Park, A., and Wang, S. (2005) Migration and rural poverty in China, *Journal of Comparative Economics* 33(4), pp. 688–709.

Duckett, J. (2001) Political interests and the implementation of China's urban health insurance reform, *Social Policy & Administration* 41(8), pp. 1965–072.

— (2011a) *The Chinese State's Retreat from Health: Policy and the Politics of Retrenchment*. London: Routledge.

— (2011b) Challenging the economic reform paradigm: policy and politics in the early 1980s' collapse of the rural co-operative medical system, *China Quarterly* 205(March), pp. 80–95.

REFERENCES

Economic Daily (5 September 2013) China widens pension coverage as population ages, www.cncaprc.gov.cn/yanjiu/35833.jhtml [in Chinese].

The Economist (24 February 2011) Comparing Chinese provinces with countries, all the parities in China, www.economist.com/content/chinese_equivalents.

— (8 September 2012) New cradles to graves, pp. 21–3.

— (4 May 2013) Chasing the Chinese dream: China's new leader has been quick to consolidate his power, www.economist.com/news/briefing/21577063-chinas-new-leader-has-been-quick-consolidate-his-power-what-does-he-now-want-his.

— (1 June 2013) Toward the end of poverty, p. 11.

— (21 November 2013) Keeping watch: economic success has given China greater weight, but not nearly enough to tip the balance, www.economist.com/news/special-report/21590099-economic-success-has-given-china-greater-weight-not-nearly-enough-tip.

Elegant, S. (2007) China's Me generation, *Time*, 5 November, http://content.time.com/time/magazine/article/0,9171,1675626-2,00.html.

Esping-Andersen, G. (1990) *Three Worlds of Welfare Capitalism*. Cambridge: Polity.

Fewsmith, J. (2004) Promoting the scientific development concept, *China Leadership Monitor* no. 11, http://media.hoover.org/sites/default/files/documents/clm11_jf.pdf.

— (2008) *China since Tiananmen*. Cambridge: Cambridge University Press.

Fisher, K., Li, J., and Fan, L. (2012) Barriers to the supply of non-government disability services in China, *Journal of Social Policy* 41, pp. 161–82.

Fong, E., and Li, C. L. (2013) Life satisfaction of the children of migrant workers in Chinese cities, in P. L. Li and L. Roulleau-Berger (eds), *China's Internal and International Migration*. London: Routledge, pp. 115–29.

Frazier, M. W. (2010) *Socialist Insecurity: Pensions and the Politics of Uneven Development in China*. Ithaca, NY: Cornell University Press.

Freeberne, M. (1964) Birth control in China, *Population Studies* 18(1), pp. 5–16.

Gagnon, J., Xenogiani, T., and Xing, C. (2009) *Are All Migrant Workers Really Worse Off in Urban Labour Markets? New Empirical Evidence from China*, OECD Development Centre Working Papers no. 278, June. Paris: OECD.

Gallagher, M., Giles, J., Park, A., and Wang, M. (2013) *China's 2008 Labour Contract Law: Implementation and Implications for China's Workers*, Policy Research Working Paper 6542. Washington, DC: World Bank.

Gao, G., and Riskin, C. (2009) Market versus social benefits: explaining China's changing income inequality, in D. Davis and F. Wang (eds), *Creating Wealth and Poverty in Post-Socialist China.* Stanford, CA: Stanford University Press, pp. 20–36.

Gao, J., Tang, S. L., Tolhurst, R., and Rao, K. Q. (2001) Changing access to health services in urban China: implications for equity, *Health Policy and Planning* 16(3), pp. 302–12.

Gao, Q. (2010) Redistributive nature of the Chinese social benefit system: progressive or regressive? *China Quarterly* 201(March), pp. 1–19.

Gao, Q., Yang, S., and Li, S. (2013) The Chinese welfare state in transition: 1988–2007, *Journal of Social Policy* 42(4), pp. 743–62.

George, V., and Manning, N. (1980) *Socialism, Social Welfare and the Soviet Union.* London: Routledge.

Gilbert, N. (2002) *The Transformation of the Welfare State: The Silent Surrender of Public Responsibility.* New York: Oxford University Press.

Giles, J., Wang, D., and Park, A. (2013) *Expanding Social Insurance Coverage in Urban China*, Policy Research Working Paper 6497. Washington, DC: World Bank.

Giles, J., Wang, D., and Zhao, C. (2010) *Can China's Rural Elderly Count on Support from Adult Children? Implications for Rural-to-Urban Migration*, Policy Research Paper 5510, December. Washington, DC: World Bank.

Global Times (2010) Hu advocates inclusive growth, 29 September, www.china.org.cn/business/2010-09/29/content_21032034.htm.

Goodman, R., and Peng, I. (1996) The East Asian welfare states in peripatetic learning, adaptive change, and nation-building, in G. Esping-Andersen (ed.), *Welfare States in Transition: National Adaptations in Global Economies.* London: Sage, pp. 192–220.

Goodman, R., White, G., and Kwon, H. J. (eds) (1998) *The East Asian Welfare Model: Welfare Orientalism and the State.* London: Routledge.

Gough, I. (2002) Globalization and national welfare regimes: the East Asian case, in R. Sigg and C. Behrendt (eds), *Social Security in the Global Village.* London: Transaction, pp. 47–65.

— (2004a) Social policy regimes in the developing world, in P. Kennett (ed.), *A Handbook of Comparative Social Policy.* Cheltenham: Edward Elgar, pp. 239–60.

— (2004b) East Asia: the limits of productivist regimes, in I. Gough, G. Wood, A. Barrientos, P. Bevan, P. Davis and G. Room (eds), *Insecurity and Welfare Regimes in Asia, Africa and Latin America: Social Policy and Developmental Contexts.* Cambridge: Cambridge University Press, pp. 169–201.

Gu, E. (2001) Market transition and transformation of the health care system in urban China, *Policy Studies* 22(3–4), pp. 197–215.

— (2010) Towards central planning or regulated marketization? China debates on the direction of new healthcare reforms, in L. Zhao and T. S. Lim (eds), *China's New Social Policy: Initiatives for a Harmonious Society*. Singapore: World Scientific, pp. 23–39.

Gu, E., and Zhang, J. J. (2006) Health care regime change in urban China: unmanaged marketization and reluctant privatization, *Pacific Affairs* 79(1), pp. 49–71.

Guan, X. P. (2003) Poverty and anti-poverty policies in urban China, in K. L. Tang and C. K. Wong (eds), *Poverty Monitoring and Alleviation in East Asia*. New York: Nova Science, pp. 15–37.

Guan, X. P., and Zhao, T. T. (2012) Policy analysis on the problems and related policy on the development of non-governmental elderly care services, *Journal of North-Eastern University* 5, pp. 52–6 [in Chinese].

Guangdong Social Workers' Association (2012) *Report on the Situation of Social Work Workforce Construction*, 6 December, www.gdsgs.org/welfare/shfl/730.html [in Chinese].

Guangming Daily (16 October 2013) Streamlining the administration and decentralization, www.gdshjs.org/shjsyw/content/2013-10/16/content_81782344.htm [in Chinese].

Guangzhou Civil Affairs Bureau (2010) *Regulations on Implementing the Assessment of Purchase of Services by Guangzhou Government*, 17 August, www.gzmz.gov.cn/publicfiles/business/htmlfiles/gzsmzj/gfxwj6/201209/972043.html [in Chinese].

Guangzhou University (2013) The situation and prospect of social work development in Guangzhou in 2013, in Z. Y. Yi (ed.), *The Analysis and Prediction on the Situation of Guangzhou in 2013*. Beijing: Social Sciences Publishers, pp. 119–37.

Guilmoto, C. (2012) Skewed sex ratios at birth and future marriage squeeze in China and India, 2005–2100, *Demography* 49(1), pp. 77–100.

Gustafsson, B., and Deng, Q. H. (2011) *Dibao* receipt and its importance for combating poverty in urban China, *Poverty and Public Policy* 3(1), pp. 116–47.

Haggard, S., and Kaufman, R. R. (2008) *Development, Democracy, and Welfare States: Latin American, East Asia, and Eastern Europe*. Princeton, NJ: Princeton University Press.

Halper, H. (2010) *The Beijing Consensus: How China's Authoritarian Model Will Dominate the 21st Century*. New York: Basic Books.

Han, J., and Luo, D. (2005) *Report of Medical Care System in Rural China*, http://mall.cnki.net/magazine/Article/FZGC200501005.htm [in Chinese].

Hand, K. (2006) Using law for a righteous purpose: the Sun Zhigang incident and evolving forms of citizen action in the PRC, *Columbia Journal of Transnational Law* 45(114), pp. 115–95.

Herd, R., Hu, Y., and Koen, V. (2010a) *Improving China's Health Care System*, Economics Department Working Papers no. 751. Paris: OECD.

— (2010b) *Providing Greater Old-Age Security in China*, Economics Department Working Papers no. 750. Paris: OECD.

Herd, R., Koen, V., and Reutersward, A. (2010) *China's Labour Market in Transition: Job Creation, Migration and Regulation*, Economics Department Working Papers no. 749. Paris: OECD.

Hillier, S., and Zheng, X. (1994) The reforms of the Chinese health care system: county level changes: the Jiangxi study, *Social Science & Medicine* 41(8), pp. 1057–64.

Holliday, I. (2000) Productivist welfare capitalism: social policy in East Asia, *Political Studies* 48(4), pp. 706–23.

— (2005) East Asian social policy in the wake of the financial crisis: farewell to productivism? *Policy and Politics* 33(1), pp. 45–62.

Holliday, I., and Wilding, P. (eds) (2003) *Welfare Capitalism in East Asia*. Basingstoke: Palgrave Macmillan.

Hsiao, W. C. (1984) Transformation of health care in China, *New England Journal of Medicine* 310(14), pp. 932–6.

Hsu, S. P., Wu, Y. S. and Zhao, S. S. (2011) *In Search of China's Development Model, Beyond the Beijing Consensus*. London: Routledge.

Hu, S. L. Tang, S. L., Liu, Y. L., Zhao, Y. X. Escobar, M.-L. and de Ferranti, D. (2008) Reform of how health care is paid for in China: challenges and opportunities, *The Lancet* 372(9652), pp. 1846–53.

Hu, X. Y. (2013) *High Level Forum of Development of China's Ageing Undertakings 2013*, 2 November, www.bj.xinhuanet.com/zt/201310/2013zglllt/index.htm [in Chinese].

Hudson, J. (2012) Welfare regimes and global cities: a missing link in the comparative analysis of welfare states? *Journal of Social Policy* 41(3), pp. 455–73.

Hudson, V., and Den Boer A. M. (2004) *Bare Branches: The Security Implications of Asia's Surplus Male Population*. Cambridge, MA: MIT Press.

Hwang, G. J. (ed.) (2011) *New Welfare States in East Asia: Global Challenges and Restructuring*. Cheltenham: Edward Elgar.

Izuhara, M. (ed.) (2013) *Handbook on East Asian Social Policy*. Cheltenham: Edward Elgar.

Jacobs, D. (2000) Low public expenditures on social welfare: do East Asian countries have a secret? *International Journal of Social Welfare* 9(1), pp. 2–16.

Jansson, B. (1990) *Social Welfare Policy: From Theory to Practice*. Belmont, CA: Wadsworth.

Jia, X. J., and Su, M. (2009) *Final Report on Government Procurement of Public Services, People's Republic of China*, ADB Technical Assistance TA 4790-PRC, June. Manila: Asian Development Bank.

Jia, Z. J. (2011) Civil organization–government relationships: functional cooperation and power dilemmas, in M. Wang (ed.), *Emerging Civil Society in China, 1978–2008*. Boston: Brill, pp. 219–23.

Jing, Y. J. (2008) Outsourcing in China: an exploratory assessment, *Public Administration and Development* 28, pp. 119–28.

Jing, Y. J., and Savas, E. S. (2009) Managing collaborative service delivery: comparing China and the United States, *Public Administration Review* 69 (supplement s1), pp. 101–7.

Johnson, C. (1982) *MITI and the Japanese Miracle: The Growth of Industrial Policy, 1925–1975*. Stanford, CA: Stanford University Press.

Jones, C. (1993) The Pacific challenge in Confucian welfare states, in C. Jones (ed.), *New Perspectives on the Welfare State in Europe*. London: Routledge, pp. 198–217.

Kamal-Chaoui, L., Leman, E., and Zhang, R. F. (2009) *Urban Trends and Policy in China*, Regional Development Working Papers no. 2009/1. Paris: OECD.

Kennedy, S. (2010) The myth of the Beijing consensus, *Journal of Contemporary China* 19(65), pp. 461–77.

Khan, A., and Riskin, C. (2001) *Inequality and Poverty in China in the Age of Globalization*. New York and Oxford: Oxford University Press.

Khor, N., and Pencavel, J. (2010) *Evolution of Income Mobility in the People's Republic of China: 1991–2002*, ADB Economics Working Paper Series no. 204, June. Manila: Asian Development Bank.

Knight, J. (2013) *Inequality in China: An Overview*, Policy Research Working Paper 6482. Washington, DC: World Bank.

Knight, J., and Gunatilaka, R. (2010) Great expectations? The subjective well-being of rural–urban migrants in China, *World Development* 38(1), pp. 113–24.

Koen, V., Herd, R., Wang, X., and Chalaux, T. (2013) *Policies for Inclusive Urbanization in China*, Working Papers no. 1090. Paris: OECD.

Law, K. T. (2013) The development of social work workforce in Guangzhou and Hong Kong, *Studies on Hong Kong and Macao* 9, pp. 5–9.

Lee, J., and Chan, K. W. (eds) (2007) *The Crisis of Welfare in East Asia*. Lanham, MD: Lexington Books.

Lee, S. (2011) *Fortune China CSR Ranking 2011 Report*, 15 March, www.fortunechina.com/rankings/c/2011-03/15/content_51879.htm.

Lei, X. Y., Giles, J., Hu, Y. Q., Park, A., Strauss, J., and Zhao, Y. H. (2012) *Patterns and Correlates of Intergenerational Non-Time Transfers: Evidence from CHARLS*. Washington, DC: World Bank.

Leung, J. (1990a) The community-based social security system in rural China: mutual help and self-protection, *Hong Kong Journal of Social Work* 25(3), pp. 196–205.

— (1990b) China, in T. Watts, D. Elliott and N. Mayadas (eds), *International Handbook on Social Work Education*. Westport, CT: Greenwood Press, pp. 403–19.

— (1994) Dismantling the iron rice bowl: welfare reforms in the PRC, *Journal of Social Policy* 23(3), pp. 341–61.

— (1995) The political economy of unemployment and unemployment insurance in the PRC, *International Social Work* 38, pp. 123–33.

— (2000) Social costs of moving toward a market economy, in J. Jones and A. Kumssa (eds), *The Cost of Reform: The Social Aspect of Transitional Economies*. New York: Nova Science, pp. 193–209.

— (2003) Social security reforms in China: issues and prospects, *International Journal of Social Welfare* 12(2), pp. 73–85.

— (2005) Social welfare reform in China: from employment-based welfare to social welfare, in A. Walker and C. K. Wong (eds), *Eastern Asian Welfare Regimes in Transition: From Confucianism to Globalization*. Bristol: Policy Press, pp. 49–72.

— (2006) The emergence of social assistance in China, *International Journal of Social Welfare* 15, pp. 188–98.

— (2007) Debate: an international definition of social work for China, *International Journal of Social Welfare* 16, pp. 391–7.

— (2010) Social education in China, in C. Noble, M. Henrickson and Y. Han (eds), *Social Work Education: Voices from the Asia Pacific*. Carlton North, Vic.: The Vulgar Press, pp. 307–40.

— (2013) The development of social work and social work education in China: issues and prospects, in C. Noble, M. Henrickson, and Y. Han (eds), *Social Work Education in the Asia Pacific*. 2nd edn, Sydney: University of Sydney Press, pp. 175–206.

Leung, J., and Lam, D. (2000) Enforcing family care obligations for the elderly in China through mediation, *Asia Pacific Journal of Social Work* 10(1), pp. 39–54.

Leung, J., and Nann, R. C. (1995) *Authority and Benevolence: Social Welfare in China*. Hong Kong: Chinese University of Hong Kong Press/St Martins.

Leung, J., and Wong, H. (1999) The emergence of a community-based social assistance programme in urban China, *Social Policy & Administration* 33(1), pp. 39–54.

Leung, J., and Wong Y. C. (2002) Community service for the frail elderly in China, *International Social Work* 45(2), pp. 205–16.
Leung, J., and Xu, Y. B. (2009) The development of social assistance in urban China: the residualization of social welfare, in J. Midgley and K. L. Tang (eds), *Poverty and Social Policy Responses in East Asia*. London: Routledge, pp. 47–65.
Leung, J., and Xu, Y. B. (2013) Initial report on the survey of social work organizations in China, October, School of Social Development and Public Policy, Beijing Normal University, unpublished.
Leung, T., Yip, N. M., and Huang, R. G. (2012) Governmentality and the politicization of social work in China, *British Journal of Social Work* 42, pp. 1039–59.
Li, B. (2006) Floating population or urban citizens? Status, social provision and circumstances of rural–urban migrants in China, *Social Policy & Administration* 40(2), pp. 174–95.
Li, P. L. (2013) The world's largest labor force migration, in P. L. Li and L. Roulleau-Berger (eds), *China's Internal and International Migration*. London: Routledge, pp. xx–xxv.
Li, P. L., and Li, W. (2013) The work situation and social attitudes of migrant workers in China under the crisis, in P. L. Li and L. Roulleau-Berger (eds), *China's Internal and International Migration*. London: Routledge, pp. 3–25.
Li, S., Sato, H., and Sicular, T. (eds) (2013) *Rising Inequality in China: Challenges to a Harmonious Society*. New York: Cambridge University Press.
Li, X. Y. (2013) What can Africa learn from China's agricultural miracle? In OECD, *Development Co-operation Report 2013: Ending Poverty*. Paris: OECD, pp. 87–94.
Liang, L. L., and Langenbrunner, J. (2013) *The Long March to Universal Coverage: Lessons from China*, UNICO Study Series 9, January. Washington, DC: World Bank.
Lieberthal, K., and Oksenberg, M. (1989) *Policy Making in China: Leaders, Structures and Processes*. Princeton, NJ: Princeton University Press.
Lin, K. (1999) *Confucian Welfare Cluster: A Cultural Interpretation of Social Welfare*. Tampere: University of Tampere.
Lin, S. L. (2011) Civil organizations and political reforms: China's logic, in M. Wang (ed.), *Emerging Civil Society in China, 1978–2008*. Boston: Brill, pp. 269–96.
Liu, Y., and Wu, F. (2006) The state, institutional transition and the creation of new urban poverty in China, *Social Policy & Administration* 40(2), pp. 121–37.

Liu, Y., He, S., Wu, F., and Webster, C. (2010) Urban villages under China's rapid urbanization: unregulated assets and transitional neighbourhoods, *Habitat International* 34(2), pp. 135–44.

Lu, M., and Feng, M. L. (2012) The evolution of China's reform and development process, in M. K. Wang (ed.), *Thirty Years of China's Reform*. London: Routledge, pp. 27–69.

Lu, X. B., and Perry, E. (1997) *Danwei: The Changing Chinese Workplace in Historical and Comparative Perspective*. Armonk, NY: M. E. Sharpe.

Lu, Y. Y. (2009) *Non-Governmental Organizations in China: The Rise of Dependent Autonomy*. London: Routledge.

Luo, C., and Sicular, T. (2013) Inequality and poverty in rural China, in S. Li, H. Sato and T. Sicular (eds), *Rising Inequality in China: Challenges to a Harmonious Society*. Cambridge: Cambridge University Press, pp. 197–229.

Ma, Q. S. (2006) *Non-Governmental Organizations in Contemporary China: Paving the Way to Civil Society?* London: Routledge.

Ma, Z. T. (2011) Key figures on the 6th population census, 28 April, www.chinanews.com/gn/2011/04-28/3004638.shtml [in Chinese].

MCA (Ministry of Civil Affairs) (1998) *1997 Annual Statistical Report on Service Development*, http://cws.mca.gov.cn/article/tjbg/200801/20080100009420.shtml [in Chinese].

— (2010) *2009 Annual Statistical Report on Service Development*, www.mca.gov.cn/article/zwgk/mzyw/201006/20100600080798.shtml [in Chinese].

— (2012a) *2011 Annual Statistical Report on Service Development*, http://cws.mca.gov.cn/article/tjbg/201210/20121000362598.shtml [in Chinese].

— (2012b) *Report on the Mid- and Long-Term Development Plan for Social Work Workforce 2011–2020*, 29 April, www.mca.gov.cn/article/zwgk/fvfg/shgz/201204/20120400302330.shtml [in Chinese].

— (2013a) *Notice of the MCA on the Situation of Social Work Workforce Construction*, 2 May, www.gdsgs.org/news/government/839.html [in Chinese].

— (2013b) *2012 Annual Statistical Report on Social Service Development*, www.mca.gov.cn/article/zwgk/mzyw/201406/20140600654488.shtml [in Chinese].

— (2014a) *Opinion on Further Promoting the Development of Non-Governmental SWOs*, 9 April, www.mca.gov.cn/article/zwgk/fvfg/shgz/201404/20140400622265.shtml [in Chinese].

— (2014b) *2013 Annual Statistical Report on Social Service Development*, 17 June, www.mca.gov.cn/article/zwgk/mzyw/201406/20140600654488.shtml [in Chinese].

— (various years) *Annual Statistical Report on Service Development*, http://cws.mca.gov.cn/article/tjbg/ [in Chinese].

McMahon, F. (2012) *Towards a Worldwide Index of Human Freedom*. Vancouver: Fraser Institute.

Midgley, J., and Tang, K. L. (2009) *Social Policy and Poverty in East Asia: The Role of Social Security*. London: Routledge.

MOH (Ministry of Health) (1987) *China Health Statistics Yearbook*. Beijing: Peking Medical University.

— (2004) *China Health Service Survey: Report of the Third National Health Service Survey*. Beijing: China Xiehe Medical University Press.

MOHRSS (Ministry of Human Resources and Social Security) (2012) *2011 Annual Statistical Report on Human Resources and Social Security*, www.mohrss.gov.cn/SYrlzyhshbzb/zwgk/szrs/ndtjsj/tjgb/201206/t20120605_69908.htm [in Chinese].

— (2013) *2012 Annual Statistical Report on Human Resources and Social Security*, 28 May, www.mohrss.gov.cn/SYrlzyhshbzb/dongtaixinwen/shizhengyaowen/201305/t20130528_103939.htm [in Chinese].

Mok, W. (2013) Price of progress, *South China Morning Post*, 13 May, p. A13.

Nanfang Daily News (21 August 2012) The difficulties behind the rising demands of social workers, cited from the website of Committee for Social Affairs of Guangdong Province, www.gdshjs.org/s/2012-08/21/content_53297185.htm [in Chinese].

— (4 June 2013) Guangzhou Blue Book on Social Development, cited from the website of Committee for Social Affairs of Guangdong Province www.gdshjs.org/shjsyw/content/2013-06/04/content_76308217.htm [in Chinese].

— (15 August 2013) Guangdong announced the first catalog on POS, http://news.xinhuanet.com/local/2012-08/15/c_123584085.htm [in Chinese].

National Health and Family Planning Commission (2013) *Statistical Report on the Development of Health and Family Planning*, 19 June, www.nhfpc.gov.cn/mohwsbwstjxxzx/s7967/201306/fe0b764da4f74b858eb55264572eab92.shtml [in Chinese].

Naughton, B. (1995) *Growing Out of the Plan: Chinese Economic Reform, 1978–1993*. Cambridge: Cambridge University Press.

— (2007) *The Chinese Economy: Transitions and Growth*. Cambridge, MA: MIT Press.

— (2010) China's distinctive system: can't it be a model for others? *Journal of Contemporary China* 19(65), pp. 437–60.

NBS (National Bureau of Statistics) (2004) *Poverty statistics in China*, September, www.nscb.gov.ph/poverty/conference/papers/4_poverty%20statistics%20in%20china.pdf [in Chinese].

— (2006) *2006 Annual Statistical Report on Labour and Social Security Development*, http://w1.mohrss.gov.cn/gb/news/2007-05/18/content_178167.htm [in Chinese].

— (2012) *Income of Urban and Rural Residents in 2011*, 20 January, www.gov.cn/gzdt/2012-01/20/content_2050056.htm [in Chinese].

— (2014) *National Data*, http://data.stats.gov.cn/normalpg?src=/lastestpub/quickSearch/y/year03.html&h=800 [in Chinese].

NBS (National Bureau of Statistics) and MOHRSS (Ministry of Human Resources and Social Security) (2012) *China Labour Statistical Yearbook 2012*. Beijing: China Statistics [in Chinese].

Ngok, K. L. (2013a) The transition of social protection in China, in J. Midgley and D. Piachaud (eds), *Social Protection, Economic Growth and Social Change*. Cheltenham: Edward Elgar, pp. 29–43.

— (2013b) Shaping social policy in the reform era in China, in M. Izuhara (ed.), *Handbook on East Asian Social Policy*. Cheltenham: Edward Elgar, pp. 105–28.

O'Brien, K. (ed.) (2009) *Popular Protest in China*. Cambridge: MA: Harvard University Press.

O'Brien, K., and Li, L. (2006) *Rightful Resistance in Rural China*. Cambridge: Cambridge University Press.

OECD (Organization for Economic Cooperation and Development) (2004) *Income Disparities in China*. Paris: OECD.

— (2006) *Challenges for China's Public Spending: Toward Greater Effectiveness and Equity*. Paris: OECD.

— (2009) *OECD Rural Policy Reviews: China*. Paris: OECD.

— (2010a) *Tackling Inequalities in Brazil, China, India and South Africa: The Role of Labour Market and Social Policy*. Paris: OECD.

— (2010b) *OECD Economic Survey: China 2010*. Paris: OECD.

— (2011) *Perspectives on Global Development 2012, Social Cohesion in a Shifting World*. Paris: OECD.

— (2012) *China in Focus: Lessons and Challenges*. Paris: OECD.

— (2013a) *Economic Survey of China*. Paris: OECD.

— (2013b) *OECD Guidelines on Measuring Subjective Well-Being*. Paris: OECD.

— (2013c) *Pensions at a Glance 2013*. Paris: OECD.

— (2013d) *The People's Republic of China: Avoiding the Middle-Income Trap: Policies for Sustained and Inclusive Growth*, September. Paris: OECD.

— (2013e) *Government at a Glance 2013*, 14 November. Paris: OECD.

— (2014) *China: Structural Reforms for Inclusive Growth*, March. Paris: OECD.

Orlik, T. (2011) *Introduction to Understanding China's Economic Indicators*. New Jersey: Pearson Education, FT Press.

Outlook (22 October 2013) Breakthrough of China social organizations in three bottle-necks, www.fjsmzt.gov.cn/xxgk/gzdt/mtgz/201310/t20131025_670677.htm [in Chinese].

Pallotta, N. (2013) CCP Third Plenum's Reform Blueprint to Confront 'Deep Water', 27 November, www.osservatorioasiaorientale.org/3plenum.

Park, D. H. (2012) *Pension Systems in East and Southeast Asia Promoting Fairness and Sustainability*. Manila: Asian Development Bank.

Parris, K. (2012) Transforming state and citizen through community building: a view from Zhejiang, in J. X. Yu and S. J. Guo (eds), *Civil Society and Governance in China*. New York: Palgrave Macmillan, pp. 189–214.

People's Daily (14 January 2013) Interpreting the policy: why there is still a need to maintain low birth rates, http://news.xinhuanet.com/politics/2013-01/14/c_124225623.htm [in Chinese].

— (25 February 2013) The difference of China's social security benefits ratio reached 0.86, http://finance.sina.com.cn/china/20130225/145614639414.shtml [in Chinese].

— (27 February 2013) Livelihood survey: why Shenzhen cannot keep its social workers, http://cpc.people.com.cn/n/2013/0227/c83083-20614444.html [in Chinese].

— (29 March 2013) *Notice on the Options of the Division of Work on Implementing the State Council Organizational Reform and Transfer of Functions*, http://finance.people.com.cn/n/2013/0329/c1004-20959955.html [in Chinese].

— (16 October 2013) Government purchase of service requires legal regulation, http://opinion.people.com.cn/n/2013/1016/c1003-23215207.html [in Chinese].

People's Network (2013) Purchase of public services promoted by Li Keqiang has deep meanings, http://politics.people.com.cn/n/2013/0802/c1001-22420756.html [in Chinese].

Perry, E. (2002) *Challenging the Mandate of Heaven: Social Protest and State Power in China*. Armonk, NY: M. E. Sharpe.

Perry, E., and Selden, M. (eds) (2010) *Chinese Society: Change, Conflict and Resistance*. New York: Routledge.

Powell, M. (ed.) (2007) *Understanding the Mixed Economy of Welfare*. Bristol: Policy Press.

Powell, B. (2009) Five things the U.S. can learn from China, *Time*, 12 November, http://content.time.com/time/magazine/article/0,9171,1938734,00.html.

Pun, N. (2005) *Made in China: Women Factory Workers in a Global Workplace*. Durham, NC: Duke University Press.

Ramo, J. (2004) *The Beijing Consensus*. London: UK Foreign Policy Centre.

Ramzy, A. (2009) The Chinese worker, *Time*, 16 December, http://content.time.com/time/specials/packages/article/0,28804,1946375_1947252_1947256,00.html.

Ravallion, M. (2009) Are there lessons for Africa from China's success against poverty, *World Development* 37(2), pp. 1–42.

Ravallion, M., Chen, S. H., and Sangraula, P. (2008) *Dollar a Day Revisited*, Policy Research Working Paper 4620. Washington, DC: World Bank.

Rimlinger, G. V. (1971) *Welfare Policy and Industrialization in Europe, America and Russia*. New York: Wiley.

Riskin, C. (1987) *Chinese Political Economy*. Oxford: Oxford University Press.

— (1994) Chinese rural poverty: marginalised or dispersed? *American Economic Review* 84(2), pp. 281–4.

— (2004) The fall in Chinese poverty: issues of measurement, incidence and cause, paper given at the Keith Griffin Festschrift Conference at Political Economy Research Institute, University of Massachusetts, Amherst, April 23–4; www.peri.umass.edu/fileadmin/pdf/conference_papers/Riskin_paperA.pdf.

Rose, R., and Shiratori, R. (1986) *The Welfare State East and West*. New York: Oxford University Press.

Ru, X., Lu, X. Y., and Li, P. L. (eds) (2009) *2009: China's Social Situation: Analysis and Prediction*. Beijing: Social Sciences Academic.

— (2013) *2013: China's Social Situation: Analysis and Prediction*. Beijing: Social Sciences Academic.

Saich, T. (2000) Negotiating the state: the development of social organizations in China, *China Quarterly* 161, pp. 124–41.

Salditt, F., Whiteford, P., and Adema, W. (2007) *Pension Reform in China*. Social, Employment and Migration Working Papers no. 53. Paris: OECD.

Salidjanova, N. (2013) *China's New Income Inequality Reform Plan and Implications for Rebalancing*, US–China Economic and Security Review Commission, 12 March, http://origin.www.uscc.gov/sites/default/files/Research/China%20Inequality%20-%203%2012%2013.pdf.

Sato, H., and Li, S. (eds) (2006) *Unemployment, Inequality and Poverty in Urban China*. London: Routledge.

Saunders, P., and Shang, X. (2001) Social security reform in China's transition to a market economy, *Social Policy & Administration* 35(3), pp. 274–89.

Saunders, P., and Sun, L. J. (2006) Poverty and hardship among the aged in urban China, *Social Policy & Administration* 40(2), pp. 138–57.

Scharping, T. (2003) *Birth Control in China 1949–2000*. London: Routledge.

Segal, E. (2010) *Social Welfare Policy and Social Programs: A Value Perspective*. Belmont, CA: Brooks/Cole.

Seldon, M., and Lippit, V. (eds) (1982) *The Transition to Socialism in China*. Armonk, NY: M. E. Sharpe.

Shallcross, D., and Huo, N. (2012) The expectations and realities of NGO registration: a study of HIV/AIDS groups in Sichuan and Yunnan, *China Development Brief*, 12 December, http://chinadevelopmentbrief.cn/?p=1353.

Shang, M. Y., and Ye, S. H. (2013) Study on social work development in Shenzhen, in X. R. Zhang (ed.), *Report on Development of Shenzhen, 2012–2013*. Beijing: Social Sciences Academic, pp. 224–34 [in Chinese].

Shanghai Civil Affairs Bureau (2011) *Report on the Development of Services for the Older People in Shanghai in 2011*, 22 November, www.shmzj.gov.cn/gb/shmzj/node8/node15/node58/node72/node99/u1ai29590.html [in Chinese].

— (31 March 2012) *Shanghai Elderly People Population and Business Information Monitoring in 2011*, www.shmzj.gov.cn/gb/shmzj/node8/node15/node55/node231/index.html [in Chinese].

Shen, C., and Williamson, J. B. (2010) China's new rural pension scheme: can it be improved? *International Journal of Sociology and Social Policy* 30(5/6), pp. 239–50.

Shenzhen Business News Network (2012) Guangdong Social Work Association to set up research base in Shenzhen, 10 July, www.gdshjs.org/s/2012-07/10/content_50482300.htm [in Chinese].

Shenzhen Civil Affairs (2007) *Opinion on Promoting Social Work and Social Work Workforce*, 25 October, www.szmz.sz.gov.cn/xxgk/ywxx/shxx/zcfg/201110/t20111018_1743928.htm [in Chinese].

Shi, S. J. (2006) Left to market and family, again? Ideas and the development of rural pension policy in China, *Social Policy & Administration* 40(7), pp. 791–806.

— (2012) Towards inclusive social citizenship? Rethinking China's social security in the trend towards urban–rural harmonization, *Journal of Social Policy* 41(4), pp. 789–810.

Shieh, S. (2011) New trends in philanthropy and civil society in China, *China Development Brief*, summer, www.chinadevelopmentbrief.cn/?p=333.

Shieh, S., and Brown-Inz, A. (eds) (2013) An overview of China's grassroots NGOs, www.cdb.org.cn/upload/userfiles/files/NGO%20Directory-3-26.pdf [in Chinese].

Shieh, S., and Knutson, S. (2012) The roles and challenges of international NGOs in China's development, *China Development Brief*, autumn, www.chinadevelopmentbrief.cn/?p=1233.

Shieh, S., and Schwartz, J. (2009) State and society responses to China's social welfare needs: an introduction to the debate, in J. Schwartz and S. Shieh (eds),

State and Society Responses to Social Welfare Needs in China. London: Routledge, pp. 3–21.

Shue, V., and Wong, C. (eds) (2007) *Paying for Progress: Public Finance, Human Welfare and Inequality in China*. London: Routledge.

Sin, Y. (2005) *Pension Liabilities and Reform Options for Old Age Insurance*, Working Paper Series on China no. 2005-1. Washington, DC: World Bank.

So, A. (2007) The state and labour insurgency in post-socialist China: implication for development, in J. Cheng (ed.), *Challenges and Policy Programmes of China's New Leadership*. Hong Kong: City University Press, pp. 133–42.

Social Work Information Network (2010) Guangzhou social work '1 + 5' policy enacted, 23 August, http://shehuigongzuo.web-12.com/Article.asp?id=103 [in Chinese].

Solinger, D. (2002) Labour market reform and the plight of the laid-off proletariat, *China Quarterly* 170(June), pp. 304–26.

Solinger, D. (2008) The *dibao* recipients: mollified anti-emblem of urban modernization, *China Perspectives* 4, pp. 36–46.

Solinger, D., and Hu, Y. Y. (2012) Welfare, wealth and poverty in urban China: the *dibao* and its differential disbursement, *China Quarterly* 211(September), pp. 741–64.

South China Morning Post (20 September 2013) Audit uncovers mass misuse of 'one-child' fines, p. A5.

— (23 September 2013) Fears grow over soaring Chinese debt, p. B1.

Spence, J. (1990) *The Search for Modern China*. New York: W. W. Norton.

State Council (2010) *The Mid- and Long-Term Development of Human Capital Planning Framework 2010-2020*, 6 June, www.chinanews.com/gn/news/2010/06-06/2326040.shtml [in Chinese].

— (2013) *The Opinion Concerning the Deepening of the Reform of the Income Redistribution System*, 3 February, www.gov.cn/zwgk/2013-02/05/content_2327531.htm [in Chinese].

Stubbs, R. (2009) What ever happened to the East Asian development state? The unfolding debate, *Pacific Review* 22(1), pp. 1–22.

Tang, J., Dong, M. Z., and Duda, M. (2007) Marginalization of laid-off stateowned enterprise workers in Wuhan, in H. Zhang, B. Wu and R. Sanders (eds), *Marginalization in China: Perspectives on Transition and Globalization*. Aldershot: Ashgate, pp. 35–54.

Tang, W. (2005) *Public Opinion and Political Change in China*. Stanford, CA: Stanford University Press.

Tian, X. Y., and Lue, W. (eds) (1991) *The Economy of Chinese Aged Population*. Beijing: Economic Press.

UNDP (United Nations Development Programme) (2008) *China Human Development Report 2007/08: Access for All: Basic Public Services for 1.3 Billion People*. New York: UNDP.
— (2010) *Human Development Report 2010: The Real Wealth of Nations: Pathway to Human Development*. New York: UNDP.
— (2013a) *Human Development Report 2013: The Rise of the South: Human Progress in a Diverse World*. New York: UNDP.
— (2013b) *China Human Development Report 2013: Sustainable and Liveable Cities: Toward Ecological Civilization*. New York: UNDP.
Vodopivec, M., and Tong, M. H. (2008) *China: Improving Unemployment Insurance*, Social Protection Discussion Paper no. 0820, July. Washington, DC: World Bank.
Vogel, E. (2011) *Deng Xiaoping and the Transformation of China*. Cambridge, MA: Belknap Press.
Wagstaff, A. (2005) *Health Systems in East Asia: What Can Developing Countries Learn from Japan and the Asian Tigers?* Policy Research Working Paper 3790, December. Washington, DC: World Bank.
Wagstaff, A., Lindelow, M., Gao, J., Xu, L., and Qian, J. C. (2007) *Extending Health Insurance to the Rural Population: An Impact Evaluation of China's New Cooperative Medical Scheme*. Washington, DC: World Bank.
Wagstaff, A., Lindelow, M., Wang, S. Y., and Zhang, S. (2009) *Reforming China's Rural Health System*. Washington, DC: World Bank.
Walder, A. (1986) *Communist Neo-Traditionalism: Work and Authority in Chinese Industry*. Berkeley: University of California Press.
— (2009) China's protest wave: political threat or growing pains? In D. Yang and L. Zhao (eds), *China's Reforms at 30: Challenges and Prospects*. Singapore: World Scientific, pp. 41–54.
Walker, A., and Wong, C. K. (2005) *East Asian Welfare State Regimes in Transition: From Confucianism to Globalization*. Bristol: Policy Press.
Wan, M. (2014). *The China Model and Global Political Economy: Comparison, Impact and Interaction*. London: Routledge.
Wang, G. W., and Zheng, Y. N. (eds) (2013) *China: Development and Governance*. Singapore: World Scientific.
Wang, H. H. (2011) The evolution into NGOs in contemporary China: the two approaches and dilemmas, in P. Hsu, Y. S. Wu and S. Z. Zhao (eds), *In Search of China's Development Model: Beyond the Beijing Consensus*. London: Routledge, pp. 204–23.
Wang, M. (2007) Emerging urban poverty and effects of the *dibao* program on alleviating poverty in China, *China & World Economy* 15(2), pp. 74–88.

Wang, S. G. (2012) Conquering poverty while in the midst of developing the nation, in M. K. Wang (ed.), *Thirty Years of China's Reform*. London: Routledge, pp. 476–512.

Weiss, L. (2000) Developmental states in transition: adapting, dismantling, innovation, not 'normalizing', *Pacific Review* 13(1), pp. 121–45.

Wen, J. B. (2010) The 2010 government report, *Xinhua*, 15 March, www.china.com.cn/policy/txt/2010-03/15/content_19612372.htm [in Chinese].

White, G., and Wade, R. (eds) (1988) *Developmental States in East Asia*. New York: St Martin's Press.

White, T. (2006) *China's Longest Campaign – Birth Planning in the People's Republic 1949–2005*. Ithaca, NY: Cornell University Press.

Whyte, M. K. (1974) *Small Groups and Political Rituals in China*. Berkeley: University of California Press.

— (ed.) (2010a) *One Country, Two Societies: Rural–Urban Inequality in Contemporary China*. Cambridge, MA: Harvard University Press.

— (2010b) *Myth of the Social Volcano: Perceptions of Inequality and Distributive Injustice in Contemporary China*. Stanford, CA: Stanford University Press.

Wilding, P. (2000) Exploring the East Asian welfare model, *Public Administration and Policy* 9(2), pp. 71–82.

Wilensky, H. (1975) *The Welfare State and Equality: Structural and Ideological Roots of Public Expenditure*. Berkeley: University of California Press.

Wong, C. K., Tang, K. L., and Lo, V. L. (2007) Unaffordable healthcare and phenomenal growth: the case of health care protection in reform China, *International Journal of Social Welfare* 16(2), pp. 140–9.

Wong, L. (2011) Chinese migrant workers: rights attainment deficits, rights consciousness and personal strategies, *China Quarterly* 208(December), pp. 870–92.

Wong, L., and Flynn, N. (eds) (2001) *The Market in Chinese Social Policy*. New York: Palgrave.

Wong, L., and Tang, J. (2008) Non-state care homes for older people as third sector organizations in China's transitional welfare economy, *Journal of Social Policy* 35(2), pp. 229–46.

Wong, Y. C., and Leung, J. (2012) Long-term care in China: issues and prospects, *Gerontological Social Work* 55(7), pp. 570–86.

Wong, Y. C., Chen, H. L., and Zeng, Q. (2014) Social assistance in Shanghai: dynamics between social protection and informal employment, *International Journal of Social Welfare* 23(3), pp. 333–41.

World Bank (1984) *China: The Health Sector*. Washington, DC: World Bank.

— (1997) *Financing Health Care: Issues and Options for China.* Washington, DC: World Bank.

— (2009) *From Poor Areas to Poor People: China's Evolving Poverty Reduction Agenda: An Assessment of Poverty and Inequality in China,* 5 March. Washington, DC: World Bank.

— (2011) *Reducing Inequality for Shared Growth in China: Strategy and Policy Options for Guangdong Province.* Washington, DC: World Bank.

— (2013) *China 2030: Building a Modern, Harmonious, and Creative High-Income Society.* Washington, DC: World Bank.

— (2014) GNI per capita, PPP, http://data.worldbank.org/indicator/NY.GNP.PCAP.PP.CD.

World Bank and DRC (Development Research Centre of the State Council) (2014) *Urban China: Toward Efficient, Inclusive, and Sustainable Urbanization.* Washington, DC: World Bank.

Wu, F. L., Webster, C., He, S. J., and Lu, Y. T. (2010) *Urban Poverty in China.* Cheltenham: Edward Elgar.

Wu, R. X. (ed.) (2013) *2013 Report on the Development of China's Elderly Businesses.* Beijing: Social Sciences Academic.

Xia, M. (2000) *The Dual Developmental State: Development Strategy and Institutional Arrangements for China's Transition.* Aldershot: Ashgate.

Xinhua (2012) Survey indicates that Chinese elderly people's desire to enter residential care is declining gradually, 7 July, http://news.xinhuanet.com/local/2012-07/10/c_112401439.htm [in Chinese].

— (2013a) Li Keqiang promotes purchase of public services has deep implications, 2 August, http://news.xinhuanet.com/politics/2013-08/02/c_116781540.htm [in Chinese].

— (2013b) WB cuts growth forecast for China, East Asia, 8 October, www.china.org.cn/business/2013-10/08/content_30223332.htm [in English].

— (2013c) China to streamline central–local gov't revenue division: Xi, 15 November, http://news.xinhuanet.com/english/china/2013-11/15/c_132892246.htm.

— (2014) China sees red in blood donation, 13 June, http://english.people.com.cn/n/2014/0613/c90000-8741205.html

Xiong, T. G., and Wang, S. B. (2007) Development of social work education in China in the context of new policy initiatives: issues and challenges, *Social Work Education* 26(6), pp. 560–72.

Xu Y. B., and Song, X. M. (2006) A study on the design and implementation of the Rural Medical Assistance Programme in China: consultation report to the Ministry of Health, unpublished.

Xu, Y. B., and Zhang, X. L. (2010) Rural social protection in China: reform, performance and challenges, in J. Midgley and K. L. Tang (eds), *Social Policy and Poverty in East Asia: The Role of Social Security*. London: Routledge, pp. 116–27.

Xu, Y. Y., and Li, X. Y. (2013) Social work organizations under government purchase of services, *Contemporary Hong Kong Macau Studies* 9, pp. 15–23.

Yang, M., and Tan, S. H. (2010) A pivot for change: the potential role of *haigui* in addressing China's social problems, in L. Zhao and T. S. Lim (eds), *China's New Social Policy: Initiatives for a Harmonious Society*. Singapore: World Scientific, pp. 211–24.

Yang, T. (ed.) (2013) *Annual Report on Philanthropy Development*. Beijing: Social Sciences Academic Press.

Ye, J., and Lu, P. (2011) Differentiated childhoods: impacts of rural labour migration on left-behind children in China, *Journal of Peasant Studies* 38(2), pp. 355–77.

Yip, W., and Hsiao, W. (2009) China's health care reform: a tentative assessment, *China Economic Review* 20, pp. 613–19.

Yu, J. X., and Guo, J. (2012) *Civil Society and Governance in China*. New York: Palgrave Macmillan.

Yusuf, S., and Nabeshima, K. (2006) *China's Development Priorities*. Washington, DC: World Bank.

Zhan, H. Y., Feng, Z. L., Chen, Z. Y., and Feng, X. T. (2011) The role of the family in institutional long-term care: cultural management of filial piety in China, *International Journal of Social Welfare* 20, pp. 121–34.

Zhang, H., Wu, B., and Sanders, R. (eds) (2007) *Marginalization in China: Perspectives on Transition and Globalization*. Aldershot: Ashgate.

Zhang, H. Q., and Shang, Y. (2013) Reflection on the situation and experiences of social work development in Guangdong, in Social Work Research Centre, MCA (ed.), *China Social Work Development Report, 2011–12*. Beijing: Social Sciences Academic, pp. 150–62.

Zhang, X., Yang, J., and Wang, S. (2011) China has reached the Lewis turning point, *China Economic Review* 22(4), pp. 542–54.

Zhang, X. L., and Xu, Y. B. (2012) Pensions and social assistance: the development of income security policies for old people in China, in S. Y. Chen and J. Powell (eds), *Aging in China: Implications to Social Policy of a Changing Economic State*. New York: Springer, pp. 43–61.

Zhang, X. L., Xu, Y. B., Leung, J., Carraro, C., and Song, X. M. (2011) Strengthening the anti-poverty function of rural social assistance system in

China, Asian Development Bank technical assistance report submitted to the Ministry of Civil Affairs, unpublished.

Zhao, H. (2011) The consultancy evaluation report submitted to the Shenzhen Civil Affairs Bureau on the performance of social work organizations, unpublished.

Zhao, L. T. (ed.) (2013) *China's Social Development and Policy: Into the Next Stage?* London: Routledge.

Zhao, L. T., and Lim, T. S. (eds) (2010) *China's New Social Policy: Initiatives for a Harmonious Society*. Singapore: World Scientific.

Zhao, X. F. (2013) Study on Government POS, 29 August, www.china-reform.org/?content_501.html [in Chinese].

Zheng, H. S. (2003) *China's Social Development Study Report 2002: Vulnerable Populations and Social Support*. Beijing: China People's University Press.

Zhuang, H. Z., Vandenberg, P., and Huang, Y. P. (2012) *Growing Beyond the Low-Cost Advantage*, October. Manila: Asian Development Bank/Peking University.

Zhuang, J. Z. (2008) Inclusive growth toward a harmonious society in the People's Republic of China: policy implications, *Asian Development Review* 25(1–2), pp. 22–33.

Index

Page numbers in *italic* refer to a table

abandonment, of babies   43, 44
abduction   46
abortion   43, 45, 46
accessibility to social welfare   4, 6, 30, *33*, *38*, 50, 55, 144, 174, 175
   health care   32, 99
   rural areas   98, 99, 120, 122
   urban areas   85, 87
accountability   144, 152, 171, 177
accuracy of official figures   8
'adjustment coefficient'   107
administration assessment   163
administrators, local   108
adoption   126
Africa   183
age-dependency ratio   41, *42*, 44, 45, 46–7, 100
aging population *see* population, aging
agricultural tax   105, 115
agricultural work   41, 47, 52, 54
agriculture   19, 36, 103, 183
AIDS patients   67, 159
All-China Women's Federation   54
Anhui province   48, 54
Asia   2, 57
Asian Development Bank (ADB)   11, 15, 35
Asian Tigers   10–11, 12

Assistance for Extremely Poor Households (AFEPH)   105, 107
Audit Department   64
authoritarianism   10, 182
autonomy   22, 153, 176

baby-boomers   46
bankruptcy   28, 77, 78, 84
Bankruptcy Law   ix, 26
'bare branches'   46
'barefoot doctors'   119, 120
Basic Medical Insurance System for Urban Employees (BMISFUE)   31, 81, 84
Beijing   48, 59, 72, 73, 139, 140, 153, 161
Beijing Normal University   161
Belarus   59
bidding, competitive   165, 168, 169
birth applications   44
birth rates   20, 39–40, *42*, 43, 44
blood donation   52, 180
Brazil   2, 57, 64
budget standard methods   89, 107
'Building a New Socialist Countryside' plan   36
business organizations   147, 150

canteens   20, 23, 138, 139
capitalism   7, 19, 27, 153–4
care workers   130, 131, 134, 139, 140
cash assistance *see* social assistance (*dibao*)
'categorical assistance'   108
census 1953   20
census 2000   40
census 2010   40, 54, 127
Central Provident Fund   11
centralization   174
   decentralization   4, 13, 32, 88, 95–6, 142, 176–7, 181, 184
charities/foundations   18, 147, 150, 151, 155, 163, 178, 179–80, 183
charity donations   116, 179–80
child care   20
child development   65
child mortality   2, 20, 98, 127
children   166
   and foster care   126, 154
   and health care   54, 55, 83, 94
   and need for care workers   154, 155
   one-child policy   38, 42–5, 52, 100, 127
   orphans   24, 43, 99, 113, 126, 128, 154
   and poverty   24, 64, 94, 104
children, abandoned   43, 44
children, adopted   126
children, homeless   154
children, left behind   50, 53–5, 67
children, second   44, 45, 52
Chile   57
China 2030 (World Bank)   6
China Association for Social Work Education   153
China Association of Social Work   153
China Health and Retirement Longitudinal Study (CHARLS)   47, 127
China Household Income Project   55, 56, 111
China Human Development Report (OECD)   15
China National Committee on Aging (CNCA)   131, 138
China Population Planning Commission   49
Chinese Academy of Social Sciences (CASS)   3, 8, 50, 51, 75–6, 183
Chinese Constitution   23, 37, 126
'Chinese dream'   36
Chongqing city   73
Circular of the Ministry of Civil Affairs (MCA) on Promoting Pilot Projects on Reforming Government-Operated Residential Institutions for Older People   142
citizenization   53
civil affairs departments
   and care of the elderly   110–11, 112, 123, 124, 135
   and social work organizations   147, 165
civil liberties   4, 150, 181
civil non-enterprise units   139, 150, 151, 160, 163
civil servants   32, 79, 123
civil society   146, 170, 178–81, 183
civil war   8, 128
clothing   19, 25, 89, 106, 113, 114
Code for Building Design for Older Persons   130

cohesion, social 2, 6, 33, 36, 146, 175
collectively owned enterprises (COEs) 22, 28, 101
collectivization viii, 19, 20, 113
  decollectivization 4, 27, 99
Committee for Social Affairs, Guangdong province 162
communes 19, 20, 22, 57, 99, 113, 119–20, 128
Communique on Decisions of the Communist Party of China (CPC) on Comprehensive Deepening of the Reforms 38
Communist Party of China (CPC)
  100th anniversary 5, 35
  16th Party Congress 33, 34, 145, 156
  17th Party Congress 102, 105, 145
  18th Party Congress xi, 35, 36, 146
    Third Plenum of 5, 37, 45, 148, 177, 178, 181, 182
  control 36–7, 182–3
  leadership 17, 25, 27, 170
  legitimacy 6, 12, 33, 181
  membership 24, 60
  and need for care workers 156, 158
  and social stability 12, 18–19, 34, 156, 181
Communist Youth Leagues 23, 149
community affairs 163
community centres 166, 167
'community democratic selection' 109–11
community monitoring 92
community service centres 157

community services 129, 138, 142, 147, 157
community work 93
compensation 78, 80
competition 22, 136, 147, 182
confidential issues 163
conflict, social 6, 38, 144, 145, 146, 148, 149, 158, 170
Confucianism 10, 34, 178–9
Congo, Democratic Republic of 60
Constructing the Social Work Workforce 165
construction, economic 25
construction, social 4, 5, 18, 34, 141, 145–7, 148, 156, 162, 165
Consumer Price Index 62
consumption 1, 63, 107, 141
contract workers' scheme 26–7
contracts, labour/employment 26, 27, 50, 73, 78, 96
Cooperative Medical System (CMS) 20, 99, 100, 119, 120, 123
  New Cooperative Medical System (NCMS) 35, 81, 84, 98, 116, 117–18, 119–22, 123, 124
corporate social responsibility (CSR) 180
corporatization 142
corruption 3, 33, 38, 64, 92, 93, 168
crime 18, 19, 155
Criminal Law 126
Cultural Revolution 4, 21, 61, 119
culture, Asian 10
Czech Republic 59

day-care centres 138, 139
de-administration 147, 168
death compensation 78

decentralization 4, 13, 32, 88, 95–6, 142, 176–7, 181, 184
Decisions of the Central Government to Strengthen Rural Health Work 120–1
Decisions on Establishing a Unified Basic Pension System for Enterprise Employees 70–1
Decisions on Establishing the BMISFUE 82
Decisions on Further Resolving the Problem of Food Adequacy in Poverty-Stricken Rural Areas 62
Decisions on Further Strengthening the Development of Poverty Alleviation 62
Decisions on Perfecting the Pension system for Employees in Enterprises 72
Decisions on the Pilot MISFUR 83–4
Decisions Regarding the Strengthening of the Construction of the Governing Capacity of the Party 145
decollectivization 4, 27, 99
delinquency 23, 24, 67, 154, 155, 159, 175
dementia 143
democracy 11, 34, 35, 36
demography 39–47
Deng Xiaoping ix, 17, 25, 27
Department of Human Resources and Social Security 93
deprivation *see* poverty
destitution 24, 126, 128, 131, 135, 142
Developing a Basic Public Service System, Five-Year Plan 146

Developing of Community Services and the Work of Civil Affairs, Five-Year Plan 157
development, balanced 26, 33–4
Development of Social Care Services for Older People, Five-Year Plan 141
Development-Orientated Poverty Reduction Programme for Rural China, White Paper 62
Development Research Centre (DRC) 31, 52, 174
dibao see social assistance (*dibao*)
disability 23, 39, 43, 67, 126, 175
 and elderly people 135, 139, 142
 and health care 84, 117
 and need for care workers 154, 155
 and rural areas 99, 104, 111, 112, 117, 127–8
 and social work organizations 159, 162, 166
 and urban areas 24, 84, 127
disasters, natural 7, 67, 92, 99, 103, 111–12, 154, 179
discrimination 50, 55
dislocation, social 2
diversification 26, 57–8, 130, 134
divorce 18
doctors, 'barefoot' 20, 119, 120
donations 18, 52, 116, 129, 150, 169, 179–80
Dongguan city 162, 165, 167
drug addiction 19, 24, 67, 154, 162, 166, 175

East Asia 9, 10–11, 12
East Europe 8–9

Economic and Social Development, Five-Year Plan 5
economic growth and development 44, 177–8
  and aging population 5, 12, 37, 125
  compared with other countries 9, 10, 12
  and inequality 61, 63, 87
  and marketization 25–32, 33, 35, 36
  rural areas 36, 62, 103
  slowdown of 3, 5, 37, 178
  and social stability 4, 33, 175
  urban areas 53, 87, 89, 96
economic growth model 6, 15, 182
economic policy 10, 11, 12, 182
economic production groups 18
Economic Reference Daily 168
economic reform ix, xi, 4, 5–6, 25–38, 39–67, 103, 172–84
  urban areas 77–8, 87, 92
economy, high-income 1, 6, 38, 65, 172, 173, 180, 182, 184
economy, mixed 178–81
education 2, 7, 10, 21, 24, 34, 44
  cost of 3, 65, 86, 87, 104, 111, 113
  inequality in 34, 55, 177
  and migrants' children 50, 55
  rural areas 27, 60, 98, 112
  spending 37, 63, 176
  urban areas 68, 85, 86, 94
education, higher 24, 40, 53, 55, 84
  see also social workers
education, political 18
education, primary 40, 54
education, secondary 40, 54
Educational Assistance 68, 85, 86, 94, 98, 112

egalitarian society 2, 4, 19, 21, 25, 56, 60, 181
elderly people 5, 7, 67, 84, 125–43, 155, 175
  and civil affairs departments 110–11, 112, 123, 124, 135
  and home care 125, 129, 134, 137–41
  and poverty 65, 94, 99, 113
  and rural areas 47, 99, 110–11, 112, 113–16, 123, 124, 127–8, 139, 141–2
  and social work organizations 159, 162, 166
  and taxation 114, 141
  and urban areas 65, 77, 83–4, 94, 99, 127, 137, 139, 140, 141–2
  and urbanization 46–7, 154
  see also pensions
elderly people, homes for 114, 115, 116, 125, 126, 128–30, 131–7, 140, 154
  registration of 135, 141
emergency relief 67, 68, 92, 99, 152, 179
emperors, little 43–4
Employee Old-Age Pension System (EOAPS) 69–73, 74, 75, 76, 77
employment 7, 35
  and *hukou* 29, 30
  job security 2, 19, 23, 27, 50, 53
  of social workers 155, 156, 157, 161, 162, 164, 166, 167, 169
  and SOEs 22, 24–5, 77–9
  see also re-employment; self-employment; unemployment
employment, informal 29, 30, 69, 75, 83, 84, 92, 94, 96, 173
employment, temporary 29, 30, 50

employment contracts   26, 27, 50, 73, 78, 96
employment opportunities   21, 34, 65
employment policy   35, 38, 184
employment rights   24, 50, 183
employment statistics   40
employment transfers   23, 85
Engel's coefficient   62, 91, 107
Enterprise Income Tax Law   169
enterprises   88, 129
  and medical insurance   27, 81, 82
  and pensions   69–70, 73, 75, 77
  and unemployment insurance   78, 79
entertainment industry   46
entrepreneurs   51, 93
environmental issues   x, 3, 5, 33, 36, 43, 183
equal rights   34, 38
Esping-Andersen, Gøsta   9
ethical guidelines for social workers   157
ethnic minority groups   42, 60, 62, 103, 104, 157, 166, 183
evaluation   148, 152
executive board members   160, 168
experience, personal   8

fairness   108, 148, 182
families, low-income   32, 60, 68, 84, 94, 110
families, single-child   117
family planning   ix, 20–1, 23, 41, 42–5
family policy   18
family relations   168
family service centres   166, 167, 168
family size   38, 40, 42–5, 52, 100, 127

family support   10, 24, 95, 154, 178–9
  for the elderly   47, 94, 126, 127, 128, 131–2, 142, 143
  rural areas   99, 100, 113, 114, 115
farmers   36, 38, 63, 101, 115, 119
farmland   33, 109, 114
fees   43
  education   55, 111, 112
  medical   31, 78, 112, 118, 119, 120
  for residential care   129, 131, 132, 135, 136–7, 141, 142
fertility rate   20, 39–40, 42, 43, 44
feudalism   19, 21
figures, official   8, 55, 61, 139, 140
financial crisis, Asian (1997)   28, 101
financial crisis, global (2008)   3, 36
financial services   36
'Five-Guarantees' programme see wubao ('Five-Guarantees' programme)
Five-Year Plans   viii, 5, 100, 114–15, 130, 141, 146, 157
  12th   137, 141, 146, 157
food   xii, 19, 22, 23, 25, 49, 62
  and dibao (social assistance)   89, 106
  and wubao   113, 114
food safety   3
food security   145
Fortune magazine   180
foster care   126, 154
Foxconn company   51
Fujian province   48
funding   173
  and elderly people   129, 134, 138, 141

rural areas   99, 100–2, 105, *106*,
    113–14, 115, 117, 119, 120,
    121–2
  and social work organizations
    152, 159, 168, 170, 171
  urban areas   74, 76, 79, 82, 88–9,
    90, 95, 97
funds, surplus   80
funeral expenses   19, 78, 80

Gansu province   59, 62, 127
GDP (gross domestic product)   2,
    11, 25, 36, 77, 172, 179
  compared with other countries   1,
    59, 176, 179
  and migration   48, 53
gender issues   18, 39, 45–6
Germany   149
Gini coefficient   21, 55, 56–7, 61
girls   43, 44, 46
globalization   5, 150, 181
governance   6, 36, 144–71, 183
government, central
  and care of the elderly   129, 134,
    135, 138–9, 142
  and *dibao* (social assistance)
    88–9, 95, 100, 105–7, 123
  and funding   53, 95, 126, 164,
    174, 176–7
  and health care/medical
    insurance   83, 84, 95, 100,
    116, 120–1
  and pensions   74, 95, 100, 102
  and rural areas   100, 102,
    105–7, 113, 115, 116, 120–1,
    123
  and social work organizations
    149, 164
  and urban areas   74, 83, 84, 88–9,
    95, 96, 123

government, local   13, 176–7
  and care of the elderly   128, 131,
    134, 135, 137, 141
  and financial capacity   13, 27, 53
  and health care/medical insurance
    83, 84, 121
  and migration   50, 53
  and need for care workers   156,
    159
  and pensions   71, 73, 74, 101,
    102
  rural areas   100, 101, 102, 105,
    107, 109, 110, 114–15, 116,
    121, 123
  and social assistance   88, 91, 92
  and social protection   95–6, 107,
    110, 114–15, 116
  and social work organizations
    149, 151–2, 160, 161, 163,
    168
  and unemployment insurance   78,
    79–80
  urban areas   91, 95–6, 97
  and medical insurance   83, 84
  and pensions   71, 73, 74
  and social assistance   88, 91,
    92
  and unemployment insurance
    78, 79–80
government bonds   101
government offices   22, 75, 117
government officials   168
government organizations   27,
    69–70, 72, 75, 79, 81, 82,
    85
Government Procurement Law   159,
    169
grandparents   54
grants   152, 165
Great Leap Forward   viii, 4, 20, 21

Guangdong province   63, 72, 111, 116, 162–7, 169, 183
   and migration   48, 51, 52, 54, 59
   and social work organizations   144, 148, 159, 161, 168, 170
Guangdong Regulations on Promoting the Development of Public Benefit Organizations   168
Guangzhou city   49, 136, 140, 162, 167, 168, 169
Guidelines for Establishing Urban ROAPS   74
Guidelines for Experimenting with the NROAPS   102
Guiding Opinion on Government Purchase of Services from the Social Sector   148
Guiding Opinion on the Government Purchase of Social Work Services   160
Guizhou province   12, 59–60

Hainan province   82, 161
Han population   40
happiness   51
health, children's   54, 55, 83, 94
health, women's   43
Health and Family Planning Commission   42, 127
health care   2, 3, 7, 11, 31, 145, 176
   access to   32, 34, 94, 99, 173
   and disability   84, 117
   and government, central   95, 100, 116
   and inequality   55, 172, 177
   and poverty   63, 87, 104, 155
   rural areas   27, 60, 98, 99, 116–22, 173
   under socialism   19, 20, 22–3
   subsidization   68, 95, 116, 121
   urban areas   68, 87, 94, 95, 173
   see also medical insurance
health care, preventive   20, 123
Henan province   45, 48, 54
Holliday, Ian   11
home care of the elderly   125, 129, 134, 137–41
homelessness   67, 126, 154
homes for the elderly   114, 115, 116, 125, 126, 128–30, 131–7, 140, 154
   registration of   135, 141
Hong Kong   10, 11, 153, 164, 166, 167
Hong Kong, University of   161
'honour homes'   128
hospitals   23, 120, 137, 166, 173
   in-patient/out-patient care   81, 83, 84, 116, 118, 121, 123
house purchasing   24
household assets   91
household income   55–6, 63, 92, 108, 111–12
   low income   32, 60, 68, 77, 84, 85, 94, 104–5, 110, 111
household registration *see hukou (household registration)*
household responsibility system   26, 57, 61
household size   60
housing   53, 56
   affordable/low-cost   3, 35, 36, 37, 50, 51, 68
   subsidized   19, 86
Housing Assistance   68, 85, 86, 94
housing provident fund   50, 68
Hu Jintao   x, 5, 17, 32, 35, 145
hukou (household registration)   23–5, 37, 164
   rural areas   54, 174

and social reform   172, 174
urban areas   33, 65, 69, 90–1, 174
  and employment   29, 30
  and migration   23–4, 47–8, 49, 51–2, 53, 65, 172
Human Development Index   1, 11, 59
human rights   44, 49, 152, 154, 182, 183
human services   7
Hunan province   48, 54

identity   22, 49, 50
illness   84, 111–12, 116, 120, 121
imperialism   19
incentives   23, 26, 57, 63, 70, 93, 95
inclusive growth   35
income
  household income   55–6, 63, 92, 108, 111–12
    low income   32, 60, 68, 77, 84, 85, 94, 104–5, 110, 111
    and inequality   2, 4, 5, 21, 30, 34, 37, 55–61, 65, 184
  see also wages
income, grey/hidden   61, 92
income, loss of   2–3
income, personal   36
income distribution   38, 61, 173
income mobility   60
income poverty   63
India   15, 39, 57, 59, 64, 149, 176
individual accounts   30
  medical insurance   31, 82, 83, 102, 123
  pensions   70–1, 72, 73, 74, 76, 77, 102, 123
  and social pooling   70–1, 82

individuals   82, 101, 129
industrialization   23, 25, 44, 57, 60, 154
Industry and Commerce Bureau   150
inequality   xii, 7, 12, 66
  and education   34, 55, 177
  and elderly people   67, 142
  and health care   55, 177
  and pensions   76, 172
  and rural areas   21, 26, 55–9, 61, 172, 174–5
  and taxation   57, 61
  and urban areas   21, 26, 55–9, 67, 96, 172, 174–5
inequality, economic/income   2, 4, 5, 21, 30, 34, 37, 55–61, 65, 184
inequality, geographic   4, 26, 59–61, 142, 167
  between urban and rural areas   26, 30, 57, 58, 67, 172, 174–5, 181
inequality, social   3, 21, 39, 182
infanticide   43, 46
informal sector   178
infrastructure   36, 63, 103, 174
Inheritance Law   126
injury, in the workplace   19, 50, 68
in-patient care   81, 83, 84, 116, 118, 121, 123
Instruction on Speeding up the Development of Community Service   138
insurance *see* social insurance
integration of migrants   50, 52–3, 67
interdependency   153
interests, collective versus individual   10, 18

Interim Administrative Measures on Social Welfare Institutions (1999) 130
Interim Administrative Measures on Social Welfare Institutions for Older Persons in Rural Areas (1997) 130
Interim Measures for Banning Illegal Social Organizations 151
International Labour Office 15
investment 41, 63, 97, 130
 foreign 4, 57, 135, 141
Iraq 59
iron rice bowl 19, 23, 26, 27

Jansson, Bruce 7
Japan 9, 11, 12
Jiang Zemin ix, 17, 27–8
Jiangsu province 59, 82, 161
Jiangxi province 45, 48, 82
Jiujiang city 82
job creation 19, 35
job security 2, 19, 23, 27, 50, 53
justice 10, 38, 154, 182, 183

Kazakhstan 59
'kick back' 168
Kunming city 73

labour camps 38
Labour Contract Law xi, 35
labour contracts 26, 27, 50, 73, 78, 96
Labour Insurance Regulations 19, 72
Labour Law 72–3
labour market 22, 25, 28
labour protection 3
labour shortages 5, 41, 44, 51, 60
labour supply 41, 42

labour surplus 28, 41, 47, 57–8, 78
'laid-off employees' (*xiagang*) 78–9, 86–7, 92
land use rights 19, 20, 37, 38, 51, 52, 183
Lao People's Democratic Republic 63
law, rule of 34, 37, 38, 49, 146, 148, 149, 170, 183
Law on the Protection of the Rights and Interests of Older People 126, 130
'left-behind' groups 53–4, 67
'Lewis Turning Point' 41
Li Keqiang 130, 148
liberalization 26, 181
life expectancy 2, 20, 40, 98
lifestyle 24, 93
literacy levels 40, 98
living standards 2, 6, 12, 25, 103, 114, 137
 rural areas 27, 51, 106, 112, 122
lotteries 138, 164, 166

Ma Yinchu 20
Mandatory Provident Fund 11
Mao Zedong viii, ix, 17, 20, 21, 25, 179
market reform 27, 39–67
marketization 2, 25–32, 38, 150, 170, 176, 178
 and social services 4, 30, 50, 53, 60, 87, 120, 125, 146, 181
marriage 21, 24, 44, 162
Marriage Law 18, 114, 115, 126
martyrs 99, 117, 128
Marxist–Leninist ideology 19
mass media 8
maternity care 44, 50, 68
'Me' generation 43–4

means-testing 68, 85, 87, 91, 92, 94, 98, 109
  see also social assistance (*dibao*)
mediation 23
Medical Assistance for Rural Residents 35, 98, 104, 112, 116–19, 123, 124
Medical Assistance for Urban Residents 35, 68, 85, 86, 94
medical insurance x, 5, 11, 22, 173
  and central government 83, 84, 120–1
  and enterprises 27, 81, 82
  and government organizations 27, 81, 82, 85
  and individual accounts 31, 82, 83, 102, 123
  and local government 83, 84
  and migrant workers 50, 81, 84
  and public institutions 27, 81, 82
  rural areas 31, 120, 122, 123
  and social pooling 81–3, 84, 120, 121
  and unemployment 78, 80
  urban areas x, 68, 81–5, 86
  see also health care
Medical Insurance System for Urban Employees 81–3
Medical Insurance System for Urban Residents 81, 83
mental health 39, 67, 126, 143, 154, 162
Methods of Migrant Workers Participating in the Basic Old-Age Pension System (Ministry of Human Resources and Social Security) 73
Methods of Setting up Homes for the Aged 130

Methods on Assessing Management of Social Organizations 151
Methods on Implementing the National Assessment on Social Organizations 151
Methods on Managing the Maintenance Fees 43
Methods on the Management of Homes for the Aged 130, 135
Methods on the Setting up of Homes for the Aged 135
Mexico 57, 176
middle classes 37
middle-income trap 9
migrant workers 47–53, 60, 96, 97, 98, 174
  and *hukou* 23–4, 30, 32–3, 47–8, 49, 51–2, 53, 65, 172
  and inequality 58, 67
  and social insurance 35, 50, 52, 80, 81, 84
  health care and medical insurance 50, 81, 84, 173
  pensions 35, 50, 69, 72–3, 75, 173
  unemployment 50, 80
  see also mobility, population
migrant workers, rights of 49, 151
migrant workers, second generation 49–50
Minimum Living Standard Guarantee System (*dibao*) see social assistance (*dibao*)
Ministry of Civil Affairs (MCA) 52, 88, 100, 104, 105, 107, 116, 117, 126
  and care of the elderly 129, 130, 131, 132–4, 135, 138, 139, 141

Ministry of Civil Affairs (MCA) (cont.)
   and need for care workers   154, 155, 156
   and social work organizations   148, 152, 160–1, 162, 167
Ministry of Finance   107, 160
Ministry of Human Resources and Social Security   73
Ministry of Labour and Social Security   86–7, 101, 130, 155
Ministry of Personnel   155
minority groups   145, 157, 166, 183
missionaries   18, 153
mobility, income   60
mobility, labour   19, 172
mobility, population   5, 26, 32–3, 37, 40, 48–9, 102, 145, 182
moderately wealthy country (*xiaokang*)   25, 35
modernization   13, 25, 144, 173
Mongolia   63
mortality, child   2, 20, 98, 127

Namibia   60
National Audit Office   43, 177
National Bureau of Statistics (NBS)   41, 50, 55
National Development Mid- and Long-Term Framework on Human Capital 2010–2020   156
national household survey   50–1, 61
National Report on the Development of China's Elderly Business   127–8
national security   38, 163
nationalization   20

New Cooperative Medical System (NCMS)   35, 81, 84, 98, 116, 117–18, 119–22, 123, 124
New National Urbanization Framework   53
New Population Theory   20
New Progress in Development-Orientated Poverty Reduction Programme for Rural China, White Paper   62
New Rural Old-Age Pension System (NROAPS)   35, 73, 102–3
New Ten Year Rural Poverty Reduction and Development Framework   62
Ningxia province   62, 89, 161
non-governmental organizations (NGOs)   179
   and care of the elderly   129, 130, 131, 134, 135, 136, 137, 139, 143
   and need for care workers   153, 155–6, 157, 158
   and social work organizations   144, 149, 152, 159
non-profit sector   7, 129, 178
non-state sector   87
Notice Concerning the Promotion of the Development of Non-Governmental SWOs   160
Notice on Deepening Reform of the Pension System for Enterprises   70
Notice on Doing a Good Job in the MISFUR   84
Notice on Setting up Rural Dibao Nationally   105, 106

INDEX

Notice on Strengthening the
 Management of Rural Dibao
 Fund 107
nurseries 20, 23

obesity 24
OECD (Organization for
 Economic Cooperation
 and Development) 2, 8, 15,
 176
 and inequality and poverty 57,
 59, 65, 66, 172
 and pensions 75, 77
 and social reform 172, 177, 182
offenders 23, 24, 67, 154, 155, 159,
 175
'off-post employees' 28–9, 78–9
old-age allowance 77
old-age 'tax' 114
one-child policy ix, 38, 42–5, 52,
 100, 117, 127
Opinion Concerning Deepening the
 Reform of the Income
 Redistribution System 37
Opinion Concerning Improving the
 Government Purchase of Pilot
 Service for the Disabled 160
Opinion Concerning Strengthening and
 Innovating Social Management
 145
Opinion Concerning the Deepening of
 the Administrative System
 Reform 145
Opinion Concerning the Development
 and Regulation of Social
 Organizations 163
Opinion Concerning the
 Implementation of the
 Socialization of Social Welfare
 129, 130

Opinion Concerning the Promotion of
 Integration of Migrant Workers
 in the Urban Community 52
Opinion Concerning the Promotion of
 the Business for Disabled People
 160
Opinion Concerning the Speeding up of
 the Development of Elderly
 Services (2013) 141, 160
Opinion on Establishing a Unified
 Urban and Rural Pension
 System 102
Opinion on Further Promoting the
 Development of Non-
 Governmental SWOs 160–1
Opinion on Further Strengthening the
 Work of the Dibao 91
Opinion on Piloting the Government
 purchase of services (POS) from
 Social Organizations 163
Opinion on Promoting the Development
 of Social Work and Social
 Work Workforce 166
Opinion on Promoting the Work of
 Home Care for Older People
 138
Opinion on Reforming the Work of
 Poverty Reduction in Rural
 Areas 62, 64
Opinion on Speeding up the
 Development of Services
 for Older People (2006)
 134
Opinion on Strengthening and
 Improving the Construction
 Work of Urban Residents'
 Committees 138
Opinion on Supporting the Operation
 of Social Welfare Institutions by
 NGOs 130

Opinion on Supporting the Society Efforts in Operating Social Welfare Organizations 160
Opinion on the Implementation of Rural MA 116, 117
Options on Reform and Transfer of Functions of the Organizations of the State Council 147
organ donation 180
Organization Department, Communist Party of China (CPC) 156
orphans 24, 43, 99, 113, 126, 128, 154
Outlook 149
out-patient care 81, 83, 84, 118, 121
ownership, industrial 26

parenthood, single 24
Party Congress
   16th 33, 34, 101–2, 145, 156
   17th 102, 105, 145
   18th xi, 35, 36, 146
     Third Plenum of 5, 37, 45, 148, 177, 178, 181, 182
passivity 24
pay-as-you-go systems 30, 70, 76, 102
Pearl River Delta 167, 169
peasants 119–20, 173
   income 27, 57–8, 63
   land ownership 19, 20, 37, 38
   and pensions 100, 101
   see also migrant workers; rural areas
peer communication 43
pension funds 27, 35, 70, 76, 96

pensions x, 3, 7, 22, 30
   compared with other countries 11, 176
   and enterprises 69–70, 73, 75, 77
   and government, central 74, 95, 100, 102
   and government, local 71, 73, 74, 101, 102
   and government organizations 69–70, 72, 75
   and migrant workers 35, 50, 69, 72–3, 75, 173
   and public institutions 69–70, 75, 77
   and reform 5, 172, 174
   Residents' Old-Age Pension System (ROAPS) 36, 69, 73–4, 75, 76, 98
   rural areas 47, 60, 61, 100–3, 123, 173
     New Rural Old-Age Pension System (NROAPS) 35, 73, 102–3
   and social pooling 27, 70–1, 72, 100
   and SOEs 27, 87
   and unemployment 69, 73–4, 173
   urban areas x, 19, 30, 35, 47, 68–77, 87, 90, 95, 173
   see also elderly people
pensions, basic x, 70, 71, 72, 73, 74, 102, 123
pensions, individual account 70–1, 72, 73, 74, 76, 77, 102, 123
pensions, pay-as-you-go 70, 76, 102
pensions, private sector 75, 77
Pensions for Employees in Government Organizations and Public Institutions 72

People's Daily 149
People's Republic of China (PRC)
    viii, 4, 17, 35, 153
petitions 183
pluralism, welfare 6, 178, 181
points system 52, 119
population, aging 5, 12, 37, 125,
    154, 181
  age-dependency ratio 41, 42, 44,
    45, 46-7, 100
  statistics 40, 46
population, mobile/floating 5, 26,
    32-3, 37, 40, 48-9, 102, 145
  see also migrant workers
population, working 40, 41, 45, 51
Population and Family Planning Law
    42, 45
population statistics 39, 40, 43, 46
Portugal 59
poverty 7, 24, 61-5, 87, 153
  alleviation of 2, 23, 62-4, 152,
    162, 179, 183
    rural areas 27, 103-13, 124,
      159
  and children 24, 64, 94-5, 104
  and economic growth 63, 87
  and elderly people 94, 99, 113
  and health care 63, 87, 104, 155
  and need for care workers 154,
    157
  rural areas 19, 27, 32, 67, 100,
    102-19, 120, 124, 152, 159
  urban areas 29, 32, 63, 67, 85,
    86-7
poverty, consumption 63
poverty, income 63
poverty, marginal 111
poverty, subsistence 19, 21, 61
poverty line 66, 104, 105, 107, 123
poverty targeting 109-11

preventive health care 20, 123
prices 19, 26, 58, 61, 120
'primitive accumulation' 19
private sector 7, 9, 173, 176, 178
  and care of the elderly 129, 130,
    132-4, 135-6, 137, 139, 141,
    143
  urban areas 75, 77, 87, 97
privatization 56, 120
privilege 19, 24, 31, 32, 57, 76
Procurement Law 169
productivity 10, 23, 27, 36
professional qualifications 125, 130,
    131, 135, 140, 144, 154-6,
    158-9, 165, 170
*Professional Standards of Carers for
    Older Persons* 130
profitability 129, 136, 143
Proposal on Establishing NCMS 121
prostitution 19, 24, 46
protest 8, 33, 183
provinces 59-61, 62
  central 28, 48, 49, 59-60, 74, 88,
    102, 123, 161, 169, 174
  coastal 12, 48, 51, 57, 59-60, 62,
    161, 169, 180
  eastern 49, 59, 74, 102, 161
  northeastern 28, 72, 169
  western 45, 59, 62, 74, 83-4,
    102, 116, 121, 161
proxy-means criteria 93
public health 20, 38, 123
public institutions 22, 27, 69-70,
    75, 77, 80, 81, 82
Public Medical Insurance System
    (PMIS) 81, 85
public opinion 3, 8, 77, 183
public sector 30, 147, 178
public services 43, 148, 152, 163,
    164, 174

public spending 176–7
Public Welfare Donation Law 169
public work projects 18, 103
purchase of services (POS) 144, 148, 149, 159–67, 169, 170–1
Purchasing Power Parity (PPP) 1, 59

Qinghai province 179
quality of life 8, 34, 37, 67, 173, 175

rationing 19
redistribution 10, 11, 15, 19, 37, 60, 184
redundancy 18, 27, 28, 77, 78–9, 84, 86–7
re-employment 23, 79–80, 93, 134
reform, economic ix, xi, 4, 5–6, 25–38, 39–67, 103, 172–84
 urban areas 77–8, 87, 92
reform, political 38
reform, social xi, 5–6, 13, 32–8, 172–84
registration, household *see* hukou (household registration)
registration of care homes 135, 141
registration of care workers 155
registration of social work organizations 147, 150, 152, 163, 170
regression 3, 15, 59, 76
Regulation on the Custody and Repatriation of Vagrants 49
Regulations on the Guarantee of the Dibao for Urban Residents 88, 89
Regulations on the Occupationalization of Social Workers 155

Regulations on the Social Workers Occupational Standard System 155
Regulations on the Work of Rural Five-Guarantees Households 114–15
Regulations on Unemployment Insurance 79, 80
reimbursement 83, 84, 86, 116, 117–18, 119, 121–2
'relationship *dibao*' 110
religion 10, 24
repatriation 49
replacement rates of pensions 75–6
Report on the Development of Social Work in China 160
Report on the Development of the Mobile Population 49
Report on the Mid- and Long-Term Development of the Social Work Workforce 157
Report on the Rule of Law 183
Report on the Transparency of Charity Organizations in China 180
residential care 114, 115, 116, 125, 126, 128–30, 131–7, 140, 154
 registration of 135, 141
Residents' Old-Age Pension System (ROAPS) 36, 69, 73–4, 75, 76, 98
Resolution on Reform of the Pension System for Enterprises 70
respite services 138, 140
responsibility, shared 6, 101
retirement *see* elderly people; pensions
retirement age 77, 173
rights 3, 6
 employment rights 24, 50, 183
 equal rights 34, 38

human rights 44, 49, 152, 154, 182, 183
land use rights 19, 20, 37, 38, 51, 52, 183
migrant workers' rights 49, 151
Rules for the Five Guarantee Work in Rural Areas 130
rural areas 19, 20, 36, 42, 98–124
  and disability 99, 104, 111, 112, 117, 127–8
  and economic growth and development 36, 62, 103
  and education 27, 60, 98, 112
  and elderly people 47, 99, 110–11, 112, 113–16, 123, 124, 127–8, 139, 141–2
  and health care 27, 60, 98, 99, 116–22, 173
    and medical insurance 31, 120, 123
  and *hukou* 54, 174
  and inequality 12, 21, 26, 38, 55–9, 61
    compared with urban areas 26, 30, 33, 57, 58, 67, 172, 174–5, 181
  and pensions 35, 47, 60, 61, 100–3, 123, 173
  and poverty 19, 27, 32, 100, 102–19, 120, 124, 152, 159
    and marketization 62, 63, 64, 67
  social welfare system 24, 27, 34
Rural Old-Age Pension System 100–1
Rural Social Assistance Programme 35, 63

SARS (Severe Acute Respiratory Syndrome) x, 33–4
Saudi Arabia 59
savings 1, 11, 30, 41, 49, 91
scarcity 103
school fees 55, 111, 112
science and technology organizations 147
'scientific development' x, 33–4
self-employment 51, 73, 78, 93
Seven-Year Priority Poverty Reduction Programme 62
sex ratio 44, 45–6
sexual disease 24
Shanghai city 87, 136, 139, 140, 153, 155–6
Shanghai province 48, 51, 52, 59, 72, 89, 116, 159, 161, 162
Shanxi province 161
Shenzhen 72, 151, 162, 165, 166, 167, 169
Sichuan province 48, 54, 179
Singapore 10, 11, 164
social assistance (*dibao*) 5, 7, 18, 23, 140
  and central government 88–9, 95, 100, 105–7, 123
  and local government 88, 91, 92
  rural areas 35, 60, 63, 98, 100, 102–19, 122–3, 124
  and social reform 172, 173, 174
  and social workers 155, 157
  urban areas 23, 28–9, 65, 68, 76, 80, 83, 85–95, 97, 104
social assistance line 89, 90, 91, 107, 108
social class 19, 21, 25, 37
social conflict 6, 38, 144, 145, 146, 148, 149, 158, 170
social development 8, 96, 98
  compared with other countries 1, 10
  reform 5–6, 33, 36, 44, 176, 182
  under socialism 7, 18

social insurance   22, 29, 35, 52, 68, 173
  and maternity care   50, 68
  and public institutions   27, 80, 81, 82
  and rural areas   98, 122–3
    medical insurance   31, 120, 122, 123
    pensions   35, 47, 60, 61, 73, 100–3, 123, 173
  and urban areas   24, 87, 93, 97
    medical insurance   68, 81–5, 86
    pensions   x, 19, 30, 35, 47, 68–77, 87, 90, 95, 173
    unemployment   28–9, 77–80, 90, 93, 173
  and work injury   19, 50, 68
  see also medical insurance; migrant workers; pensions; unemployment insurance
Social Insurance Law   xi, 35, 79
Social Insurance Scheme for Migrants   35
social maintenance fees   43
social policy, Asian   10
social policy, China   5, 11, 12, 14, 30, 38
social pooling   27, 70–1, 72, 78, 81–3, 84, 96, 97, 100
  village/township-based   120, 121
Social Protection Index   11
social protection system   2–3, 4, 5, 11, 22, 27, 32, 68–97, 98–124, 125
  reform   34, 38, 172, 173, 184
social reform   xi, 5–6, 13, 32–8, 172–84
social sciences, as university subject   7, 18, 153–4

social sector   146, 148, 149–53
social security   2–3, 7, 14, 26, 29–30, 32, 52
  and inequality and poverty   55, 65
  and reform   34, 35, 37, 38, 46, 87, 173–4, 177, 181
  and rural areas   59, 100, 111, 124
  under socialism   19, 22–3
  and urban areas   59, 68, 73, 74, 77, 87, 93, 95, 97
social services   4, 13–14, 20, 27, 53
  and elderly people   125, 138
  and *hukou*   30, 33
  and marketization   4, 30, 50, 53, 60, 87, 120, 125, 146, 181
  and reform   32, 33, 172, 174, 177, 181, 184
  and rural areas   60, 110, 114
  and social work organizations   144, 146, 149–50, 152
  and urban areas   77, 87
social work   xiii, 153–9
Social Work Association of the Guangzhou Civil Affairs Bureau   165
social work education   xiii, 153–9, 165, 169
social work organizations (SWOs)   144–71
social workers   xiii, 131, 153–9, 160, 167, 169, 170
  education and training   144, 152, 153–4, 157, 161, 164, 165–6, 169
socialism   4, 18–25, 153, 181
socialist society, harmonious   x, 34, 35, 96–7, 156, 178, 181, 184
socialization   30, 129, 159
societies   150, *151*, 163
'society sector'   132–4, 141, 148

soldiers and ex-soldiers   7, 24, 99, 117, 128, 155, 166
South Africa   2, 57, 64
South Korea   9, 11
Soviet Union   18
special economic zones   26
spending, education   37, 63, 176
spending, public   176–7
spending, social   5, 10–11, 12, 173, 175–8
stability, political   6, 173, 184
stability, social   6, 10, 52–3, 92, 95, 115, 144, 146
  and Communist Party of China   12, 18–19, 34, 156, 181
  and economic growth and development   4, 33, 175
standard-setting   143, 158
Standards of Social Welfare Institutions for the Elderly   130
Star Light project   138
state control   24, 26, 178
State Council   37
  and care of the elderly   130, 141
  and *dibao* (social assistance)   88, 89, 91, 92, 105
  and medical insurance   82, 83–4
  and pensions   70–3, 74
  rural areas   102, 103, 105–6, 114, 120–1
  and SOEs   147, 148, 156
  and unemployment   78, 79, 80
State Council Leading Group of Poverty Alleviation and Development   103
state-owned enterprises (SOEs)   28, 57, 173
  contributions to welfare system   37, 68, 87, 95, 173
  and employment   22, 24–5, 77–9

management of   26–7, 28
  and pensions   27, 70, 74, 87
  and redundancy   27, 84, 86–7
  restructuring   77–9, 86–7, 95
  and State Council   147, 148, 156
State Population and Family Planning Commission   50
status, social   21, 22, 23, 24, 32
stock markets   28, 57
students   83, 84, 94, 102, 166, 183
  social workers   xii, xiii, 158
subsidization   19, 23, 24, 28–9, 64, 83–4, 140, 164–5
  and health care   68, 95, 116, 121
  and pensions   74, 77, 95
  and social assistance   95, 106
subsistence   19, 21, 61
Sun Yat Sen University   164
Sun Zhigang   49
survivors' compensation   78, 80
sustainability, financial   76–7, 96, 97

Taiwan   10, 11
'take home your own child' approach   88
Tang, Jun   136
taxation   18, 26, 63, 93
  and elderly people   114, 141
  and inequality   57, 61
  rural areas   105, 114, 115
  and social reform   173, 174, 184
  and social work organizations   163, 165, 169
'tax-for-fee' policy   105, 115
technology   4, 63, 130
Temporary Assistance   68, 85, 98, 105, 112–13
Temporary Method on Social Assistance   92

Temporary Methods on Government purchase of services POS from Social Organizations   163
Temporary Regulations on Establishment of Insurance for Employees in SOEs Waiting for Job Assignment   78
Temporary Regulations on the Collection of Social Insurance Premiums   72–3
'three lines of defence'   28
'three nos'   24, 49, 86, 88, 99, 128, 129, 130, 134
Tiananmen Square protest   ix, 150
Tianjin city   136
Tibet   42, 59, 62, 161
Tigers, Asian   10–11, 12
Time magazine   43, 51, 126
township government   113–14
township village enterprises (TVEs)   26, 61, 100, 103
trade, foreign   4
trade unions   149
trafficking   46
training   29, 35, 78, 80, 93
   care workers   130, 131, 134, 140
   social workers   144, 152, 153–4, 157, 161, 164, 165–6, 169
transfer of function (*zhuan*)   147, 148, 149, 163
transfers, employment   23, 85
transfers, financial   88–9, 90, 95, 106–7, 116, 126, 127, 142, 174, 176–7
transparency   177, 179–80
trust   179, 182–3
Tsinghua University   52
Turkey   57

turning points   4–6
   first   4, 17–25, 181
   second   4, 25–32, 181
   third   5–6, 32–8, 172–84

unemployment   27, 32, 65, 154
   'laid-off employees' (*xiagang*)   65, 78–9, 86–7, 92
   under socialism   19, 23, 153
   and urban areas   28–9, 69, 73–4, 77–80, 90, 92, 93, 173
   see also employment
unemployment insurance   x, 23, 27, 28, 80
   and migrant workers   50, 80
   and pensions   69, 73–4, 173
   and urban areas   28–9, 77–80, 90, 93, 173
unemployment rate   29, 32, 40, 80
unions   23
United Kingdom   ix, 149, 180
United Nations Development Programme (UNDP)   1, 15
United Nations Millennium Development Goals   64
United States   ix, 126, 149, 179, 180
universities   7, 18, 55, 153–4, 158, 164, 165
unrest, social   52
urban areas   27, 34, 42, 68–97
   and central government   74, 83, 84, 88–9, 95, 96, 123
   and disability   24, 84, 127
   and economic growth and development   33, 53, 77–8, 87, 89, 92, 96
   and elderly people   65, 77, 83–4, 94, 99, 127, 137, 139, 140, 141–2
   and employment   29, 30

and health care   68, 81–5, 86, 87, 94, 95, 173
and *hukou*   33, 65, 69, 90–1, 174
and inequality   12, 21, 26, 55–9, 67, 96, 172, 174–5
  compared with rural areas   26, 30, 33, 57, 58, 67, 172, 174–5, 181
and migration   23–4, 47–8, 49, 51–2, 53, 65, 172
and poverty   29, 32, 63, 65, 67, 85, 86–7
and social assistance   23, 28–9, 65, 68, 76, 80, 83, 85–95, 97, 104
and social insurance   24, 87, 93, 97
  medical   x, 68, 81–5, 86
  pensions   x, 19, 30, 35, 47, 68–77, 87, 90, 95, 173
  unemployment   28–9, 77–80, 90, 93, 173
and social security   59, 68, 73, 74, 77, 87, 93, 95, 97
and social services   77, 87
and unemployment   28–9, 69, 73–4, 77–80, 90, 92, 93, 173
Urban Resident Basic Medical Insurance   35
urban residents' committees   149, 162
urban villages   51
urbanization   37, 44, 46–7, 52–3, 98, 154, 174, 181
urbanization rate   23, 40

vagrancy   49
Vanuatu   59
Vietnam   63

Views on Deepening the Reforms on Income Distribution System   173
village committees   109–10, 111, 113–14, 149
violence, against women   46
violence, domestic   154, 175
volunteering   52, 179
vouchers   140
vulnerable people   3, 4, 7, 31–2, 65, 111–12, 184
  see also children; migrant workers

wage, minimum   37, 61, 90, 91, 174
wage bill   96
wages
  care workers/social workers   140, 154, 157, 161, 164, 169
  increases   36, 41, 60, 61
  low   19, 23, 51, 65, 77, 86, 87, 140
  under socialism   19, 20, 23
Wan Jiabao   146–7
Wang, Gungwu   2
Wang Sibin, Professor   158
welfare, collective   23, 114
welfare, personal   23
welfare dependency   24, 93–4, 108
welfare states   9, 10–11, 12, 24, 125, 172–5, 181
Wen Jiabao   35
Western model of modernization   13, 173
westernization   153–4, 183–4
Whyte, Martin K.   21, 60
Wilding, Paul   11
women   18, 43, 46, 51, 60
Women's Federation   23, 149
Wong, Linda   136
work ethic   10

work injury insurance 19, 50, 68
work permits 52
work placements xiii, 18, 93, 157
work units (*danwei*) 19, 22–3,
    29–30, 68, 82, 86, 128, 138,
    149, 180
workers, guest/temporary 48
workers, low-income 65
workforce, declining 37, 51
working classes 19
working conditions 164, 169
working population 40, 41, 45, 51
World Bank 6, 15, 33, 35, 70, 111
  and migration 52–3, 174
  and poverty 61, 63, 64
World Giving Index 179
World Health Organization (WHO)
    31, 180
wubao ('Five-Guarantees' programme)
    x, 19, 92, 98, 99, 104,
    113–16, 124, 128
  and medical insurance 117, 118

Xi Jinping xi, 15, 17, 36
xiagang ('off-post' employees) 28–9,
    78–9
Xi'an city 73
xiaokang (moderately prosperous
    society) 5, 25, 35

Yunnan province 59, 62

Zhang, Xiaobo 109
Zhejiang province 48, 127, 161
Zheng, Yong-Nian
Zhenjiang city 82
Zhu Rongji 31
zhuan see transfer of function (*zhuan*)